A Guide to International Monetary Economics, Third Edition

Exchange Rate Theories, Systems and Policies

Hans Visser

Professor of Money and Banking and International Economics, Vrije Universiteit, Amsterdam, The Netherlands

Edward Elgar

Cheltenham, UK • Northampton, MA, USA

Published by
Edward Elgar Publishing Limited
Glensanda House
Montpellier Parade
Cheltenham
Glos GL50 1UA
UK

Edward Elgar Publishing, Inc.
136 West Street
Suite 202
Northampton
Massachusetts 01060
USA

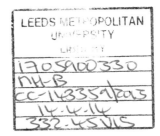

A catalogue record for this book
is available from the British Library

Library of Congress Cataloguing in Publication Data
Visser, H. (Herschel), 1943–
    A guide to international monetary economics : exchange rate theories, systems and policies / Hans Visser.—3rd ed.
        p. cm.
    Includes bibliographical references.
    1. Foreign exchange. 2. Foreign exchange rates. I. Title.

HG3851.V57 2005
332.4'5—dc22

2004050644

ISBN   1 84376 595 0

Printed and bound in Great Britain by MPG Books Ltd, Bodmin, Cornwall

A Guide to International Monetary Economics, Third Edition

Contents

Figures

Tables and boxes

TABLES

BOXES

Acronyms and symbols

BIS   Bank for International Settlements
CAC   Collective Action Clauses
CIP   Covered Interest Parity
ECB   European Central Bank
ESCB   European Systems of Central Banks
EEC   European Economic Community
ERM   Exchange Rate Mechanism
EMS   European Monetary System
EMU   Economic and Monetary Union
EU   European Union
GDP   Gross Domestic Product
GNP   Gross National Product
IMF   International Monetary Fund
LDCs   Less-Developed Countries
LOP   Law of One Price
PPP   Purchasing Power Parity
REH   Rational Expectations Hypothesis
RER   Real Exchange Rate
SDRM   Sovereign Debt Restructuring Mechanism
SGP   Stability and Growth Pact
UIP   Uncovered Interest Parity
URR   Unremunerated Reserve Requirement
e spot exchange rate
ex export volume
g growth rate of national income or national product
g_{Ms} growth rate of the money supply
go real government expenditure
i rate of interest
im import volume
k 'Cambridge' k, or the ratio between cash balances and nominal income
m money multiplier
md real money demand
p probability

q	relative price of nontradeables in terms of tradeables
r	risk premium
s_{ex}	price elasticity of export supply
s_{im}	price elasticity of import supply
u	residual
v	speed of change
w	real wealth
x	expected change in the rate of exchange
y	real income
ys	real product
z	real private expenditure (Appendix 2.1); total real expenditure (Chapter 3)
A	nominal value of assets
B	bonds
Bd	demand for domestic bonds
Bs	supply of domestic bonds
C	base money
CA	surplus on the current account of the balance of payments
D	domestic credit supply
D_{ex}	demand for exports
D_{im}	demand for imports
E	expectations operator
Ex	nominal exports, or receipts on the current account of the balance of payments
F	forward rate of exchange
G	government expenditure
H	open-market purchases
I	investments
Im	imports
J	Jacobian
K	net (non-bank) capital inflow
M, Ms	money supply
Md	money demand
Mf	foreign exchange held by residents
Nd	demand for nontradeables
Ns	supply of nontradeables
P	price level
P_{ex}	price of exports
Ph	price level of domestic production
P_{im}	price of imports
P_N	price of nontradeables
P_T	price of tradeables

Q	number of foreign bonds at one foreign currency unit per bond
Qd	domestic demand for foreign bonds
Qs	domestic supply of foreign bonds
S_{ex}	supply of exports
S_{im}	supply of imports
T	taxes
Tb	trade balance
Td	demand for tradeables
Ts	supply of tradeables
V	foreign-exchange reserves
W	nominal wealth
X	balance-of-payments surplus (of the non-bank sector)
Y	nominal national income
Z	nominal private expenditure
ε_d	domestic price elasticity of demand for imports
ε_{Ex}	elasticity of export earnings in foreign exchange with respect to the exchange rate
ε_f	foreign price elasticity of demand for imports
ε_{Im}	elasticity of import value in foreign exchange with respect to the exchange rate
ε_t	elasticity of terms of trade with respect to exchange rate
ε_{Tb}	elasticity of trade balance with respect to exchange rate
π	rate of inflation
*	expected value
◆	values associated with momentary equilibrium

NOTE

Subscripts not shown in this list represent partial derivatives, except for t, $t-1$, $t+1$, and so on, which denote points in time or periods of time, and e which denotes equilibrium level.

The superscript f denotes foreign value.

A dot over a variable denotes a growth rate.

Foreword

This text, aimed at third-year undergraduate and first-year graduate students, is the fruit of quite a long period of teaching international monetary economics. It focuses on the economics behind exchange-rate models, leaving the econometrics of testing models to one side. Also, exchange-rate policy in a broad sense, including capital controls, dollarisation and monetary unions, is discussed.

It is highly satisfactory that the publisher continues to see a market for the product and asked for a third edition. If my students complain about the complexity of the subject and I tell them that 'this swift business I must uneasy make, lest too light winning make the prize light' (*The Tempest*, I. ii), they can at least console themselves with the thought that the stuff they are wrestling with has stood the test of the market.

The third edition is the result of a continuous process of updating. In this I was helped by my student Niels Visser, who noted a number of mistakes and confusing phrases from an earlier version. Hopefully, the clarity of exposition has benefited from the revisions.

Hans Visser, January 2004

Introduction

When the Bretton Woods system of fixed-but-adjustable exchange rates foundered in March 1973, exchange rates apparently went their own merry way, independent of differences in inflation rates between countries or of the current account of the balance of payments. A decisive factor was that capital movements developed to such an extent that they soon seemed totally to swamp international payments on account of trade in goods and services. Surveys conducted in April 2001 by 48 central banks and other monetary authorities put the average daily turnover in so-called traditional foreign-exchange (or forex) markets (including spot, outright forward and foreign-exchange swap transactions and adjusted for double counting) at $1200 billion, of which $387 billion was made up of spot transactions (BIS 2002, p. 5).[1] Against that, the aggregate value of world exports of goods and services reached $7465 billion in 2001 (IMF 2002, p. 185), equal to the volume of foreign exchange traded in slightly more than six days. So the experience since 1973 has been characterised by a dominance of capital movements over payments on the current account (though the figures may give a somewhat distorted picture, as $689 billion or 59 per cent of daily turnover was between forex dealers, who shift funds among themselves in order to spread their risks). International economists were sent back to their studies to rethink exchange-rate theory. The result has been a spate of models that venture to explain the erratic behaviour of exchange rates after 1973. The variety of models is quite bewildering.

In order to discern some method in the model madness, or to impose some method on it, we will follow de Roos (1985) and group the various theories according to the period for which their explanation of the exchange rate is relevant. This appears to be a useful criterion, even if other criteria are also possible. First, we discern a *very short period*, during which exchange-rate movements are explained by capital flows. The relevant models are known as *asset models*. In the *short period* the movements of the rate of exchange are explained by both capital flows and payments and receipts on the current account. The same goes for the *long period*, but there is an additional equilibrium condition in this case, namely that the current account and the capital account separately be in equilibrium. Finally, in the *very long period*, all possible adjustment processes have run their

1

course and ideally *purchasing power parity* (PPP) prevails, with factor prices internationally equalised. The rates of exchange that follow from the longer-term models can be regarded as trends around which movements take place that are explained by shorter-term models. Capital flows dominate in the short term, but as the period studied grows longer, the current account gains in importance.

Where relevant we also discuss the fixed-rate version of the various models. These variants explain fluctuations in foreign-exchange reserves or the balance of payments rather than exchange-rate movements. Chapter 1 covers the asset models, short-term models are tackled in Chapters 2 and 3, and long-term and very-long-term models are discussed in Chapter 4. The remaining two chapters do not deal with the explanation of exchange rates or foreign-exchange reserves, but with other aspects of the exchange-rate system. Chapter 5 discusses the policies which are required either to maintain fixed exchange rates or to prevent a flexible-rate system from exhibiting excessive volatility. A central topic is whether, and if so, how, capital movements should be controlled. Monetary unions and optimal currency area theory form the subjects of Chapter 6, with special attention being paid to European monetary integration.

A few caveats are in order concerning the exchange-rate models. First, the various models differ as to their premises and it is very important to bear those premises in mind in order not to get confused. The different premises mean that the models apply to different situations. Within each period, in particular the very short and short periods, models differ as to their assumptions about the degree of price flexibility and the degree of substitutability between foreign and domestic titles. It is a question of horses for courses.

Second, one should not entertain too high expectations of the predictive powers of exchange-rate models. The finding by Meese and Rogoff (1983) that these models did not outperform a random-walk model has proved hard to refute (see Sarno and Taylor 2002, ch. 4 for a survey of the literature). These findings pertain to one- to twelve-month horizons and for longer periods the picture is less bleak. Still, there are many reasons why exchange-rate models may generate poor forecasts.

In the following chapters, reference is made to 'the' equilibrium exchange rate. However, economic agents do not agree on the exchange-rate model that is relevant in any specific situation, nor are economic theorists unanimous on which relationships are fundamental. In addition, expectations figure prominently in exchange-rate models but it has proved extremely difficult to model expectations in an empirically satisfying way. In practice, investors' expectations as to the future course of a currency may be swayed by the relative 'strength' (real growth or perceived growth potential) of an economy during one period, by relative inflation rates during another period, and by current-account imbalances during yet another period.

More generally, there may be speculative forces at work not included in the usual menu of macroeconomic fundamentals (Taylor 1995, p. 30). Things may even get more complicated if the fundamental relationships are unstable. In particular, the linchpin of virtually every exchange-rate model, the money-demand function, appears to be unstable, at least in the short term. This might be one reason behind the fact that exchange-rate movements are largely unpredictable over periods of up to two years (Kilian and Taylor, 2003). Alternatively, money demand may be stable but money-market equilibrium may take a considerable time to re-establish after a shock. Kontolemis (2002) found that adjustment may take more than two years (for a survey of money demand studies, see Sriram 1999). That would do little to improve the predictability of exchange rates.

We can probably best view exchange-rate models (and their fixed-but-adjustable rate balance-of-payments variants) as logical exercises of the *if–then* variety. If they are of limited value in making short-term or even medium-term forecasts, at least they can be of some help in the interpretation of history and in the preparation of policy measures, as they help identify the possible sources of exchange-rate movements.

On a more general level, we should always bear in mind that models are no more than attempts to get a mental grip on the world around us. As McCloskey wrote, 'We humans must deal in fictions of our own making. Whether or not they correspond to God's Own Universe is something we cannot know' (McCloskey 1994, p. 195). Models are not 'true' descriptions of the world; they should rather be seen as metaphors that we develop in order to try and understand the world, however imperfectly. This means that we adopt an *instrumentalist* view of economic theory, in which models are devices for the description and prediction of phenomena but the entities in the models or the relationships between them need not refer to anything that exists in the 'real world'. Milton Friedman, too, takes an instrumentalist position in his famous 'methodology of positive economics', when he argues that a theory is satisfactory if the phenomena described by the theory behave *as if* the theory's assumptions about the working of the system were correct (Friedman 1953).

The instrumentalist approach at least goes back to the eighteenth-century English philosopher George Berkeley (1685–1753) and was also propagated by the physicist Ernst Mach (1838–1916). Berkeley and Mach went one step further and even have no use for metaphors; they want science (in their case physical science) to restrict itself to a mathematical description and prediction of phenomena (Berkeley 1951; Losee 2001, ch. 11). Such an approach may be fine for phenomena such as the speed of a falling object, which was what Berkeley was writing about, but not for most economic phenomena. In order to explain developments in, say, the current account of the balance of payments or the rate of exchange, one first has to work out how these entities might be linked to other entities, which means that one cannot do without a model.

Our view of the role of economic models means that we have no qualms neglecting the New Open Economy models recently developed to give international macroeconomics a robust microeconomic foundation, in particular Obstfeld and Rogoff's Redux model (Obstfeld and Rogoff 1996; see also Lane 2001; Mark 2001). These are general-equilibrium models with optimising agents; the models accommodate imperfect competition and nominal rigidities. Models lacking a strong microeconomic foundation are often quite satisfactory as vehicles to trace and interpret real-world developments and the mathematics of the New Open Economy models might well obscure the economics which they are supposed to describe. Put another way, these models are fine for Ph.D. courses, but in their present state of development they would probably leave undergraduate students bewildered.

NOTE

1. Note that this represents a fall from a total of $1490 billion and $568 billion respectively in April 1998. The BIS attributes this fall to the introduction of the euro, which eliminated trading between European currencies; to the growing share of electronic broking in the spot interbank market, which eliminated trade between forex dealers; and to consolidation in the banking industry, with similar results.

1. Asset models

1.1 INTRODUCTION

In the very short period, it is only capital movements that explain the balance of payments or exchange-rate changes. It can be imagined that changes in the data of the system that bear on capital flows influence the balance of payments or the rate of exchange within hours or even minutes or seconds, while the current account needs more time to react. The balance of payments or the rate of exchange then is determined by the demand for and supply of financial assets, not by payments associated with flows of goods and services. The models explaining exchange-rate movements in the very short period are therefore called *asset models*. It is, in particular, the existing stock of financial assets that is decisive. Developments in the real economy that would make the stock of financial assets change play no role in the time period under consideration.

Asset models can be broadly divided into two categories: one in which domestic and foreign titles are perfect substitutes and the interest-elasticity of capital flows is infinite, and one in which they are imperfect substitutes and the interest-elasticity of capital flows is finite. The former are known as *monetary models* and the latter as *portfolio models*. The monetary models are subdivided into *flexprice monetary models*, with fully flexible goods prices, and *sticky-price monetary models*, with sticky goods prices. We first apply the monetary model to the situation of fixed rates, where the balance of payments rather than the rate of exchange is the variable to be explained.

A common point of departure for asset models is the assumption that the foreign-exchange market is an *efficient market*. A market is efficient if asset prices fully reflect all available information. Consequently, no profits can be made by trading on the basis of the available information and new information is immediately reflected in prices. In the finance literature three forms of efficiency are usually distinguished:

1. weak efficiency, with the information set made up of past prices;
2. semi-strong efficiency, with the information set including all publicly available information;

3. strong efficiency, with the information set including all information, both public and private.

The difference between semi-strong and strong efficiency does not seem very important in the case of exchange rates. Private information or insider information could only play a major role in the case of secret plans to change parities or to manipulate a floating exchange rate. Efficiency in exchange-rate models is generally of the (semi-)strong variety. Expectations about the future value of the exchange rate are formed using present information on the future values of the fundamental determinants or *fundamentals* of exchange rates, such as future money growth and future real income growth. With weak efficiency, today's spot exchange-rate would be the best predictor of future spot rates and exchange rate movements would essentially be expected to follow a random walk, depending on unforeseen shocks.

Two elements are involved in the concept of market efficiency. First, *rational expectations* are assumed, which means that economic agents make no systematic mistakes when making forecasts on the basis of the available information or, in other words, that they apply the correct model. Under this Rational Expectations Hypothesis (REH) agents may make mistakes, but these are assumed to average out. Second, any differences between countries in (risk-adjusted) net returns on different assets are assumed to be swiftly arbitraged away, that is, capital mobility is high. In other words, transaction costs are negligible. Note that high capital mobility is something different from high interest-elasticity of capital flows. High mobility is a feature both of monetary and portfolio models.

It should be recognised that the assumption of rational expectations is rather problematic. It is based on the idea that people use 'the correct model' of the economy and that people who do not are swiftly and surely eliminated as players in the market, because they run up losses. This is, however, dubious. There are various problems:

- The model admits of random shocks and losses may result both from incomplete knowledge of the relevant model and from a random shock. Rational expectations imply that people will on average be right, but that is not of much help in the case of a negative shock. Bad luck can land you in bankruptcy as much as poor knowledge of the model and the dumb may fare better than the smart.
- The model is subject to continuous change. In order to fully know the 'correct' model, an infinite number of observations would be called for. REH seems to imply that those observations are indeed made and that new information is immediately digested. Implicitly, REH

presumes an inductivist theory of learning, which is rather problematic (cf. Boland 1982, ch. 4). Moreover, even if it were possible to learn the 'correct' model, it would seem reasonable to assume that people can make systematic mistakes after a shock has hit the system, because they need time to find out how the fundamentals have changed (see Garretsen, Knot and Nijsse 1998 for the case of an exchange-rate regime shift).

- Unlike a model of, say, the probability of meteorites hitting the Earth, an economic model is not something given exogenously. If exchange rates are determined by expectations entertained by economic agents, those agents themselves create the model. If there were something like a 'correct' model, but some agents do not behave in accordance with REH, that in itself would change the model (Harvey 1996; see also Harvey 2001 for a critique of basing analysis of foreign-exchange markets on fundamentals).

What we in fact do when applying REH is to assume that there is such a thing as a correct model and that people act (circumventing the problem of the validity of inductive reasoning) *as if* they know this model, following Friedman (1953). Rational expectations mean that economic agents act in conformity with the model of which they form part. This is done in order to avoid ad-hocery in the modelling of expectations. Perhaps it can best be seen either as a kind of benchmark from which real-world situations will deviate to a greater or lesser extent or, following Gale (1982, pp. 30–1), as an equilibrium condition, meaning that under REH people have no incentive to make different or better use of their information. REH in this way functions as a short cut to a complete and consistent model of expectations formation ('consistent' meaning that people have no incentive to change their expectations).

If everybody applied the same model and used the same information, the commonly agreed fundamentals would determine exchange rates. If there is no such homogeneity, we could distinguish between *fundamentalists*, who base their expectations on the fundamentals of exchange rates, and *noise traders*, who do not (Shleifer and Summers 1990). It may be remarked in passing that without such heterogeneity there would be significantly less trade in financial markets. Noise traders may follow the advice of some guru or act on regularities they detect in exchange-rate time series; in the latter case they are called *chartists* (on the technical analysis which chartists rely on, see Neely 1997). Chartists do not act on fundamentals; moreover, such regularities as they detect are at odds with the idea of efficient markets, as these imply that people pass up opportunities to earn a profit.[1] Exchange-rate expectations could then be modelled as a weighted average of the expectations of fundamentalists and those of chartists. In such an approach exchange rates may easily take some time to adjust to a change in fundamentals (van Hoek 1992).

It does not come as a surprise that a simulation by Pilbeam (1995a) did not show any better performance by fundamentalists than by noise traders. Pilbeam simulated the yields and the variability of $1000 invested, under different investor behaviour, for three-month periods in pounds sterling, yen, D-Mark and French francs over the 1974–94 period, giving fundamentalists the advantage of perfect foresight with regard to fundamentals. Noise traders were divided into chartists and so-called simpletons. The latter followed a very simple rule: they placed funds into the currency that provided the highest return in the previous period. They did not perform worse on average than the others. Pilbeam (1995b) also found that in the short term extrapolative and adaptive expectations predict exchange-rate movements better than static, regressive or rational expectations. This fits in with Takagi's finding that for periods shorter than one month expectations tend to respond to lagged exchange-rate movements, whereas for a time horizon over three months they tend to be dominated by fundamentals (Takagi 1991).

Whatever the way expectations are formed, it is a sobering exercise to compare expectations with outcomes. *Wall Street Journal* surveys among top US macroeconomic forecasters revealed for instance that from 1991 to 1994 the panellists predicted each year in December that next year the dollar would reverse its slide against the yen and every time they were proved wrong (Greer 1999). Remember what we said in the Introduction: models are attempts to get a mental grip on reality. For shorter terms, in particular, these attempts have not so far been too successful.

All this does not mean that the idea of efficient markets is fully discredited. Students of stock-market prices and yields notice that professional investment fund managers, who spend most of their time collecting and assessing market information, are unable to systemically outperform the market. In line with this, it turns out that any predictable pattern in stock prices, the basis of chartism, disappears after it has been published in the finance literature (Malkiel 2003). There is little reason to believe that things are different for exchange rates.

1.2   GLOBAL MONETARISM

In the global monetarist approach (developed by Johnson 1972a) the balance of payments of a country depends on money demand and supply in that country and in the rest of the world. In a small country, any discrepancy between the amount of money demanded and the amount of money supplied will be met through capital imports without production volume, interest rates or the price level being affected. The price level is equal to the foreign price level at the going rate of exchange, that is, Purchasing Power Parity (PPP) prevails. As in the monetary models of exchange-rate behaviour, domestic and foreign interest rates are equal and international capital flows are infinitely interest-elastic. Any upward pressure on the rate of interest caused by money demand exceeding money supply thus will induce capital inflows and any downward pressure caused by money supply exceeding money demand triggers off capital outflows.

Domestic money is created through domestic credit granting, open-market purchases or a surplus in international payments. The surplus or deficit in international payments adjusts, through capital imports or exports, to the amount of money demanded. The monetary authorities are thus unable to control the money supply, nor can they influence the rate of interest or the price level, as these are fully determined by the foreign interest rate and the foreign price level respectively. The only magnitude they can regulate is foreign-exchange reserves, by manipulating domestic credit creation or through open-market policy. If they wish to increase reserves, they resort to imposing a higher reserve ratio on commercial banks (inducing the banks to slow down credit expansion) or to open-market sales. Economic agents will then borrow abroad. They sell the foreign exchange which they borrowed to domestic banks and their accounts are credited in domestic currency.

A perhaps unexpected implication of the model is that economic growth may result in higher foreign-exchange reserves, that is, in a surplus on the balance of payments on the money account. Economic growth increases the volume of money demanded and if domestic credit creation does not meet this demand, the money supply will expand via the balance of payments.

1.3 MONETARY MODELS

1.3.1 Interest Parity

We now turn to the determination of exchange rates. We first analyse the relationship between domestic and foreign interest rates on the one hand and exchange-rate movements on the other hand, without at this stage explaining the *level* of the exchange rate.

We postulate a fully free-floating exchange-rate system. The *exchange rate*, denoted by e and defined as the price of one unit of foreign exchange in terms of domestic currency, is determined by demand and supply. A fall in the exchange rate means that foreign exchange becomes cheaper. This is equivalent to an appreciation of the domestic currency. Conversely, a rise in the exchange rate is synonymous with a depreciation of the domestic currency (note that an appreciation of the domestic currency is sometimes called a rise in the rate of exchange and a depreciation a fall, especially in Britain; when reading the literature one must always first find out which definition is followed). Movements in the rate of exchange ensure that the foreign-exchange market always clears. The banks, including the central bank, are assumed only to act as brokers in the foreign-exchange market and not as net buyers or sellers of foreign exchange. The domestic money supply consequently is not affected by international payments. In the monetary models it is furthermore assumed that domestic and foreign interest-bearing titles are perfect substitutes.

Economic agents are indifferent as to the shares of domestic and foreign titles in their portfolios, provided these yield the same return. The return on foreign titles is made up of the foreign interest rate plus any profit or loss on exchange-rate movements. Given competitive markets with negligible transaction costs (that is, swift arbitrage) and either exchange-rate expectations that are held with certainty or risk-neutral investors, the foreign interest rate plus the expected profit from exchange-rate movements equals the domestic interest rate and *uncovered interest parity* (UIP) prevails. This idea dates back at least to an 1896 article by Irving Fisher (Levich 1978, p. 131) and is sometimes dubbed the *Fisher Open* theory or condition (McKinnon 1981, p. 548). At the same time there will be *covered interest parity* (CIP), which means that the yield on foreign investments which are covered in the forward market equals the yield on domestic investments.[2] Any difference between domestic and foreign interest rates is balanced by a premium or discount on the forward rate. This relationship can be derived as follows. One unit of domestic money invested at the domestic interest rate i will have grown after one period to $(1 + i)$ units. One unit of domestic money exchanged into foreign currency at the spot rate e results in an amount $1/e$ of foreign currency, which, if invested at the foreign interest rate i^f, will have grown after one period to $(1 + i^f)/e$ units of foreign currency. Under CIP, the forward rate F will make this amount equal to $(1 + i)$:

$$(1 + i) = (1 + i^f).F/e$$

or

$$(1 + i)/(1 + i^f) = F/e$$
$$(1 + i)/(1 + i^f) - 1 = F/e - 1$$
$$(F - e)/e = (i - i^f)/(1 + i^f) \tag{1.1}$$

If i^f is small and $(i - i^f)/(1 + i^f) \approx i - i^f$, equation 1.1 simplifies to

$$(F - e)/e = i - i^f \qquad (1.2)$$

which says that *the forward premium is equal to the difference between domestic and foreign interest rates.*

Given foreign and domestic assets that are identical as to default risk and time to maturity, deviations from CIP point to transaction costs (including information costs), (fear of) capital controls or a finite elasticity of the supply of arbitrage funds. Not surprisingly, the CIP assumption fares quite well in empirical tests involving Eurocurrency markets, where assets are comparable in all respects except currency of denomination, trade volume is high and information and other transaction costs are low (from an extensive literature we mention Dufey and Giddy 1978, pp. 86–96, who provide a survey of empirical studies; Sarno and Taylor 2002, pp. 7–9 for another discussion of empirical research). For Australia, Hong Kong and Singapore, de Brouwer (1999, pp. 68–75) reports that capital liberalisation and technological advances in trading technology have made interest differentials move very close to CIP over the period 1985–94.

It may be noted that forward cover is not usually available for periods longer than two years (but *currency swaps*, involving the exchange of specific amounts of two different currencies for a specified period of time between two parties, can be negotiated for much longer periods; these will, however, have higher transaction costs and carry a higher default risk). Apparently, banks do not have a very elastic supply of arbitrage funds for comparatively long periods (see McKinnon 1979, ch. 5 on the supply of arbitrage funds). Possible reasons mentioned by Levich (1985, p. 1027) are the loss of liquidity involved in supplying funds for such long periods, credit risks and an adverse impact on balance sheet ratios. What deviations from CIP there are for shorter periods, say up to one year, can to a great extent be explained by transaction costs, at least for the leading currencies (Clinton 1988; Maasoumi and Pippenger 1989).

Under UIP, the foreign interest rate plus the expected exchange-rate change equals the domestic interest rate, or $(1 + i) = (1 + i^f)E_t \, e_{t+1}/e_t$ (subscripts denote points in time, E = expected value, F is the forward rate for one period ahead). CIP says that $(1 + i) = (1 + i^f)F_t/e_t$. Given that CIP holds very generally if financial markets are well developed, it follows that *under UIP the forward exchange rate equals the expected future spot rate*, so that $E_t \, e_{t+1} = F_t$ or $E_{t-1}e_t = F_{t-1}$.

UIP says that any difference between domestic and foreign interest rates equals the expected change in the rate of exchange. This means that the current spot exchange rate depends on the expected future exchange rate and on domestic and foreign interest rates. Any shock in one of these three variables will make the spot rate adjust. We study two such shocks, starting from a situation in which domestic and foreign interest rates are equal and the exchange rate is not expected to change.

(i) Speculators suddenly expect a future rise in the rate of exchange. They will buy foreign exchange spot in the expectation of being able to sell it at a higher price in the future. They themselves thus bring about the rise in the exchange rate they expected, a case of a self-fulfilling prophecy. Instead of buying foreign exchange spot, they could also buy foreign exchange on the forward market, with a view to selling it upon delivery at a profit. The arbitrageurs (banks) who offer forward exchange to the speculators cover their position by buying foreign exchange on the current spot market, again pushing up the current spot exchange rate. The activities of the speculators thus see to it that both the current spot rate and the forward rate adjust to the expected future spot rate.

(ii) The domestic (short-term) interest rate increases, but the expected future exchange rate stays put. At the original exchange rate, investment in domestic securities promises higher returns than foreign investments. People want to invest in domestic rather than in foreign securities. They sell foreign exchange and buy domestic currency. The exchange rate falls. The expected future exchange rate has not fallen, the exchange rate is, therefore, expected to rise again. Foreign investments offer the prospect of a gain from an exchange-rate increase in addition to the interest yield. The fall in the exchange rate goes on until the expected future rise plus the foreign interest rate equals the domestic interest rate.

Under UIP the expected future exchange rate equals the forward rate. Realised spot rates then should on average equal the lagged forward rate. UIP is therefore often tested by regressing realised spot rates on the lagged forward rate:

$$\ln e_t = a + b \ln F_{t-1} + u_t \qquad (1.3)$$

u is a residual.

The error term u should be serially uncorrelated and $Eu_t = 0$ if the foreign exchange market is efficient. Under risk neutrality, the condition for the monetary approach, the constant a should not differ significantly from 0 nor should coefficient b differ much from 1. The forward rate is in that case an *unbiased predictor* of future spot rates (see Taylor 1995, pp. 14–17 for the problems and ambiguities of econometric testing). This implies that the expectation of excess profits of investing in one currency rather than another is zero.

Empirical research does not provide much support for the forward rate as an unbiased predictor of the future spot rate and thus for UIP (see King 1998, for Australia and East Asia see de Brouwer 1999, pp. 75–89). The divergence is often quite substantial, especially over shorter periods. Possible explanations are given in Section 1.3.5. Nevertheless, there is evidence that over longer periods, covering several years, differences in interest rates to a greater or lesser degree reflect exchange-rate changes. This after all provides support, if only weak, for UIP (see Lothian and Simaan 1998 in a study covering 23 OECD countries over the period 1973 to 1994; Berk and Knot 2001, employing long-term interest rates and exchange-rate expectations derived from PPP for five currencies *vis-à-vis* the US dollar 1975–97; Flood and Rose 2001, using high-frequency data from the 1990s for a large number of countries).[3]

1.3.2   The Basic Flexprice Monetary Model

UIP and CIP show how the current exchange rate and (expected) future rates are interconnected, under certain assumptions. They are not sufficient to explain the *level* of the exchange rate. In the basic monetary model of exchange-rate determination UIP is to this end combined with three other building blocks: the quantity theory, PPP and Irving Fisher's theory of inflation-corrected interest rates (it will presently be shown that any two of the building blocks UIP, PPP and inflation-corrected interest rates imply the third one; there are thus three independent building blocks in total).

First, prices are, in quantity-theory fashion, assumed to be determined by the (exogenous) nominal money supply and a real money demand which is a function of (exogenous) real national income and the rate of interest:

$$Ms = Md = kPy^{\alpha}i^{-\beta} \tag{1.4}$$

Ms = money supply, Md = money demand, P = price level, y = real income.

Taking logs and solving for the price level:

$$\ln P = -\ln k - \alpha\ln y + \beta\ln i + \ln Ms \tag{1.5}$$

Assuming, for the sake of simplicity, that k, α and β have the same value abroad as at home, we find for the foreign price level:

$$\ln P^f = -\ln k - \alpha\ln y^f + \beta\ln i^f + \ln Ms^f \tag{1.6}$$

The superscript f denotes foreign countries.

PPP provides the link between the domestic and the foreign price levels: the domestic price level is assumed to equal the foreign price level at the going rate of exchange:

$$e.P^f = P$$

or

$$\ln e = \ln P - \ln P^f \tag{1.7}$$

from which it follows, after differentiating with respect to time, that movements in the rate of exchange reflect the difference between domestic and foreign inflation:

$$\dot{e} = \pi - \pi^f \tag{1.8}$$

π = the rate of inflation.

Equations 1.5, 1.6 and 1.7 tell us that the rate of exchange is determined by the stock demand for and supply of money at home and abroad:

$$\ln e = \alpha(\ln y^f - \ln y) + \beta(\ln i - \ln i^f) + (\ln Ms - \ln Ms^f) \tag{1.9}$$

Before we add expected values of the various variables to the model, let us first apply the model as formulated in equation 1.9 to two simple cases:

(i) The domestic money supply increases to a higher level. This immediately feeds into a higher domestic price level, leaving real cash balances M/P and thus the domestic interest rate unchanged. Given PPP, the exchange rate will increase.

(ii) Domestic national income jumps to a higher level. At first sight slightly surprising, perhaps, is that this causes a fall in the rate of exchange (an appreciation of the domestic currency). The economic reasoning behind this result is that a higher level of y increases the volume of money demanded, which, given the nominal money supply, makes the price level fall. In terms of equation 1.4, a rise in y causes a fall in P. Given Ms, an increase in the demand for money caused by a higher real income has to be offset by a fall in money demand from some other cause, and in the quantity theory it is the price level that has to give way. A fall in the price level makes the rate of exchange fall too, given PPP. The *real exchange rate* (RER), that is, the nominal exchange rate corrected for relative price-level movements, is constant (even unity) under PPP: $RER = eP^f/P$ and $P = eP^f$, so that $RER = 1$. Nominal exchange-rate movements exactly offset diverging price-level movements under PPP, so that the relative price of a bundle of domestic goods and a bundle of foreign goods at the going nominal rate of exchange does not change.[4]

Note that a fall in the real exchange rate, or a real appreciation, means that a country's price level increases *vis-à-vis* another country, as when domestic inflation is higher than foreign inflation under fixed exchange rates or when the rate of exchange falls and the domestic currency appreciates with unchanged domestic and foreign prices. As in the case of the nominal exchange rate, this definition has not been universally adopted: a real appreciation of the currency is sometimes called a rise in the real exchange rate.

BOX 1.1. REAL INTEREST RATE PARITY

Equality of real interest rates at home and abroad, or *real interest rate parity*, requires that

$$i - \pi = i^f - \pi^f$$

This is equivalent to

$$(i - i^f - \dot{e}) + (\dot{e} - \pi + \pi^f) = 0$$

where a dot denotes a rate of change. The expression between the first pair of brackets is zero if uncovered interest parity holds. Real interest rate parity then requires that the expression between the second pair of brackets also be zero. In other words, exchange-rate movements counterbalance differences in inflation rates, which means that purchasing power parity holds, at least in its relative variant.

Let us now revert to the distinguishing feature of the monetary approach, the UIP assumption (or Fisher Open condition).

According to UIP, the value of $(i - i^f)$ reflects the expected rise in the rate of exchange. We also found, from PPP (equation 1.8), that the change in the rate of exchange equals the difference between domestic and foreign inflation (note that we use continuous time here, whereas in the preceding section we used discrete time). Expected future exchange-rate changes will correspondingly equal the difference between expected domestic and expected foreign inflation, given rational expectations. With perfect capital markets and consequently a uniform expected real rate of interest this implies that the Fisher inflation–interest relationship, which says that the nominal rate of interest equals the real rate plus the expected inflation rate, holds.[5] The real rate of interest is assumed exogenous; it can be thought to be determined by the marginal efficiency of capital. Real interest rates therefore are equal across countries in this model. *Real interest rate parity* holds, a result which requires both uncovered interest parity and PPP to hold (see Box 1.1).

PPP, UIP and Fisher's inflation-corrected interest rates are not independent. Any two of them implies the third. This will be immediately apparent if we remember that PPP says that

$$\dot{e} = \pi - \pi^f \tag{1.8}$$

UIP says that

$$\dot{e} = i - i^f \tag{1.10}$$

and Fisher that

$$\pi - \pi^f = i - i^f \tag{1.11}$$

It can now be shown that not only the present values of the exogenous variables but also their expected future values determine the present exchange rate. We have seen that $(i - i^f)$ reflects the expected rise in the rate of exchange, which can be written as $(E_t\, e_{t+1} - e_t)$, so that the second term between brackets in equation 1.9 can be changed into $(\ln E_t\, e_{t+1} - \ln e_t)$. Economic agents are assumed to entertain rational expectations, that is, to know the relevant economic model and use all available information. E_t is the expectational operator conditional on the available information at date t. For the sake of convenience, denote $[\alpha(\ln y^f - \ln y) + (\ln Ms - \ln Ms^f)]$ by $\ln z$ and drop the $\ln$'s. Equation 1.9 can then be rewritten as

$$e_t = z_t + \beta(E_t\, e_{t+1} - e_t)$$

or

$$e_t = [1/(1 + \beta)](z_t + \beta E_t\, e_{t+1}) \tag{1.12}$$

From equation 1.12 it follows that

$$E_t\, e_{t+1} = [1/(1 + \beta)](E_t\, z_{t+1} + \beta E_t\, e_{t+2}) \tag{1.13}$$

Substituting equation 1.13 in equation 1.12 we find

$$e_t = [1/(1 + \beta)][z_t + \beta/(1 + \beta).E_t z_{t+1} + \beta^2/(1 + \beta).E_t e_{t+2}].$$

Repeating this forward iteration for the next date yields

$$E_t e_{t+2} = [1/(1 + \beta)](E_t z_{t+2} + \beta E_t e_{t+3})$$

so that

$$e_t = [1/(1 + \beta)].[z_t + \beta/(1 + \beta).E_t z_{t+1} + \beta^2/(1 + \beta)^2.E_t z_{t+2} \\ + \beta^3/(1 + \beta)^3.E_t e_{t+3}]$$

and so on *ad infinitum*:

$$e_t = [1/(1 + \beta)][z_t + \beta/(1 + \beta). E_t z_{t+1} \\ + \beta^2/(1 + \beta)^2.E_t z_{t+2} + \beta^3/(1 + \beta)^3. E_t z_{t+3} + . . .] \\ = [1/(1 + \beta)] \sum_{j=0}^{\infty} [\beta/(1 + \beta)]^j E_t z_{t+j} \qquad (1.14)$$

So the current exchange rate in this *equilibrium exchange-rate model* or monetary model with rational expectations hinges not only on the present values but also on the expected values of the exogenous variables at all future dates (Bilson 1978, 1979; Hoffman and Schlagenhauf 1983; Vander Kraats and Booth 1983).

Changes in expectations as to future monetary policy, future real growth or any other exogenous variable immediately feed back into the current spot rate, before the expected change actually takes place. Two further cases may help us to grasp the mechanics of the system.

(iii) Consider an expected future discrete jump in the domestic money supply (higher values for $E_t z_{t+j}$). Rational agents know that the price level will be higher in the future and demand a temporarily higher rate of interest on loans as a compensation for the expected loss in the purchasing power of money. A higher rate of interest reduces the demand for money. Given an unchanged present money supply, an excess supply of money develops that drives goods prices up. Thanks to PPP, the current spot exchange rate moves up too. It will increase to such a level that the expected additional rise in the exchange rate matches the difference between domestic and foreign interest rates (UIP). Part of the exchange-rate and price-level changes associated with the expected future jump in the money supply, therefore, take place immediately.

(iv) Consider an increase in the expected future growth rate of money. This raises the expected rate of inflation, which feeds into the current rate of interest, as lenders demand a higher rate of interest in order to get compensation for the expected fall in the real value of the capital sum of the loan (Fisher). A higher current rate of interest decreases the volume of money demanded. Given the money supply, this leads to an excess supply of money at the original current price level and thus to a higher current price level. Given PPP, a higher rate of exchange will result. Again, UIP implies that further depreciations are expected to take place in the future. Note that the real rate of interest does not change; the change in the nominal rate of interest therefore does not trigger capital flows that in their turn might make exchange rates change.

We may conclude that expected future events are linked to the present via the rate of interest. Note that the increase in the rate of interest does not lead to capital imports and through those imports to a lower exchange rate, as the *real* rate of interest is not affected.

A few final remarks on price flexibility are in order. The price of foreign exchange in this model is formed in very much the same way as the prices of other financial assets and may therefore be highly volatile. Changes in expectations about the future immediately feed into the current spot rate. However, it should be kept in mind that the monetary model is based on some extreme assumptions. Obstfeld (1985, p. 431) found for the February 1976 to February 1985 period for the United States, Japan and Germany that the variability of the effective (that is, trade-weighted) nominal exchange rate lay between the variability of the wholesale price index and the variability of the stock-market price index.

It has also been found that the consumer price index was significantly less volatile, whereas some commodity price indices, particularly the petroleum price index, exhibited even higher variability than equity prices (for figures over 1973–80 and 1981–90 for the same three countries, see Goldstein and Isard 1992, pp. 16–18). Commodity prices may adjust very quickly to a change in circumstances, but wholesale prices are much less volatile, whereas consumer prices are apparently quite sticky. The assumption that the price level immediately adjusts is, therefore, far removed from reality. PPP is at best a reasonable approximation for price and exchange-rate developments in the long run (see Chapter 4). Only under hyperinflation, when monetary disturbances swamp any other influences on prices and exchange rates, does PPP fit the facts in the short run too, say on a quarterly or annual basis (Frenkel 1978). No wonder then that the monetary model, implying as it does real-interest-rate parity, that is, not only PPP but also UIP, does not fare too well in econometric tests (see the surveys mentioned in the Introduction, and in addition Cushman 2000; Groen 2000; Neely and Sarno 2002 and explicitly for real-interest-rate parity Fujii and Chinn 2001). PPP holds better in the long term (say, ten years) than in the short term (say one or two years), and the same goes for UIP. It is only for periods of hyperinflation that the monetary model provides a close description of what happens (Frenkel 1978; Moosa 2000). UIP can, however, be combined with prices that are sticky in the short run and with short-term deviations from PPP. This is the subject of the next section.

This leaves the question of why real exchange rates under a floating-rate system are much more volatile than under a fixed-but-adjustable-rate system. For Diboglu and Koray (2001), capital flows are the culprit. These may attract speculators (Flood and Rose 1999). Sticky nominal prices provide another possible explanation. For instance, if prices are pre-set in the buyer's currency, a change in the nominal exchange rate will also make the real exchange rate change. If monetary-policy changes do not immediately affect prices we have another case of sticky prices.

1.3.3   Dornbusch's Sticky-Price Monetary Model

Dornbusch's *exchange-rate dynamics model* (Dornbusch 1976, 1980, ch. 11; Bilson 1979) differs from the flexprice monetary model in that prices do not adjust immediately after a shock. The quantity theory applies only in the longer term. Consequently, changes in the money supply first exert a Keynesian liquidity effect affecting the rate of interest, whereas in the equilibrium exchange-rate model they immediately feed into higher or lower prices with the interest rate remaining constant (or, if we analyse changes in the *rate of growth* of the money supply, in higher or lower inflation and in Fisherian interest-rate adjustments). PPP also applies only in the longer term, but UIP holds continually. The model can perhaps not be seen as an ultra-short-term model in the strict sense. Nevertheless, we cover the model under this heading because it is capital flows that drive the system whereas the current account of the balance of payments is neglected.

Assume that, starting from an equilibrium with full employment in an economy with a given and constant production capacity, the money supply expands (in the form of a discrete jump, so that there is no ongoing inflation and consequently no Fisherian inflation compensation in nominal interest rates). Prices adjust slowly. The real money supply M/P therefore increases at first, depressing the rate of interest. Investors send their money abroad, not only in order to benefit from the higher foreign interest rate, but also in anticipation of the future increase of the exchange rate (which they know will happen, thanks to rational expectations). At the level of the new equilibrium exchange rate they go on sending money abroad, because of this temporary interest differential between foreign and domestic financial markets. They will only stop driving up the exchange rate in this way at the point where the expected fall in the exchange rate (to its new equilibrium level) just balances the interest differential.

Given uncovered interest parity, the initial fall of the domestic interest rate leads to a discount on the forward exchange rate, which should correspond with an expected future fall in the rate of exchange. However, the increased money supply implies a higher future domestic price level and, consequently, a future rise in the rate of exchange. These two movements are only compatible if the rate of exchange first moves beyond its new long-term equilibrium level and gradually returns to it later. This phenomenon is known as *overshooting* (see Figure 1.1).

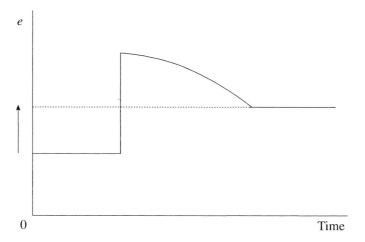

Figure 1.1   Overshooting

Real cash balances *M/P* have increased and the domestic rate of interest has fallen. This results in a higher demand for goods. Moreover, the exchange rate has increased while domestic prices have not gone up, or only slightly. Real depreciation has taken place (the real exchange rate rises) and net export demand can be assumed to grow as well. All this puts upward pressure on the domestic price level. As this price level increases, real balances fall and the rate of interest goes up until finally both real balances and the rate of interest are back at their original levels, albeit at a higher price level. As the rate of interest returns to its original level, both the gap between the domestic and the foreign interest rate and the discount on the forward rate diminish, while the exchange rate moves towards its new equilibrium level.

In the new equilibrium situation prices and the exchange rate have changed proportionately to the money supply and the real exchange rate has returned to its initial value. During the transition from one equilibrium to another, however, PPP is violated and the real exchange rate moves first up, then down.

> It is worth noting that overshooting in the present model hinges on the combination of slow price adjustment and high substitutability of foreign and domestic assets, with a high speed of adjustment. The lower the degree of substitutability, the smaller the increase in the rate of exchange brought about by a fall in the domestic rate of interest. Below some degree of substitutability, or below some speed of adjustment, overshooting will not occur. However, a situation like that is, of course, not within the compass of the monetary model. It is also assumed that a monetary impulse first results in a liquidity effect on the rate of interest. It can be imagined, though, that rational agents who understand that prices will rise, take advantage of the opportunity to borrow at interest rates that for a while are low in real terms. The demand for credit rises temporarily and with it the demand for money (Lüdiger 1989). This works against the fall in nominal rates that overshooting in the Dornbusch models rests upon.

In Dornbusch's sticky-price model, exchange-rate volatility is caused by monetary-policy actions. Empirical tests of the model have not been very successful, but Rogoff argues that the model does capture the effects of at least some major turning points in monetary policy, in particular Margaret Thatcher's deflation policy in Britain from 1979 and the American deflation policy in the early 1980s (see Rogoff 2002, which also considers empirical testing of the model).

The Dornbusch mechanism can only explain mild exchange-rate fluctuations. If adjustments are expected to take one year and monetary policy makes the 12-month interest rate in a country change initially by, say, 4 per cent, this would also lead to an initial amount of overshooting of also 4 per cent that would gradually be reduced to zero in the course of the year. Nonetheless, Dornbusch's model is important because it focuses on the interaction of goods markets characterised by slow adjustment mechanisms and asset markets with very fast adjustment. Furthermore, it showed that exchange-rate volatility, including overshooting, could occur even with economic agents who were perfectly rational and well informed.

Overshooting does not only occur in the Dornbusch model. Other cases of overshooting will be dealt with later.

1.3.4   Frankel's Real-Interest-Rate-Differential Model

Dornbusch studied the effects of a once-and-for-all change in the money supply in a non-growing economy. Consequently, only price-*level* changes rather than changes in the rate of inflation occur in his model. Frankel

(1979) generalised the sticky-price monetary model, allowing for changes in the *growth* rate of money and in the rate of inflation.

Again, we start from UIP, which says that the (expected) relative change in the rate of exchange equals the difference between domestic and foreign interest rates:

$$\dot{e} = i - i^f \qquad (1.10)$$

In the flexprice monetary model this equalled the difference between domestic and foreign inflation rates, hence real interest rates were equal. In the Frankel model, as in the Dornbusch model, the rate of exchange adjusts with a lag to changes in the equilibrium rate of exchange e_e:

$$\dot{e} = -\Theta(e - e_e) + \pi - \pi^f \qquad (1.15)$$

Equations are in logs.

During the adjustment process, real interest parity does not hold. Hence the real-interest-rate-differential moniker.

Combining equations 1.10 and 1.15 we find

$$e - e_e = -(1/\Theta)[(i - \pi) - (i^f - \pi^f)] \qquad (1.16)$$

The expression in square brackets is the real interest differential (which equals zero in the case of real interest parity, as we know from Box 1.1).

The equilibrium exchange rate can be taken from equation 1.9, with $(i^f - i)$ replaced by $(\pi^f - \pi)$:

$$e_e = \alpha(y^f - y) + \beta(\pi^f - \pi) + (Ms - Ms^f) \qquad (1.17)$$

The inflation rates are the expected long-run rates. In the sticky-price model the actual interest-rate differential need not correspond with the long-run inflation-rate differential, hence the replacement.

Substituting equation 1.17 in equation 1.16 we find

$$e = -(1/\Theta)(i - i^f) + [(1/\Theta) - \beta](\pi - \pi^f) + \alpha(y^f - y) + (Ms - Ms^f) \qquad (1.18)$$

This is a general expression which yields as special cases the Dornbusch model, if $\pi = \pi^f = 0$, and the flexprice monetary model, if $[(i - i^f) - (\pi - \pi^f)] = 0$. The model works in the same way as the Dornbusch model. Consider a tightening of monetary policy, that is, a fall in the growth rate of the money supply. The equilibrium rate of inflation and the equilibrium nominal rate of interest fall, as does the equilibrium rate of exchange. In the short term, however, goods prices do not fall or decline only slightly and the rate of interest rises, because of the initial fall in real balances. Capital imports move the rate of exchange past its new (lower) equilibrium level. As the domestic price level falls, i declines again and e rises to its new equilibrium value, or rather to its new equilibrium path, as it will move over time if $\pi \neq \pi^f$ (see Figure 1.2).

In Frankel's view, the equilibrium exchange-rate model provides a good description of what happens during hyperinflations, when prices are extremely flexible, whereas the Dornbusch model would be relevant in the case of a low and stable inflation differential. His own model, which he applied to the D-Mark–US dollar rate over the July 1974–February 1978 period, was meant to describe a situation of moderate inflation differentials. Later research suggests that Frankel's validation of the real-interest-rate-differential model was an historical accident (Isaac and de Mel 2001).

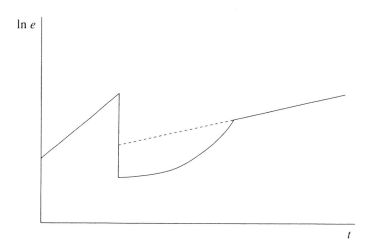

Figure 1.2   Overshooting in the Frankel model

1.3.5   *Ex Post* Deviations from UIP

Empirical tests generally do not support UIP, at least not for shorter periods. A very conspicuous case of the failure of UIP was that of the US dollar in the early 1980s. On a trade-weighted basis, the dollar appreciated by about 50 per cent between autumn 1980 and February 1985 (Mussa 1990, p. 31), but the appreciation occurred in the face of a discount in the forward rate of the dollar and a positive difference between US interest rates and European and Japanese rates. Forward rates were not unbiased predictors of future spot rates and there were persistent *ex post* excess returns on holding dollars over other currencies. Realised values clearly differed from expected values. Especially in 1984, there was a general feeling that the dollar was overvalued, but still the appreciation went on until the early months of 1985. Such a failure of UIP *ex post* can mean different things:

(a)   UIP does not hold *ex ante* because markets are not efficient.
(b)   UIP does not hold *ex ante* because the portfolio model applies.
(c)   Government intervenes.
(d)   UIP is rejected *ex post* but the monetary model still applies and UIP does hold *ex ante*.

(a) UIP does not hold *ex ante* because markets are not efficient. This may, but does not necessarily, mean that economic agents are irrational. The finding by Ngama (1994) that there is an error-correction mechanism at work, such that systematic prediction errors are eliminated over time, could explain why UIP does not hold in the short term. This agrees with the non-instant adjustment to a change in fundamentals mentioned in Section 1.1.

(b) UIP does not hold *ex ante* because the portfolio model applies, that is, investors, though rational, are not risk neutral.

(c) Government intervenes. Meredith and Ma (2002) found that currencies that command a forward premium tend, on average, to depreciate, whereas currencies with a forward discount tend to appreciate. This relationship, known in the literature as the *forward premium anomaly*, conflicts with UIP and could be the result of policy reactions to random exchange-rate changes. If, for example, the domestic currency depreciates for some reason, output and inflation would tend to rise. It is natural for the monetary authorities to react by tightening monetary policy. Short-term interest rates increase and the domestic currency will command a forward discount. Nonetheless, if the policy bites, the domestic currency appreciates. Interventions in the foreign-exchange market can also provide an explanation (Mark and Moh 2003). This stands to reason, as, for instance, interventions to halt a depreciation of a currency are made up of sales of foreign exchange by the central bank against domestic currency and this tightens the money market.

(d) UIP is rejected *ex post* but the monetary model still applies and UIP does hold *ex ante*. This means that a failure of UIP to be corroborated in econometric tests is not necessarily disastrous for the monetary model. There appear to be three explanations:

(i)   asymmetric shocks;
(ii)   the peso problem;
(iii)   speculative bubbles.

We shall discuss these three cases in turn. However, first we should note that there does not always seem to be a satisfactory way of distinguishing between the three explanations by econometric methods. As so often when competing theories or models are involved, a choice between them is made difficult because of *observational equivalence*, the phenomenon that the empirical evidence is compatible with several competing models.

(i) *Asymmetric shocks.* One explanation that is consistent with the monetary model is that *ex post* divergences from UIP are attributable to *news*, that is, developments or shocks that were impossible to foresee when expectations were originally formed and that make economic agents revise their expectations (see Frenkel 1981a; Edwards 1983; Goodhart 1988a; MacDonald 1988a, ch. 12; Gruijters 1991). These shocks could well be asymmetric, that is, they do not neutralise each other, causing unforeseeable and unforeseen autocorrelation of the error term in equation 1.3 (cf. Roberts 1995). In the case of the dollar in the first half of the 1980s two such shocks were the repatriation of loans to Latin America by American banks in the wake of the 1982 foreign-exchange and debt crises and the ongoing liberalisation of Japan's financial markets, which got into higher gear thanks to American pressure which led to the 1984 US–Japan accord and helped sustain capital flows to the United States (Osugi 1990).

(ii) *The peso problem.* With rational expectations, agents use a correct model and make no systematic mistakes. UIP holds *ex ante*. *Ex ante* validity of UIP is compatible with *ex post* deviations from UIP when a change in the government's macroeconomic policy and a concomitant movement in the (equilibrium) exchange rate are expected, but the exact moment is not known and the change fails to materialise for a period of time, or if a policy change has been announced but takes time to be implemented (Krasker 1980; Borenszstein 1987, pp. 34–7; Kaminsky 1993). An expected devaluation, for instance, will go hand in hand with domestic interest rates that are higher than foreign rates and will result in high *ex post* returns on investments not covered in the forward market during the period before it actually occurs. Realised spot rates for a period of time differ systematically from lagged forward rates. The phenomenon is known as the *peso problem*. This expression refers to the situation in Mexico in the 1970s, when an expected devaluation of the peso was reflected in high domestic interest rates and a discount on the forward peso, long before the devaluation in fact took place in August 1976.

If there is a peso problem, the market may be efficient, but the usual tests fail to corroborate efficiency. Economic agents appear to make autocorrelated forecasting errors, but this is because there is no well-behaved error variable; isolated policy changes do not make a large sample and forecasting errors need not average out.

(iii) Speculative bubbles.   In the flexprice monetary model, exchange rates are determined by the fundamentals, including firmly held expectations about future values of these fundamentals. It has been argued by several authors that the rate of exchange may be influenced by other variables as well, even when retaining the efficiency condition that the expected excess return of holding foreign assets over the return on domestic assets is nil: the rate of exchange may be determined by rational expectations of (other market participants') whims, that is, my expectation of what other people's expectations will be. Those expectations may be governed by factors other than fundamentals. What we then have is a *rational bubble*. We are back with Keynes's gloomy view of (in his case, stock) market valuation as a game of musical chairs (Keynes 1961, pp. 155–6).

A rational bubble occurs when market participants weigh some expected chance of a continuing rise of a currency, for instance the dollar, against the probability of a crash. The expected rise may be totally unconnected with fundamentals. If this is to be called rational, it can only be seen as rational on the level of the individual agent and hardly as collective rationality. Assume that people know that in the long run fundamentals determine the rate of exchange, but that they expect the rate of exchange for some period of time to deviate from its fundamentals-determined equilibrium value (Blanchard 1979; see also the discussion in Krause 1991, pp. 35–42). The expected rise in the rate of exchange (which may be negative, of course) is $E_t\, e_{t+1} - e_t$. Denote the rate of increase for any period t by v_t. Speculators expect the increase to continue for a period of time at rate v_t with a probability $(1-p)$. Expected profits from speculation are $(1-p)v_t$. The probability of a return of the exchange rate to its equilibrium value e_e is p and the associated loss amounts to $p(e_e - e_t)$. Under (*ex ante*) UIP, it follows that

$$E_t\, e_{t+1} - e_t = i - i^f = (1-p)v_t + p(e_e - e_t) \qquad (1.19)$$

or the interest-rate differential equals the weighted average of possible exchange-rate movements. Equations are in logs again.

G.W. Evans (1986) found evidence of a speculative bubble in the US dollar–pound sterling rate over the period 1981–84. In this case, with the US dollar seen as the foreign currency, $i^f > i$ and there was a discount on the forward dollar. Thus, $E_t\, e_{t+1} - e_t = i - i^f < 0$. Still, it happened that the variable $v_t > 0$. This may have been, apart from asymmetric shocks, because of the expectation of individual investors to be able to pull out of the dollar just before its inevitable crash, which translates into a small value of the variable p. It seems somewhat far-fetched, though, to assume that the dollar was driven by a speculative bubble over a four-year-plus period. Speculative bubbles may explain short-term exchange-rate movements, but it is hard to believe that they could occur over periods spanning more than a few months.

A curious corollary of the analysis which led to equation 1.19 is that, if a currency is overvalued and still appreciating, the rate of appreciation must pick up speed all the time. This is because the loss per unit of currency which the crash in the end will entail also increases over time, as the rate of exchange moves further and further away from the equilibrium exchange rate (as perceived by the market participants). In terms of equation 1.19,

$$v_t = (i - i^f)/(1 - p) + (e_t - e_e).p/(1 - p) \qquad (1.20)$$

As long as the spot rate increases, given the interest rates and p, the value of the variable v_t must rise faster and faster in order to make speculators hold on to their foreign exchange. If, moreover, the probability of the bubble bursting grows over time, p rises, $(1 - p)$ falls and v_t must rise even faster. These results are conditional on a generally shared idea of what the equilibrium rate of exchange should be. If and when the pace of increase of variable v_t starts to slow down, the bubble will burst.

In the speculative-bubble model, investors weigh the probability of a continued rise in the rate of exchange against the probability of a crash. There is *ex ante* uncovered interest-rate parity. The interest-rate differential between home and abroad reflects the expected exchange-rate change, that is, the mathematical expectation of the change in the rate of exchange. As long as the bubble does not burst, however, yields on foreign financial assets are higher than on domestic assets and as soon as the bubble bursts they are lower. In this model there are, at any moment, two possible outcomes. Neither outcome will conform to UIP; only their probability-weighted average does. Thus, UIP holds *ex ante* but not *ex post*. It's like cars approaching a T-junction. Every car turns either left or right, but on average they follow a way in between.

It should be emphasised that bubbles do not hinge on zero expected excess returns. They can also occur when a risk premium applies. In that case they properly fall under the heading of portfolio analysis.

1.4 PORTFOLIO MODELS

1.4.1 Risk Premiums and Exchange Rates

Portfolio models differ from monetary models in that domestic and foreign titles are not perfect substitutes. CIP holds but (*ex ante*) UIP does not.

Rational expectations still apply. The forward rate no longer necessarily equals the expected future spot rate nor do expected exchange-rate movements correspond with interest differentials across countries. Portfolio analysis in a very-short-term setting studies the effects on the rate of exchange of decisions on the allocation of a given volume of wealth. In the very short term, changes in accumulated wealth can be taken as negligible in comparison to the stock of wealth (apart from deliberate changes in the money supply as a result of monetary policy). Again, the current account of the balance of payments is neglected.

If domestic and foreign titles are imperfect substitutes, the composition of portfolios, the rate of interest and the rate of exchange interact. The basic idea of portfolio analysis is that economic agents are risk averters, who demand a higher expected return if they are to add some risky asset to their portfolios, *ceteris paribus*, but are willing to give up some expected yield if the inclusion of an asset reduces the expected risk of their portfolio. Risk is commonly measured as the standard deviation of possible future returns and assets are assumed to be identical as to maturity, taxability and default risk. The usual assumption is that the *risk premium* or required excess return increases with the share of the asset in question in the portfolio, but that diversification of a portfolio over a variety of assets, both domestic and foreign, may reduce risk. On the one hand, wealth holders will demand a higher expected yield on foreign assets if the share of those assets in their portfolios is to grow; on the other hand, they may be satisfied with a lower expected yield if there is no perfectly positive correlation between expected returns on domestic and foreign assets and diversification over domestic and foreign assets consequently reduces risk. The risk premium may thus be negative. UIP does not prevail with a non-zero risk premium, but there is no reason why CIP should not hold. CIP simply results from hedging foreign-exchange risks in competitive financial markets. The risk premium can be measured by the difference between required returns on assets denominated in different currencies or by the difference between the expected future spot rate and the forward rate: $r_t = E_t\,e_{t+1} - F_t$ or $F_t + r_t = E_t e_{t+1}$, where r = the risk premium.

What impact does the introduction of a (positive) risk premium have on the rate of exchange? Consider US investors who find sterling investments risky. They buy sterling assets with some specific time to maturity and they may cover their foreign-exchange risk by selling sterling (the sterling that they will receive when their investment matures) forward. Let us assume, to keep matters simple, that the relevant interest rates in the UK and the US are equal. Under CIP the forward exchange rate will then be equal to the current spot rate. What happens if investors do not cover their foreign-exchange risk? To clearly see the mechanisms at work, assume that people at first do not demand a risk premium, but start doing so at some point in time. At a zero risk premium, expected yields in the US and the UK are equal. If interest rates are also equal, this implies that the expected future rate of exchange of sterling in terms of the US dollar is equal to the current spot rate: American investors will receive the same interest yield, whether they invest in the US or the UK, and do not expect to make a profit or suffer a loss on their present purchase and future sale of sterling. When they start demanding a positive risk premium, this means that sterling investments have become less attractive. The demand for sterling decreases and the spot rate falls. More sterling is received for every dollar, while the expected rate at which sterling can be changed back into dollars has remained unchanged, so that a higher return is expected from investing in sterling than from investing in dollars.

Alternatively, the American investors may seek cover on the forward market, either with banks in Britain or with banks in the US. If they seek cover with banks in Britain, they buy dollars forward and the banks will cover their own exchange-rate risk by buying dollars spot and investing these in the US. If they seek cover with banks in the US, they again buy dollars forward against sterling. The banks will neutralise their long position in sterling by borrowing sterling and converting it into dollars (the forward sterling bought from the investors will be used to amortise the sterling loan). Either way, the demand for dollars against sterling in the spot market increases and the exchange rate of sterling in terms of the US dollar falls.

If interest rates stay put, the forward rate will fall in step with the current rate, whereas the expected future rate is assumed to remain unchanged. The forward rate thus falls below the expected future rate. American investors have a choice between covering the foreign-exchange risk by selling sterling forward, in which case they are sure of receiving the same amount of dollars for each pound sterling as they have paid, and not covering that risk, in which case they expect to receive more dollars per pound sterling than they have paid but cannot be sure they will. Against the risk there is the mathematical expectation of a higher yield.

We see that with a risk premium the spot exchange rate moves in such a way that the expected return from unhedged investments in the United Kingdom becomes higher than from investments in the United States and from hedged investments in the UK. The risk premium is measured by the difference between the expected future spot rate and the current forward rate. It can also be seen as the expected profit from buying forward foreign exchange and selling the foreign-exchange spot upon delivery (note that definitions of the risk premium vary: sometimes it is defined as the forward rate minus the expected future spot rate rather than the other way round).

If a positive risk premium makes the current exchange rate fall, it follows that variations in risk premiums can be a cause of exchange-rate fluctuations. Such variations may result from changes in the shares of different assets in the wealth holders' portfolios or, given those shares, from fluctuations in risk aversion. Given domestic and foreign interest rates and the expected future spot rate, an increase in the risk premium r will depress the current spot rate and the forward rate and a diminution of the risk premium will make them rise. Diebold and Pauly (1988) found evidence of a varying risk premium in the D-Mark–dollar rate, but noted that it is hard to empirically separate this effect from market irrationality or rational bubbles.

A simple representation of the portfolio model is the following:

$$Ms = Md = a_1(i, i^f + x)\ W \tag{1.21}$$
$$Bs = Bd = a_2(i, i^f + x)\ W \tag{1.22}$$
$$eQs = eQd = a_3(i, i^f + x)\ W \tag{1.23}$$
$$a_1 + a_2 + a_3 = 1 \tag{1.24}$$

with x = expected change in the exchange rate,
W = nominal wealth,
Bs = supply of domestic bonds,
Bd = demand for domestic bonds,
Qs = domestic supply of foreign bonds, expressed in the number of bonds,
Qd = domestic demand for foreign bonds.

In order to avoid complications resulting from the impact of interest-rate changes on bond prices, it seems best to define both domestic and foreign bonds as floating-rate notes, the prices of which for all practical purposes are fixed. An alternative is to assume a very short time to maturity of the titles.

The fractions a of their wealth that domestic economic agents invest in the various assets are a function of domestic and foreign interest rates and of exchange-rate expectations. Perceived risk on domestic and foreign titles and preferences as to combinations of risk and expected return do not explicitly figure in the equations, but changes in these variables will change the functions. We now further explore the demand for and supply of foreign bonds with an eye to their impact on the exchange rate. Any combination of e and Qs that has the value $a_3.\ W$ (expressed in domestic currency) will fulfil the wishes of the economic agents. The product of the rate of exchange and the number of bonds is a constant. In a diagram with the number of bonds Qs on the abscissa and the rate of exchange on the ordinate, the demand for foreign bonds as a function of the rate of exchange is represented by an orthogonal hyperbola (see Figure 1.3). The number of foreign bonds can be taken as given in the very short term. The current account of the balance of payments is neglected and with free-floating exchange rates the central bank does not intervene in the foreign-exchange market; nor do commercial banks, for that matter. Neglecting the current account and with the official settlements account in equilibrium, the capital account cannot but be in equilibrium as well. Hence, the supply of foreign bonds cannot change. The demand schedule and the given supply of foreign bonds determine the rate of exchange. In this basic model residents hold foreign non-monetary financial assets but not foreign money and non-residents do not hold domestic financial assets.

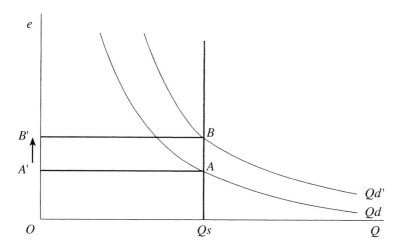

Figure 1.3   The rate of exchange and the demand for foreign bonds

In order to show the workings of the system we analyse what happens after a shock. We look at two cases:

(i) The domestic money supply increases (for example, as a result of monetary financing of government budget deficits). Total wealth increases and portfolio balance at unchanged interest rates and an unchanged exchange rate would require higher volumes of domestic and foreign bonds. However, bond supplies are fixed. An excess supply of domestic money and an excess demand for domestic bonds and foreign bonds ensue. The rate of interest on domestic bonds is driven down, but the foreign rate of interest and foreign bond prices are given for domestic economic agents. The only variable they can influence is the rate of exchange. An increase in the demand for foreign bonds drives up the rate of exchange from OA'

to OB'. The demand curve Qd for foreign bonds shifts upwards (for any given volume of foreign bonds a higher rate of exchange is offered) and to the right (at any rate of exchange more foreign bonds are demanded) (see Figure 1.3).

(ii) The perceived risk of investment in foreign bonds falls. This will affect demand for these bonds in a similar way as the first shock. They will become more attractive to the normal risk-averse investor. For any combination of i, i^f and x the variable a_3 in equation 1.23 increases and the demand curve again shifts upwards. In the case of an increase in the perceived risk of foreign investment, as discussed above, the demand curve conversely shifts downward of course.

The basic specification of the model admits of variants. One simplifying specification is to model the demand for money as a demand for transactions purposes only (see Branson 1985, p. 145). In that case, portfolio considerations are absent in money demand and wealth is not an argument in the money-demand function.

An interesting case presents itself when net holdings of foreign bonds are negative, as Masson (1981) has shown (see also de Jong 1983 and Branson 1985, p. 152). This means that domestic economic agents have a foreign-currency-denominated net debt *vis-à-vis* non-residents. Unlike the situation with positive net holdings, equilibrium situations may now be unstable. Let us first look what happens after a random shock when net holdings are positive. Consider a random upward shock of the exchange rate. The value of e, and therefore of eQs, rises above its equilibrium value. In the normal case, we see an excess supply of foreign bonds which will make the rate of exchange return to its equilibrium value. If $Qs < 0$, however, an increase in e will increase the value of foreign-currency-denominated net debt *vis-à-vis* non-residents. Economic agents want to reduce the share of this net debt in their portfolios and demand foreign-currency-denominated bonds (to offset foreign-currency debt with foreign-currency assets) or foreign currency (in order to pay off their debt). As a result, the rate of exchange is pushed further upward.

If expectations as to the future rate of exchange are stable, such destabilising processes need not occur. A rise of the exchange rate will be intensified if $Qs < 0$, but economic agents may expect a return to the original level or some level not too much higher in the future. After the exchange rate has passed that level, economic agents will therefore expect a future fall. The value of x in equations 1.21 to 1.24 will turn negative and the expected costs of having a foreign-currency debt fall. Debtors expect the foreign exchange needed to amortise their debt to be cheaper in the future. This reduces and finally brings to an end the net demand for foreign-currency-denominated bonds, or may even lead to an excess supply as investors wish to expand the volume of foreign-currency-denominated debt *vis-à-vis* non-residents. The rate of exchange stops rising or may fall again (see Branson and Henderson 1985, pp. 777ff. for a more formal analysis).

A problem with the theoretical portfolio models for the very short term is that the rate of exchange is a rate at which no exchange need take place at all. In the case of a free float, exchange-rate movements ensure that the existing volumes of domestic and foreign debt are willingly held by investors. As there are no net capital movements and the current account, including payments of capital income, is neglected, no international payments have to be made. The rate of exchange is not the price at which foreign currency is bought and sold; it is nothing but a numeraire linking the domestic and foreign-currency prices of foreign bonds. This problem disappears if we not only allow domestic agents to hold foreign debt but also foreign agents to hold domestic debt. The volume of foreign debt held by domestic agents need no longer be constant in that case, even if there are no net capital inflows or outflows: the volume of foreign debt held by domestic agents can increase if they succeed in selling domestic debt to foreign agents and decrease if they buy back domestic debt. Another possibility is that domestic agents hold both foreign debt and foreign currency. In that case it is again possible to change the volume of foreign debt held by domestic agents even in the very short term, this time not against domestic debt but against foreign money (see Section 1.4.3).

1.4.2 Safe-Haven Effects

A special kind of portfolio effect on exchange rates is the *safe-haven effect*. In the case of the safe-haven effect, domestic and foreign titles differ as to political risk and CIP no longer holds. Residents of a country may fear high future taxes. They may also hedge against future changes of government that may bring confiscation of their property, or they may prefer to hold funds abroad not only to evade taxes but also to escape the police. In general, the safe-haven effect does not so much concern a comparison between rates of return that induces people to invest abroad as a wish to keep the principal safely out of the hands of the domestic authorities or a fear of disturbances. Of course, confiscation can be seen as a negative return and a useful way of looking at safe-haven effects may be to view these as caused by a highly skewed subjective probability distribution of returns on domestic investment, that is, a high subjective probability of an extremely negative outcome. Safe-haven effects are a case of *capital flight*, but not all capital flight, however defined, is motivated by safe-haven considerations. Much of it, in particular from Latin America, resulted from a fear of negative real returns on domestic investments in a situation of double- or triple-digit inflation. Whatever the cause, fraction a_3 in the portfolio model represented by equations 1.21 to 1.24 rises at the expense of a_1 and a_2.

The idea that political factors play a role in capital flight has been corroborated in empirical research. A direct link between capital flight and various political risk variables, such as the number of assassinations per million of inhabitants per year and the extent of civil liberties, was made by Lensink, Hermes and Murinde (2000; see that article also on the question of how to measure capital flight). Collier, Hoeffler and Pattillo (2001) study capital flight in the context of the portfolio model and relate the share of flight capital in a portfolio to exchange-rate overvaluation, adverse investment risk ratings and high indebtedness of a country. All these factors add to the risks of domestic investments.

Apart from affecting the exchange rate, safe-haven phenomena and capital flight in general have another negative effect. As wealth owners cannot be expected to give the tax authorities a truthful report of their wealth or their capital income abroad, the country concerned will have lower tax income.

1.4.3   Currency Substitution

Another special case of portfolio diversification is the holding of both domestic and foreign currencies by a country's economic agents. If we include foreign money in domestic agents' portfolios, we have to add an equation to system 1.21–1.24. The expected rate of change of the exchange rate is also included as an argument in the various demand functions. This is because the demand for foreign money is first of all a function of expected exchange-rate changes; x reflects the expected return on holding foreign money. The system now becomes as follows:

$$Ms = Md = a_1 \, (i, \, i^f + x, \, x) \, W \qquad (1.25)$$
$$Bs = Bd = a_2 \, (i, \, i^f + x, \, x) \, W \qquad (1.26)$$
$$eQs = eQd = a_3 \, (i, \, i^f + x, \, x) \, W \qquad (1.27)$$
$$eMfs = eMfd = a_4 \, (i, \, i^f + x, \, x) \, W \qquad (1.28)$$

$a_1 + a_2 + a_3 + a_4 = 1$; $Mf =$ foreign exchange held by residents.

Apart from the aim of portfolio diversification, a reduction in transaction costs may be an important motive for firms engaged in foreign trade to hold foreign exchange (see Handa and Bana 1990 on transaction costs and their importance for currency substitution; obviously, the volume of foreign trade would be more important than wealth as a scale variable in this case; indeed, trade, along with interest differentials, was found to be an important determinant of currency substitution by Milner, Mizen and Pentecost 2000).

Shifts from domestic into foreign currency and vice versa can be an independent source of exchange-rate instability. Empirical research suggests, however, that currency substitution has not been a significant factor in exchange-rate movements between the currencies of the rich countries with comparatively stable currencies, that is, low inflation (Cuddington 1983; Laney, Radcliffe and Willett 1984; Batten and Hafer 1984). In countries with very unstable currencies, though, rampant inflation could induce people to replace domestic by foreign currency (unless financial institutions offer indexed deposits, as in Brazil; see Sahay and Végh 1995).

In many countries (Latin American countries, Vietnam) the US dollar functions as the substitute for the national currency. Currency substitution is also called *dollarisation* in such cases (sometimes this term is used to describe the use of the dollar as a means of payment, but it is also used to describe its use as a unit of account and a store of value). In Central and Eastern Europe the D-Mark, followed by the euro, has also been popular. Note that what is discussed here is *unofficial dollarisation*. The case of *official dollarisation*, where a foreign currency is adopted as legal tender, will be discussed in Chapter 6, Section 6.6.

A full picture is hard to come by, because there are no reliable statistics on currency (notes and coin) circulation, but researchers at the Federal Reserve System estimate that foreigners hold 55 to 70 per cent of US dollar notes, which, given that about $480 billion circulated in 1999, works out at some $300 billion. In 1995 a Bundesbank study put the percentage of German mark notes in the hands of foreigners at about 40 (Joint Economic Committee 2000). The share of foreign-currency-denominated bank deposits in broad money (M2) is another useful measure of dollarisation. Available data show that the flight from domestic currency on this measure may take quite substantial proportions. A few examples are Bolivia: 92.5 per cent, Peru: 78.2 per cent and Uruguay: 84.2 per cent, all at the end of 2000 (Berg, Borensztein and Mauro 2003). Obviously, currency substitution to the degree found in these countries may create quite a number of problems:

• Currency substitution means an increase in the demand for foreign exchange and thus can hardly fail to put upward pressure on exchange rates. On the one hand, this makes a country's exports more competitive. On the other hand, though, it gives an extra impetus to inflation as measured in the domestic currency, which was already high to start with (otherwise there would have been no currency substitution).

• More serious, perhaps, the volatility of exchange rates is likely to increase. With two currencies in circulation, the demand for domestic currency may become more sensitive to changes in its expected opportunity costs. In other words, the interest-elasticity of domestic money demand may become higher, leading to substantial shifts into and out of foreign money (IMF 1997b, p. 93).

• *Seigniorage*, that is, the revenue accruing to the government from the creation of base money (see Chapter 6, Section 2.2), falls. This is caused by a decline in the real balances held in domestic money under inflation, a decline which is steeper if there is currency substitution.

• Closely connected with this last result is the phenomenon that a money-financed government deficit will be more inflationary if the demand for real balances held in domestic money falls. This is because a given relative increase in M/Py requires a higher increase in P to restore real balances to the low level preferred by economic agents. A numerical example may help to clarify the point. Let $Py = 2$ and $M = 0.5Py = 1$ without inflation, $Py = 200$ and $M = 0.05Py = 10$ at some point during an inflationary process. The government runs a budget deficit of 10 per cent of Py and resorts to monetary financing. In the first case, M increases by $0.1\ Py$ or 20 per cent and, given real income, prices will rise in the same proportion. In the second case, by contrast, a 10 per cent increase in terms of nominal income, $0.1\ Py$, means a 200 per cent increase of the money supply and the price level will treble as well.

• The money-supply process becomes more expensive. If domestic economic agents want to add to their foreign-currency money balances and the domestic banking system (including the central bank) is unable to satisfy this need, foreign exchange has to be earned by running a surplus on the current account of the balance of payments or by foreign borrowing, both of which are more costly in terms of real resources than domestic money creation. The costs will be lower if domestic banks offer foreign-currency-denominated deposits without full cover by foreign-currency-denominated assets, but in that case the banks will be exposed to serious exchange-rate risks which may jeopardise their solvency. A depreciation of the domestic currency would increase their liabilities without a matching rise in their assets.

• Monetary policy becomes more difficult to plan and execute. This is because the demand for domestic money becomes less stable, so that the impact of monetary-policy measures on spending is harder to predict.

• Monetary policy becomes less effective, because changes in the domestic money supply or the domestic monetary base have less impact on domestic expenditure.

• Exchange rates between other currencies may be affected if people switch from one foreign currency to another. It has been argued, in particular by Hans-Werner Sinn of the Ifo Institute in Munich, that the fall of the euro *vis-à-vis* the dollar during the first three years after the euro's introduction in 1999 was partly caused by people in Eastern Europe and Turkey shifting from D-Mark banknotes into dollars (D'Amato 2001). This was because of uncertainty about the transition to the euro. In addition, individuals inside and outside euroland are reported to have bought dollars in order to get rid of their black-market holdings of the predecessor currencies of the euro.

If currency substitution takes the form of switching to deposits held abroad, monetary policy will be even less effective than in the case of a switch to foreign-currency-denominated deposits held at domestic banks. In the latter case, the monetary authorities can after all still try to influence the banks' activities, for example by setting required liquidity ratios, and the effects can be forecast with a somewhat higher degree of accuracy. Money-income relationships with monetary aggregates including cross-border deposits tend to outperform relationships including only domestic monetary assets (Angeloni, Cottarelli and Levy 1994). Under high inflation and a serious degree of currency substitution this is likely to be even more the case. It will be harder then to forecast the effects of monetary-policy measures.

Finally, it should be noted that if a steep increase in the rate of inflation may lead to currency substitution, the reverse is not generally true. The experience in a country such as Bolivia has been that even if inflation falls from a five-digit level (11,750 per cent in 1985) to a one-digit level (9 per cent in 1993), the foreign currency remains in use. This has been a common experience in dollarised countries (Reinhart, Rogoff and Savastano 2003). Possible explanations are a credibility problem for the domestic currency and the costs of again switching to another currency. Dollar inflows from drug trafficking may have played a role as well in some countries (Melvin and Peiers 1996), but it has also been suggested that a continuing high share of dollars in the money supply after a fall in the domestic inflation rate may reflect shifts in residents' portfolios from dollars held abroad to dollars held in domestic banks, following a return of confidence in the domestic banking system (IMF 1997b, pp. 92–3).

1.5 CONCLUSION

Asset models can explain the high volatility of exchange rates, even under the assumption of rational expectations. The possible causes are many and diverse. Current changes in the 'fundamentals' obviously play a role, but changes in expectations about future values of the fundamentals also immediately feed into the current exchange rate. The volatility of exchange rates can be further increased by the phenomenon of overshooting, speculative bubbles, varying risk premiums and currency substitution.

With efficient markets it cannot, within the framework of these models, be said that volatility is excessive, for with excessive volatility speculators would move in and make profits. Speculative bubbles, though, would seem to qualify this statement. If they are based on rational behaviour, it is not collective rationality. However convenient efficient markets and rational expectations may be as modelling devices, as representations of the real world they leave something to be desired. A fundamental problem is that there may be no such thing as a 'true' model that economic agents can discover. Nonetheless, 'fundamentals' seem to have reasonable explanatory power for exchange-rate movements over longer periods (see also Chapter 4). Portfolio models are much less restrictive than monetary models. Without a model for the real side of the economy, it will be difficult to use them for forecasting purposes, but they provide a framework for analysing which processes may have been at work in specific situations.

Of course, asset models are either incomplete models of exchange-rate determination or very extreme ones (in the case of the essentially friction-less monetary model). For more complete models we turn to Chapters 2 and 3.

APPENDIX 1.1. JENSEN'S INEQUALITY AND SIEGEL'S PARADOX

In our discussion of UIP we stated that the forward exchange rate equals the expected future spot rate, or $F_t = E_t e_{t+1}$. There is a snag here. If, for instance, this equality holds for the exchange rate of the euro in terms of yen, one would also expect the forward rate for the yen in terms of euro to be equal to the expected future spot rate of the yen in terms of euro, ds $1/F_t = 1/(E_t e_{t+1})$. This, however, is not generally true. That is because the expected future spot rate of the yen in terms of euro is $E_t(1/e_{t+1})$ and *Jensen's inequality* tells us that generally

$$E_t(1/e_{t+1}) > 1/(E_t e_{t+1}) \qquad (1.29)$$

This means that, if the forward rate of the euro in terms of yen equals the expected future spot rate of the euro in terms of yen, it generally cannot also be true that the forward rate of the yen in terms of euro equals the expected future spot rate of the yen in terms of euro. This phenomenon is called *Siegel's paradox*.

We will not provide a formal proof; a numerical example may be more helpful to grasp the point. Consider agents attaching a 30 per cent probability to a value of 125 for the future spot rate of the euro in terms of yen, a 20 per cent probability to a value of 160 and a 50 per cent probability to a value of 200. The expected future spot rate then will be 0.3 x 125 + 0.2 x 160 + 0.5 x 200 = 169.5. Under UIP the forward rate too will be 169.5. If the forward rate of the euro in terms of yen is 169.5, the forward rate of the yen in terms of euro is its obverse, or $1/169.5 \approx 0.0058997$. Is this equal to the expected future spot rate of the yen in terms of euro? There is a 30 per cent probability that the future spot rate of the yen in terms of euro will be $1/125$, a 20 per cent probability that it will be $1/160$ and a 50 per cent probability that it will take the value of $1/200$. The expected future spot rate of the yen in terms of euro will thus be $0.3 \times 1/125 + 0.2 \times 1/160 + 0.5 \times 1/200 = 0.00615$ and we see Jensen's inequality confirmed.

Underlying Siegel's paradox is the assumption that Japanese investors act in such a way that expected returns from holding uncovered rather than covered euro are zero in terms of yen, whereas European investors are assumed to act in such a way that expected euro returns are zero. No equilibrium can be found in this way (see Obstfeld and Rogoff 1996, p. 587).

NOTES

1. There is evidence that any predictable pattern in stock prices, the basis of chartism, disappears after it has been published in the finance literature (Malkiel 2003). Markets are efficient after all. There is little reason to believe that things are different for exchange rates.
2. Instead of tailor-made forward purchases or sales of foreign exchange, standardised transactions on futures markets are possible. On 16 May 1972, the world's first futures market in international currencies officially opened for business, the IMM or International Monetary Market, an offshoot of the Chicago Mercantile Exchange (Steinherr 1998, p. 166).
3. Berk and Knot (2001) find that UIP fares better in the 1980s than in the 1970s, thanks to increased capital liberalisation, but that there is no further improvement to be found in the 1990s. Flood and Rose (1999), however, argue that UIP works better than it used to do and especially that countries with a high interest rate tended to have depreciating currencies, which was far from the case in earlier periods.
4. A thorough discussion of real exchange rates and PPP, interpreted as an equilibrium relationship, can be found in De Grauwe (1989); see IMF (1990) for the calculation of various empirical real exchange-rate indices.
5. Irving Fisher himself found that it may take more than 20 years before the effects of inflation or deflation have fully worked their way into changes of the nominal rate of interest, and even then there is no 100 per cent adjustment (Fisher 1930, ch. XIX). Adjustment will have become faster over the years, but the interest rate on liquid financial instruments is less likely to adjust fully to inflation than the interest rate on less liquid assets. This is because liquid instruments are attractive substitutes for money, so that people will substitute non-monetary liquid assets for money under inflation (Coppock and Poitras 2000). Taxes levied on nominal rather than real interest income may also distort the picture. Still, in a study for ten countries over the January 1978–February 1997 period, Booth and Ciner (2001) found that generally a one-point increase in the expected inflation rate was associated with a one-point increase in the nominal one-month eurocurrency interest rate.

2. *IS/LM* for an open economy

2.1 THE BASIC MODEL

We study two small monetary macromodels for an open economy: the dependent-economy model in Chapter 3 and the *IS/LM* model in the present chapter. Both are models for the short term, that is, overall equilibrium in international payments does not necessarily imply equilibrium on the current account and the capital account of the non-bank sector separately.

We start from a standard Keynesian *IS/LM* model with rigid wages and prices and under-employment as the normal state of affairs. This implies that PPP does not hold in this model and that a nominal exchange-rate change is at the same time a change in the real exchange rate. The country in question is a small one, so if we extend the model to incorporate international transactions, export demand at any given rate of exchange and the rate of interest in international capital markets are taken as given.[1]

This tried and trusty workhorse of open-economy macroeconomics is known as the *IS/LM/EE* model (as we add an *EE* curve to the *IS* and *LM* curves) or *Mundell–Fleming* model.[2] It can be deployed for analysing how national income, the rate of interest and the rate of exchange or, in fixed-rate models, the money supply, react to various policy measures and to (other) domestic and foreign shocks. A number of simplifying assumptions have been made. In order not to unduly complicate our analysis, for instance, we abstract from the real-balance effect. Changes in the money supply consequently only make the *LM* curve shift; they do not work directly on the *IS* curve. In Appendix 2.1, this restriction and other restrictions and imperfections are discussed. In this chapter, only policy measures taken by an individual country are studied. The analysis of coordinated actions by several countries will be taken up in Chapter 5. We look at *permanent* shifts in the policy instruments, that is, movements to another level of the money supply or government expenditure. The impact of *temporary* shifts in the money supply and government expenditure is touched upon in Appendix 2.1. Finally, in the model there is only one rate of interest, to wit the interest rate on government bonds. It is assumed that other interest rates move in step with the government bond rate.

The basic version of the *IS/LM/EE* model is made up of three equations. It can be graphically represented by a diagram with three curves:

- the *IS* curve, representing the equilibrium conditions for the real side of the economy, or investment–savings equilibrium;
- the *LM* curve, representing the equilibrium conditions for the monetary side of the economy, or liquidity preference–money supply equilibrium;
- the *EE* curve, representing the equilibrium conditions for the market for foreign exchange, or external equilibrium.

The *IS* curve in the model for an open economy differs from its counterpart in the model for a closed economy in that its position and slope are also determined by imports and exports or, to be more exact, by payments and receipts on the current account of the balance of payments:

$$Y = Z(Y, i, T) + G + Ex(e) - Im(Y, e) \qquad (2.1)$$

Y = national income,
Z = private expenditure (consumption and investment),
i = interest rate,
T = taxes,
G = government expenditure,
Ex = receipts on the current account of the balance of payments,
e = rate of exchange,
Im = payments on the current account of the balance of payments.

The *LM* curve likewise is influenced by the balance of payments, as disequilibria in international payments affect the money supply:

$$Md = Ms$$
$$Md = Md(Y, i)$$
$$Ms = m.C$$

where Md = money demand,
Ms = money supply,
m = money multiplier,
C = volume of base money.

Base money is created through domestic credit granting by the central bank and through purchases of foreign exchange by the central bank (see Box 2.1). We abstract from foreign-exchange holdings of the commercial banks; international payments disequilibria of the non-bank sector are fully reflected in changes in the official foreign-exchange reserves.

The base money supply at any moment in time equals the base money supply one period back plus the change in the domestic credit supply D during that period and the change in the foreign-exchange reserves V. That change in its turn equals the balance-of-payments balance X of the non-bank sector.

$$C = C_{-1} + \Delta D + \Delta V$$
$$\Delta V = X$$

The instrument of monetary policy is open-market transactions through sales or purchases of domestic debt instruments by the central bank. The volume of open-market transactions (purchases) is denoted by $H = \Delta D$.

BOX 2.1.   BASE MONEY CREATION

Central bank balance sheet

assets	*liabilities*
D	C
V	

Notes:
D = domestic money supply
V = official foreign-exchange reserves
C = base money

We now have

$$C = C_{-1} + X + H$$
$$Ms = m(C_{-1} + X + H)$$

which leads to the following equation for the LM curve:

$$Md(Y, i) = m(C_{-1} + X + H) \qquad (2.2)$$

The equations for the IS curve and the LM curve represent the *equilibrium conditions* for the real sector and the monetary sector respectively. We add a *definition* of the balance of international payments:

$$X = Ex(e) - Im(Y, e) + K(Y, i) \qquad (2.3)$$

K = net non-bank capital inflow.

Equation 2.3 turns into an equilibrium condition if we put $X = 0$. With $X = 0$ the equation thus represents the EE curve.

2.2 MACROECONOMIC POLICY IN A FIXED-BUT-ADJUSTABLE PEG SYSTEM

2.2.1 Elaboration of the Model

With the help of equation system 2.1–2.3 we can study the impact of fiscal policy, monetary policy and exchange-rate policy on national income, the rate of interest and the balance of payments. In order to study the changes in the variables, we first take total differentials of the various equations. Diagrams showing the relevant shifts in the IS, LM and EE curves will be used throughout in order to get a clear picture of the various economic mechanisms at work. It is assumed that the economy returns very swiftly to the intersection of the IS and LM curves after a shock. If at that intersection $X \neq 0$, the money supply changes. Consequently, the LM curve, and with it the intersection of the IS and LM curves, shifts. Full equilibrium therefore is only reached when the LM curve cuts the IS curve at the intersection of the IS and EE curves. In order to be able to analyse situations where the real side and the monetary side of the economy are in equilibrium, but the balance of payments or market for foreign exchange is not, we use definition equation 2.3 and not the equilibrium condition with $X = 0$.

We start from a situation of full equilibrium with $X = 0$ and $H = 0$ and analyse the effects of a policy measure by taking total differentials of equation system 2.1–2.3:

$$dY = Z_Y.dY + Z_i.di + dG + Ex_e.de - Im_Y.dY - Im_e.de$$
$$Md_Y.dY + Md_i.di = mdX + mdH$$
$$Ex_e.de - Im_Y.dY - Im_e.de + K_Y.dY + K_i.di = dX$$

Subscripts denote partial derivatives.

Note that the variable T has disappeared. In our model, taxes T are a lump sum and fiscal policy solely consists of changing government expenditure G.

Fiscal policy consists of changing variable G, monetary policy implies a non-zero value of variable H and exchange-rate policy means a change in variable e. The variables G, H and e represent the instruments of macroeconomic policy and are thus *instrument variables*. Rearranging terms, with the dependent variables to the left of the equals sign and the instrument variables to the right, we find:

$$(1 - Z_Y + Im_Y)\mathrm{d}Y - Z_i\mathrm{d}i = \mathrm{d}G + (Ex_e - Im_e)\mathrm{d}e \qquad (2.4)$$
$$Md_Y\mathrm{d}Y + Md_i\mathrm{d}i - mdX = mdH \qquad (2.5)$$
$$(K_Y - Im_Y)\mathrm{d}Y + K_i\mathrm{d}i - \mathrm{d}X = (Im_e - Ex_e)\mathrm{d}e \qquad (2.6)$$

The slopes of the IS, LM and EE curves follow if we fill in zeros for $\mathrm{d}G$, $\mathrm{d}e$ and $\mathrm{d}H$, and in addition $\mathrm{d}X$ (non-zero values of the instrument variables will make the various curves shift, but do not impact on their slopes). For the slope of the IS curve we obtain

$$\mathrm{d}i/\mathrm{d}Y = (1 - \overset{+}{Z_Y} + \overset{+}{Im_Y})/\overset{-}{Z_i} \qquad (2.7)$$

Generally, this slope will be negative, unless Z_Y is much larger than 1. A negative slope means that, when national income increases, spending would increase by a smaller amount, *ceteris paribus*. A fall in the rate of interest would be called for in order to stimulate spending and maintain equilibrium in the real sector. If there is a high positive correlation between investment and national income, however, with $Z_Y \gg 1$, the IS curve has a positive slope. An increase in income leads to a sharp rise in investment in such a situation, and the rate of interest has to increase in order to restrain this rise and maintain equilibrium in the real sector.

For the slope of the LM curve we obtain, at any given money supply,

$$\mathrm{d}i/\mathrm{d}Y = -Md_Y/Md_i \qquad (2.8)$$

Generally, this slope is positive. The LM curve is vertical if $Md_i = 0$, that is, if money demand is interest-inelastic. The slope is zero and the LM curve runs horizontally if money demand is infinitely interest-elastic, that is, if Md_i tends to minus infinity. This is the case of the Keynesian *liquidity trap*. Note that the slope of LM will also be zero if not money demand but money supply, Ms, is infinitely interest-elastic. In that case, i = constant and the money supply adjusts to the volume of money demanded at the given rate of interest. The money supply is infinitely elastic if the monetary authorities want to keep the rate of interest constant and adjust H to that end any time equilibrium at the desired interest rate is disturbed, or if international capital flows are infinitely interest-elastic. In the latter case, any deviation of the domestic rate of interest from the international interest rate, or world interest rate, calls capital inflows or outflows into being that, through their impact on X, make the money supply adjust to the demand for money at the internationally determined rate of interest.[3]

The slope of the *EE* curve is

$$\overset{+}{}\quad\overset{?}{}\quad\overset{+}{}$$
$$\mathrm{d}i/\mathrm{d}\,Y = (Im_Y - K_Y)/K_i \tag{2.9}$$

In general, this slope is positive: a rise in national income makes imports grow; maintaining equilibrium in the foreign-exchange market implies (an increase in) net capital inflows and an increase in the rate of interest. A strongly positive correlation between capital inflows and national income ($K_Y > Im_Y$) will, however, make the slope of *EE* negative: with national income increasing, the inflow of capital has to be curbed by a fall in the rate of interest in order not to exceed the rise in import payments. In a small open economy, the *EE* curve may also run horizontally. This is the case if capital flows are infinitely interest-elastic. Again, a deviation of the domestic rate of interest from the world interest rate will trigger huge capital flows which will continue until the domestic rate of interest has adjusted to the world rate. K_i approaches infinity and the *EE* curve runs horizontally. The current account of the balance of payments is no longer important in this respect, as any imbalance will be swamped by capital flows.

With an eye to manipulating our system of equations and finding more exact outcomes for the results of the various policy measures to be discussed below, it is convenient to apply Cramer's rule. To this end, we write the system 2.4–2.6 in matrix form:

$$\begin{bmatrix} 1 - Z_Y + Im_Y & -Z_i & 0 \\ Md_Y & Md_i & -m \\ K_Y - Im_Y & K_i & -1 \end{bmatrix}\begin{bmatrix} \mathrm{d}Y \\ \mathrm{d}i \\ \mathrm{d}X \end{bmatrix} = \begin{bmatrix} \mathrm{d}G + (Ex_e - Im_e)\mathrm{d}e \\ m\mathrm{d}H \\ (Im_e - Ex_e)\mathrm{d}e \end{bmatrix}$$

We deploy Cramer's rule to calculate the effects of policy measures. We first have to calculate the Jacobian determinant, that is, the determinant of the matrix of first derivatives, which we denote as J_1:

$$\overset{+}{}\;\overset{+}{}\;\overset{-}{}\;\overset{-\,+}{}\;\overset{?}{}\;\overset{+}{}\;\overset{++}{}\;\overset{+}{}\;\overset{+}{}\;\overset{-\,+}{}$$
$$J_1 = -(1 - Z_Y + Im_Y)Md_i + Z_i m(K_Y - Im_Y) + mK_i(1 - Z_Y + Im_Y) - Z_i Md_Y$$

Generally, J_1 will be positive, but with a very large value for Z_Y (strong positive reaction of investment to changes in income) or K_Y (strong reaction of net capital imports to income changes) it may become negative. We will ignore this case.

2.2.2   Fiscal Policy

We now want to establish the impact of fiscal policy, that is, a change in *G*, on national income. We start from equilibrium in all three markets. *EE* cuts *LM* and *IS* in the intersection of *LM* and *IS*. An increase in government expenditure *G* will shift the *IS* curve to the right. A new momentary equilibrium is found at the intersection of the *IS* and *LM* curves at a higher level of national income and, unless the *LM* curve runs horizontally, a higher rate of interest. The position of full equilibrium depends on the balance of payments, that is, on the *EE* curve.

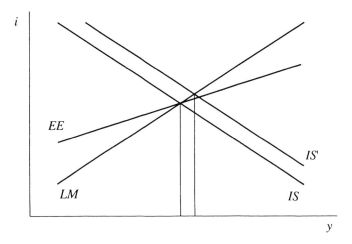

Figure 2.1   Fiscal policy with LM *steeper than* EE

First consider the case of the *LM* curve running more steeply than the *EE* curve (Figure 2.1). The shifted *IS* curve cuts the *LM* curve in a point above and to the left of the *EE* curve. At the given level of income, the rate of interest is above the rate at which international payments are in equilibrium. Capital imports exceed the equilibrium level. Alternatively, we could say that at the given rate of interest, income is below the level at which international payments are in equilibrium. Imports of goods and services, or more generally payments on the current account of the balance of payments, are below the equilibrium level. There are net receipts of foreign exchange which increase the money supply and make the *LM* curve shift to the right until it cuts the shifted *IS* curve in its intersection with the *EE* curve. After the first-round effect of the fiscal impulse, there is a second-round effect of the increase in the money supply, which is larger the smaller the slope of the *EE* curve.

We now turn to the case where the *EE* curve is steeper than the *LM* curve. The momentary equilibrium after the fiscal impulse is one of a deficit in international payments (Figure 2.2). The money supply decreases and the *LM* curve shifts to the left. The first-round effect of the fiscal impulse is partially undone by the deficit in international payments. Neglecting the income sensitivity of capital flows, it turns out that *the larger the interest-elasticity of capital flows, the larger are the effects of fiscal policy*. As for the interest rate, the larger the interest-elasticity, the smaller the change in the rate of interest that results from fiscal policy measures, thanks to the changes in the money supply associated with capital inflows and outflows.

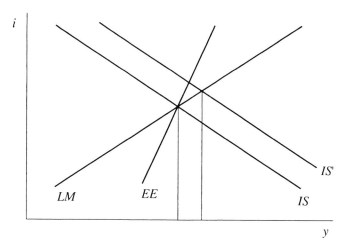

Figure 2.2   Fiscal policy with EE *steeper than* LM

It is worth noting that the coefficients of the system may differ between different situations. If a country for instance enters into an economic union with other countries, we may expect the marginal propensity to import to rise as the openness of the economy increases. That implies a faster leaking away of a fiscal impulse: Im_y increases and from equations 2.7 and 2.9 we see that the slopes of the *IS* and *EE* curves become steeper, making for a smaller change in income after a shift of the *IS* curve. Against this, capital flows will become more interest-elastic and in the final analysis fiscal policy may prove to have become more effective: the increased interest-elasticity of capital flows may swamp the effect of a higher propensity to import and make the *EE* curve flatter.

The system may also change through the actions of the authorities. When M. François Mitterrand became President of France in 1981, for instance, he embarked on an aggressively expansive fiscal policy, which shifted the *IS* curve to the right and led to current-account deficits. The policy package also kindled fears of inflation and thus of a future loss of competitiveness and a further worsening of the current account. The rhetoric of the government added to the public's fears that the government was not committed to maintaining the exchange rate. The end result was capital flight, leading to a shift to the left of the *EE* curve through a fall in the values of K_Y and K_i. The mounting deficit in international payments rapidly depleted the reserves of the Banque de France, the French franc devalued three times in less than two years and French macroeconomic policies had to make a U-turn (Sachs and Wyplosz 1986; Gros and Thygesen 1992, pp. 72–82).

Employing Cramer's rule, we want to calculate dY/dG and put both de and dH at zero. In the matrix of coefficients we substitute the first column by the vector of instrument variables:

$$\begin{vmatrix} dG & -Z_i & 0 \\ 0 & Md_i & -m \\ 0 & K_i & -1 \end{vmatrix} = -Md_i dG + K_i dG \tag{2.10}$$

In order to find dY we divide this outcome by J_1:

$$dY = [(-Md_i + mK_i)dG]/J_1$$

so that

$$dY/dG = (-Md_i + mK_i)/J_1 \geq 0 \tag{2.11}$$

This is the first-round effect resulting from the fiscal impulse (including the initial effect of X on the money supply and thus on the *LM* curve). Note that with $Md_i = 0$ and $K_i = 0$ the *LM* curve runs vertical and dY/dG = 0. With $K_i \rightarrow \infty$ we find dY/dG = $m/[m(1 - Z_Y + Im_Y)]$.
For the impact on the balance of payments, and with it the impact on the *LM* curve, we calculate dX/dG with the help of Cramer's Rule:

$$dX = \begin{vmatrix} 1 - Z_Y + Im_Y & -Z_i & dG \\ Md_Y & Md_i & 0 \\ K_y - Im_y & K_i & 0 \end{vmatrix} / J_1$$

$$= [Md_Y K_i dG - Md_i(K_Y - Im_Y)dG]/J_1$$
$$dX/dG = [Md_Y K_i - Md_i(K_Y - Im_Y)]/J_1 \tag{2.12}$$

dX/dG is positive if $Md_YK_i > Md_i(K_Y - Im_Y)$, or $-Md_Y/Md_i > (Im_Y - K_Y)/K_i$, that is, if *LM* is steeper than *EE* (see equations 2.8 and 2.9). If so, the *LM* curve will shift further to the right until $X = 0$.

2.2.3 Monetary Policy

We now turn to monetary policy. Monetary policy implies a shift of the *LM* curve. Normally, national income will increase after a positive monetary impulse, that is, open-market purchases. If the *IS* curve is vertical, however, a shift of the *LM* curve does not affect national income; there will only be an effect on the rate of interest. With a horizontal *LM* curve resulting from a liquidity trap, neither national income nor the rate of interest will change. With a positively sloping *LM* curve and a negatively sloping *IS* curve national income first increases after a positive monetary impulse. Whether *LM* is steeper or less steep than the *EE* curve, however, a shift to the right of the *LM* curve will move the intersection of *LM* and *IS* to the right of and/or below the *EE* curve. A positive monetary impulse in that way results in a balance-of-payments deficit of the non-bank sector (starting from equilibrium). The authorities may try to undo the impact of the deficit on the money supply, or *sterilise* the balance-of-payments effect, by further open-market purchases. If this goes on period after period the country's foreign-exchange reserves dwindle and it may become impossible to defend the existing exchange rate. Without sterilisation the *LM* curve will sooner or later return to its original position.

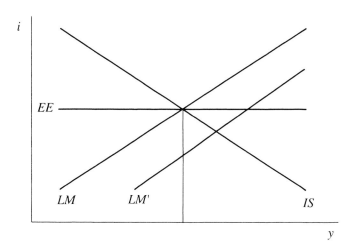

Figure 2.3   Monetary policy with fully interest-elastic capital flows

In the special case of perfect capital mobility (and swift adjustment), monetary policy is without any effect on the rate of interest and national income. Any tendency of the rate of interest to fall after an increase in the money supply immediately calls capital outflows into being which make the money supply return to its original volume. Every monetary impulse is neutralised by an opposite balance-of-payments change. Sterilisation becomes impossible. The *EE* curve runs horizontally and after a shock the *LM* curve immediately returns to the intersection of the *IS* and *EE* curves. Alternatively, it could be said that *LM* runs horizontally as well, as the money supply has become fully interest-elastic in this case and equilibrium on the Walrasian money market is only possible at the world interest rate (Figure 2.3). We find that *with fixed exchange rates, monetary policy is normally frustrated to a greater or lesser degree by cross-border money flows and in the case of perfect capital mobility it is even made fully ineffective.* Normally, not always: if the *IS* curve has an algebraically larger slope than the *EE* curve but a smaller one than the *LM* curve, a rise in the money supply will turn the non-bank balance of payments into surplus (Figure 2.4). If *IS* has a negative slope and *EE* a steeper negative slope we have a similar case. An *EE* curve with a negative slope follows from a high positive income elasticity of capital inflows, requiring a fall in the rate of interest for equilibrium to be maintained. If *LM* and *IS* then intersect to the right of *EE*, the balance of payments is in surplus. In both cases the money supply goes on increasing and the model explodes (until full employment is reached and the assumption of fixed prices has to be abandoned; further

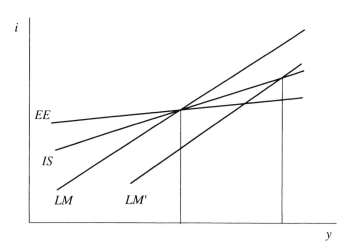

Figure 2.4   Monetary policy with IS *between* LM *and* EE

increases of the money supply then translate into inflation, which makes the curves shift).

As in the global monetarist model in Chapter 1, with perfect capital mobility the monetary authorities are unable to control the domestic money supply or the rate of interest. Monetary policy does, however, affect foreign-exchange reserves. A positive monetary impulse leads to capital outflows and a fall in the reserves of foreign exchange, while a monetary contraction leads to capital inflows and an increase in foreign-exchange reserves. On the central bank's balance sheet any change in the open-market portfolio (variable D in Box 2.1) will lead to an opposite change in the foreign-exchange reserves (variable V). The central bank's liabilities, that is, the volume of base money, remain unaffected. Monetary policy, therefore, is an important instrument for controlling foreign exchange reserves and, in particular, for preventing a steep fall in reserves, which would kindle fears of devaluation and so might spark off speculative attacks on the currency.

Reverting to Cramer's rule, we calculate dY/dH:

$$dY = \begin{vmatrix} 0 & -Z_i & 0 \\ mdH & Md_i & -m \\ 0 & K_i & -1 \end{vmatrix} / J_1 = -Z_i m.dH / J_1$$

$$dY/dH = -mZ_i/J_1 \qquad (2.13)$$

With a vertical *IS* curve, $Z_i = 0$ and, as a result, $dY/dH = 0$. In the case of a liquidity trap, with the *LM* curve horizontal, Md_i in J_1 approaches minus infinity and $dY/dH = 0$.

With dY/dH we have found the first-round effect. What is the effect on the non-bank sector's balance of payments? We calculate dX/dH:

$$dX = \begin{vmatrix} 1 - Z_Y + Im_Y & -Z_i & 0 \\ Md_Y & Md_i & mdH \\ K_Y - Im_Y & K_i & 0 \end{vmatrix} / J_1$$

$$= [-K_i(1 - Z_Y + Im_Y)m.dH - Z_i(K_Y - Im_Y)m.dH]/J_1$$
$$dX/dH = m[-K_i(1 - Z_Y + Im_Y) - Z_i(K_Y - Im_Y)]/J_1 \qquad (2.14)$$

$dX/dH < 0$ if $K_i(1 - Z_Y + Im_Y) > Z_i(Im_Y - K_Y)$, that is, if $(1 - Z_Y + Im_Y)/Z_i < (Im_Y - K_Y)/K_i$ (remember that $Z_i < 0$ and dividing by Z_i changes the sign of the inequality). From equations 2.7 and 2.9 it follows that the slope of the *IS* curve is smaller than the slope of the *EE* curve under this condition. With the normal, negative, slope of the *IS* curve and a positive slope of the *EE* curve this condition is fulfilled and a positive monetary impulse results in a balance-of-payments deficit of the non-bank sector (starting from equilibrium). This will move the system back to the point of departure.

With fully interest-elastic capital flows, K_i in the Jacobian J_1 approaches infinity and $dX/dH = -1$. Monetary policy is ineffective as far as the money supply is concerned and the *LM* curve runs horizontally.

2.2.4 Exchange-Rate Policy

Exchange-rate changes influence national income via the current account of the balance of payments. Consider a devaluation of the domestic currency, that is, a rise in the exchange rate e. The products of the country in question become more competitive in world markets and exports expand. On the other hand, foreign products become more expensive and spending on imports expressed in domestic currency may increase. National income increases and the *IS* curve shifts to the right if the increase in export earnings exceeds the increase in spending on imports: $Ex_e > Im_e$ (see equation 2.1 above). If we start from current-account equilibrium so that $Ex = Im$, we may divide the left-hand term of the inequality by Ex/e and the right-hand term by Im/e. For the left-hand term we write $-\varepsilon_f$, with ε_f the foreign price elasticity of the demand for imports (domestic prices are constant, so that $\delta Ex/Ex$ represents a relative change in volumes; remember that $Ex_e = \delta Ex/\delta e$ and $Im_e = \delta Im/\delta e$). Next substitute Im by $P.q$, with P the price of imports in terms of domestic currency and q the volume of imports. Given a constant foreign price level, the relative change in P is equal to the relative change in e. Furthermore, for marginal changes we may write the relative change in $P.q$ as the relative change in P plus the relative change in q. For the right-hand term we get:

$$(\delta Im/Im)/(\delta e/e) = (\delta P/P + \delta q/q)/(\delta e/e) = (\delta e/e + \delta q/q)/(\delta e/e)$$
$$= 1 + \varepsilon_d$$

with ε_d the domestic price elasticity of demand for imports.

For $Ex_e - Im_e > 0$ we now can write

$$-\varepsilon_f > 1 + \varepsilon_d$$

or

$$\varepsilon_f + \varepsilon_d < -1 \qquad (2.15)$$

This is the *Marshall–Lerner condition*. The Marshall–Lerner condition is predicated on the assumption of a constant domestic price level, that is, a fully elastic supply of goods, and current-account equilibrium at the point of departure. In Appendix 2.2 the *Metzler–Robinson condition* or *Bickerdike condition* is derived. This is a generalisation of the Marshall–Lerner condition providing for finite supply elasticities and current-account disequilibria to start with. Empirical research suggests that the Marshall–Lerner condition generally is satisfied at least in the long run (Boyd, Caporale and Smith 2001).

It should be noted that real income may fall as a result of a devaluation, even if nominal income and real production do not fall. After a devaluation, to pay for one unit of import good one must part with more export goods. This *terms-of-trade loss* is not reflected in our formulae.

A few examples may serve to show that the Marshall–Lerner condition should not be applied mechanically. Let us assume that a country starts with imports and exports both to the tune of 400,000 bn domestic currency units, say rupiahs, a year. The price elasticity of demand for imports in that country is –0.6. After a 1 per cent devaluation the volume of imports drops by 0.6 per cent, given a constant foreign price level. Rupiah prices of imports have risen by 1 per cent, the volume has fallen by 0.6 per cent, so the rupiah value of imports increases by 0.4 per cent, or Rp 1,600 bn. Let the price elasticity of exports likewise be –0.6. Foreign-currency prices of exports fall by 1 per cent and the volume of exports grows by 0.6 per cent. As rupiah prices of exports do not change, the rupiah revenue of exports also grows by 0.6 per cent, or Rp 2,400 bn. The current account improves by Rp 800 bn. With the price elasticity of export demand –0.4 and the sum of import and export elasticities –1, the increase in export earnings would equal the increase in import payments and the current account would remain in equilibrium. Using other values for our elasticities it will be easily seen that the current account will deteriorate if the Marshall-Lerner condition is not fulfilled.

We started from equilibrium. However, in the real world devaluations usually take place when the current account is in serious deficit. Let us assume that imports again amount to Rp 400,000 bn per year, but exports only reach Rp 250,000 bn. A 1 per cent devaluation makes imports again rise by Rp 1,600 bn, but this time around export earnings only increase by 0.6 per cent of Rp 250,000 bn, or Rp 1,500 bn. The current account deteriorates, even if the elasticities still sum to < –1.

So far, the current-account balance has been expressed in domestic currency. It should be noted that a deterioration of the current account in terms of domestic currency need not mean a deterioration in terms of foreign currency. This is because, after a devaluation, more units of domestic currency go into one unit of foreign currency. In the last numerical exercise, the deficit grew from Rp 150,000 bn to Rp 150,100 bn, or by two-thirds of 1 per cent. In terms of foreign currency the deficit by contrast decreased, by nearly 1 per cent. Let the relevant foreign currency be the US dollar. Before devaluation, the rate of exchange was, say, $1 = Rp 10,000. Imports amount to $40 bn and fall by 0.6 per cent or $24 million. Exports grow by 0.6 per cent but are sold at a lower dollar price, so total export earnings in terms of the dollar fall by 0.4 per cent of $25 bn, or $10 million. The current account improves to the tune of $14 million. Apparently, if we start with a current-account deficit the current account in terms of foreign currency may improve even if the Marshall–Lerner condition is not fulfilled and the current account in terms of domestic money deteriorates. Foreign currency may be the relevant unit of account for expressing the results of a devaluation if the aim of a devaluation is to ease the burden of debt in terms of foreign currency.

With the Marshall–Lerner condition we have, again, found a first-round effect. If national income increases, imports will tend to grow further and if supply is not fully elastic, prices will rise. The *absorption approach* tells us that, when all is said and done, the current account of the balance of payments will only stay in surplus if aggregate expenditure rises less than national income, or $\Delta Z + \Delta G < \Delta Y$ (cf. equation 2.1). The relationships implied can be quite complicated, depending as they do on such quantities as terms-of-trade effects on spending and saving and the monetary policy followed (see Tsiang 1989 for a painstaking exposition). A restrictive monetary policy, for instance, helps to prevent the initial improvement in the current account leaking away in too high an increase in imports. A devaluation will in that case, through higher prices of imports, reduce real balances. Depending on capital inflows, the rate of interest increases and both a higher interest rate and possibly the real-balance effect work to reduce domestic spending. Even if prices do not rise but national income increases, a fall in the ratio of real balances to national income M/Y will have similar effects.

The impact of exchange-rate changes on national income is found by:

$$dY = \begin{vmatrix} (Ex_e - Im_e)de & -Z_i & 0 \\ 0 & Md_i & -m \\ (Im_e - Ex_e)de & K_i & -1 \end{vmatrix} / J_1$$

$$= (-Md_i - mZ_i + mK_i)(Ex_e - Im_e)de$$
$$dY/de = (-Md_i - mZ_i + mK_i)(Ex_e - Im_e)/J_1 \qquad (2.16)$$

If e rises, national income, or at least real production, increases, provided $(Ex_e - Im_e) > 0$. Even if the Marshall–Lerner condition is fulfilled, a non-bank balance-of-payments deficit is possible instead of a surplus if capital outflows have a high income elasticity. The impact of an exchange-rate change on the non-bank balance of payments is found by Cramer's rule:

$$dX/de = [-Md_i(1 - Z_Y + Im_Y) + K_iMd_Y - Md_i(K_Y - Im_Y) - Z_i Md_Y]/J_1 \quad (2.17)$$

Equation 2.17 shows that dX/de will only turn negative if K_Y is strongly negative, or if the marginal propensity to import Im_Y is improbably high. Only first-round effects are considered in this approach.

2.3 MACROECONOMIC POLICY WITH FREE-FLOATING EXCHANGE RATES

2.3.1 The Model

Fully free floating means that the central bank does not intervene in the foreign-exchange market. As we assume that the commercial banks are not net buyers or sellers of foreign exchange either, we have $X \equiv 0$. *There is no balance-of-payments surplus or deficit influencing the domestic money supply.* A current-account surplus is always matched by net capital exports and a current-account deficit by net capital imports.[4] Equation system 2.1–2.3 changes into

$$Y = Z(Y, i, T) + G + Ex(e) - Im(Y, e) \qquad (2.1)$$
$$Md(Y, i) = m(C_{-1} + H) \qquad (2.18)$$
$$Ex(e) - Im(Y, e) + K(Y, i) \equiv 0 \qquad (2.19)$$

The endogenous variables now are Y, i and e, instead of Y, i and X. Note that equation 2.19 is an identity, unlike equation 2.3, which is a definition. Taking total differentials, we obtain

$$dY = Z_Y dY + Z_i di + dG + Ex_e de - Im_Y dY - Im_e de$$
$$Md_Y dY + Md_i di = m.dH$$
$$Ex_e de - Im_Y dY - Im_e de + K_Y dY + K_i di \equiv 0$$

The slopes of the *IS* and *LM* curves can be derived in the same way as in the fixed-but-adjustable rate case. An *EE* curve representing the pairs of i and Y for which equation 2.19 holds could also be drawn. It should be realised, however, that this model differs from the fixed-but-adjustable rate case in that we cannot hold the exchange rate fixed. We can no longer have a momentary equilibrium in an intersection of the *IS* and *LM* curves with the market for foreign exchange in disequilibrium. Every combination of i and Y at which the foreign-exchange market would be in disequilibrium makes the exchange rate change, which causes both the *IS* curve and the *EE* curve to shift in the i–Y plane. With infinitely interest-elastic international capital flows, though, the *EE* curve runs horizontally at the world interest rate, independent of the exchange rate. For every value of e there is another position of the *IS* curve and of the *EE* curve or, put differently, instead of curves in the i–Y plane, we have *IS* and *EE* surfaces in three-dimensional e–i–Y space. Only the position of the *LM* curve appears to be independent of the exchange rate, but this is because the price level is held constant. A change in the rate of exchange can, however, hardly fail to have an impact on the price level, as it makes domestic prices of imported goods change. If the domestic price level is a function of the rate of exchange, e should enter the money-demand function and the position of the *LM* curve would not be independent of the exchange rate. In most of the discussion, we ignore this complication. In order not to clutter up the diagrams we will leave out the *EE* curves and, in order to determine the shift of the *IS* curve after a shock, just ask ourselves which way the exchange rate moves.

When comparing model simulations for the free-floating system with those for the fixed-but-adjustable peg system, it should be borne in mind that the various coefficients may well have different values in the two cases. Volatile exchange-rate fluctuations in the free-floating system may, for instance, make business firms less eager to engage in international trade. Consequently, Im_Y and, perhaps, Im_e may possess a smaller value than in a fixed-but-adjustable peg system. This phenomenon should be kept in mind when analysing the possible effects of a shift in the exchange-rate system.

With an eye to applying Cramer's rule we rewrite equation system 2.1, 2.18, 2.19 in matrix form:

$$\begin{bmatrix} 1 - Z_Y + Im_Y & -Z_i & Im_e - Ex_e \\ Md_Y & Md_i & 0 \\ K_Y - Im_Y & K_i & Ex_e - Im_e \end{bmatrix} \begin{bmatrix} dY \\ di \\ de \end{bmatrix} = \begin{bmatrix} dG \\ mdH \\ 0 \end{bmatrix}$$

The Jacobian J_2 is:

$$J_2 = (Ex_e - Im_e)[Md_i(1 - Z_Y + Im_Y) - Md_Y K_i + Md_i(K_Y - Im_Y) + Z_i Md_Y]$$
$$= (Ex_e - Im_e)[Md_i(1 - Z_Y + K_Y) + Md_Y(Z_i - K_i)]$$

If the Marshall–Lerner condition is fulfilled, J_2 generally is negative, unless K_Y has a large negative value.

2.3.2 Fiscal Policy

Consider a positive fiscal impulse and fully interest-elastic capital flows. What will happen to national income and the exchange rate? The fiscal impulse will shift the *IS* curve to the right. However, the rate of interest will come under upward pressure and, capital mobility being perfect, capital starts to flow in. With full floating, the money supply is not affected and capital inflows will instead make the rate of exchange fall. This is a case of *real exchange rate appreciation*: the domestic currency appreciates, and as prices are sticky there is not only nominal but real appreciation. The current account of the balance of payments deteriorates, provided the Marshall–Lerner condition holds. The *IS* curve consequently shifts back to its original position.

With perfect capital mobility, there is only one possible level for the domestic rate of interest, to wit, the world rate of interest. Given that money demand is a monotonously decreasing function of the rate of interest, for any given money supply the economy is in equilibrium at one and only one level of national income. A change in G in that case cannot but be neutralised by an opposite change in the current account $Ex - Im$. *In a floating-rate system the effects of fiscal policy are weakened by capital flows, and with perfect capital mobility they are fully neutralised.*

In the absence of capital flows the rate of exchange will increase and the domestic currency will depreciate, as imports increase at the old exchange rate. A rise in the exchange rate serves to curb the rise in imports and to stimulate exports, maintaining equilibrium in the foreign-exchange market while giving a further boost to national income. Cases with finite elasticities of capital flows fit between these two extremes.

These results can be checked mathematically as follows. We first calculate dY/dG again:

$$dY = \begin{vmatrix} dG & Z_i & Im_e - Ex_e \\ 0 & Md_i & 0 \\ 0 & K_i & Ex_e - Im_e \end{vmatrix} / J_2$$

$$= Md_i(Ex_e - Im_e)dG/J_2$$
$$dY/dG = Md_i(Ex_e - Im_e)/J_2 \qquad (2.20)$$

If the Marshall–Lerner condition is fulfilled, we have $dY/dG \geq 0$. With perfect capital mobility, K_i approaches infinity. Divide both the numerator and the denominator of the right-hand term of equation 2.20 by K_i. It will be seen that, with perfect capital mobility, $dY/dG = 0$.

The movement of the rate of exchange can be found by calculating de/dG:

$$de/dG = [K_i.Md_Y - Md_i(K_Y - Im_Y)]/J_2 \qquad (2.21)$$

With perfect capital mobility both the numerator and the denominator on the right-hand term of equation 2.21 have to be divided by K_i. If the Marshall–Lerner condition is fulfilled, this yields $de/dG = -1/(Ex_e - Im_e) < 0$. The rate of exchange falls and the fiscal expansion causes an appreciation of the currency.

If there are no capital flows, we have

$$de/dG = Md_i.Im_Y/J_2 > 0$$

and the currency depreciates.

The domestic price level has been assumed constant. If it is a function of the rate of exchange, as in the model in Appendix 2.2, perfect capital mobility will not fully undo the results of fiscal policy: an appreciation of the currency makes the domestic price level fall and shifts the *LM* curve to the right. National income increases. Another point is that, whether the domestic price level falls or not, an appreciation of the currency makes real income increase because of an improvement in the terms of trade. More foreign goods are received in exchange for one unit of the domestic good.

2.3.3   Monetary Policy

Consider a monetary expansion. The *LM* curve shifts to the right, the rate of interest falls and national income increases, barring the case of the Keynesian liquidity trap where Md_i tends to minus infinity and the *LM* curve runs horizontally. The fall in the rate of interest induces capital outflows while the increase in national income would, at an unchanged rate of exchange, make for higher imports. At an unchanged rate of exchange more foreign exchange would have been demanded both on the current account and on the capital account. As a result, the rate of exchange will rise (the domestic currency depreciates). If the Marshall–Lerner condition is fulfilled, the current account will improve as a result of the depreciation and the *IS* curve shifts rightward as well. With perfect capital mobility it is easily seen how far the *IS* curve shifts. The rate of interest cannot change; the *IS* curve therefore will move until it cuts the *LM* curve in its new position at the given rate of interest (Figure 2.5). *Unlike the situation with fixed exchange rates, monetary policy is effective in the case of free-floating exchange rates,* provided that money demand shows finite interest-elasticity. With infinite interest-elasticity of money demand, the *LM* curve runs horizontal and a change in the money supply will not make the rate of interest move. Note that capital outflows in a fully floating system imply a current-account surplus to the same amount.

If capital flows have finite interest-elasticity and a high income-elasticity, a monetary expansion will lead to a higher income level, through the effect of a lower rate of interest on domestic spending (a shift along the *IS* curve). The income-induced capital inflows may, at the old rate of exchange, lead to an excess supply of foreign exchange. The rate of exchange will in that case fall and the *IS* curve shifts to the left.

If there are no capital flows, an increase in the money supply will make national income increase and imports will tend to rise. The current account of the balance of payments will worsen and equilibrium in international payments will be disturbed. The rate of exchange will rise to preserve equilibrium, exports will increase and the *IS* curve shifts to the right. So, if the Marshall–Lerner condition is fulfilled and there are no strong income-induced capital inflows, a monetary expansion will result in a depreciation and an increase in national income (abstracting from terms-of-trade effects), whatever the interest-elasticity of capital flows.

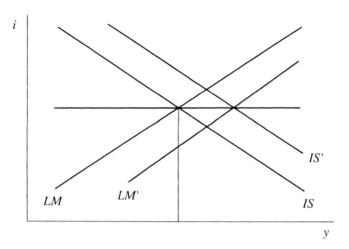

Figure 2.5 *Monetary policy with fully interest-elastic capital flows and free-floating exchange rates*

In the early 1980s the US dollar appreciated strongly against most other currencies. Within the framework of the *IS/LM* model explanations can readily be provided. To start with, the Reagan administration's fiscal policy was expansionary, whereas the Fed followed a restrictive monetary policy. The *IS* curve shifted to the right but the *LM* curve stayed put or shifted to a lesser extent. The rate of interest increased. Capital inflows proved highly interest-elastic and the dollar appreciated, while the current account deteriorated. The curious thing is that the dollar remained high, till February 1985, even after the high interest differential *vis-à-vis* the rest of the world had largely disappeared.

Possibly foreign investors expected a high growth rate of the US economy, making for a high value of K_Y (strictly speaking, Y should here be seen as *expected* rather than actual national income). Other possible contributing factors have been discussed in the preceding chapter.

Again, we check our statements. For dY/dH we find:

$$dY = \begin{vmatrix} 0 & -Z_i & Im_e - Ex_e \\ mdH & Md_i & 0 \\ 0 & K_i & Ex_e - Im_e \end{vmatrix} / J_2$$

$$= [(Im_e - Ex_e)K_i m.dH + (Ex_e - Im_e)Z_i m.dH]/J_2$$
$$dY/dH = m(Ex_e - Im_e)(Z_i - K_i)/J_2 \geq 0 \qquad (2.22)$$

The larger the sensitivity of money demand with respect to the rate of interest, the smaller the effect of monetary policy measures on national income at any given value of the interest-sensitivity of capital flows: the absolute value of J_2 increases and dY/dH becomes smaller. In the Keynesian liquidity trap, when Md_i and therefore also J_2 tend to minus infinity, $dY/dH = 0$.

With fully interest-elastic capital flows, K_i approaches minus infinity and dY/dH approaches m/Md_Y (divide both the numerator and the denominator of equation 2.22 by K_i to get this result).

For the movement of the exchange rate we find:

$$de/dH = [-mZ_i(K_Y - Im_Y) - mK_i(1 - Z_Y + Im_Y)]/J_2 \qquad (2.23)$$

If the Marshall–Lerner condition is fulfilled (see the formula for the Jacobian), $de/dH > 0$, unless K_Y is extremely large.

BOX 2.2. EFFECTS OF MONETARY AND FISCAL POLICIES WITH FULLY INTEREST-ELASTIC CAPITAL FLOWS

	Fixed exchange rates	Fully floating exchange rates
Monetary policy	ineffective	very effective
Fiscal policy	very effective	ineffective

2.3.4 Insulation against Shocks

Fully free-floating exchange rates have been advocated as a means to insulate an economy from foreign shocks. The *IS/LM* diagram helps in showing that the character of a shock is decisive in this respect. We consider a few cases.

(i) Assume first that foreign demand increases. Exports rise (the export function changes: at any level of the exchange rate exports assume a higher volume and value). The *IS* curve shifts to the right and the current account improves. Also, the rate of interest rises, inducing capital inflows. At the original rate of exchange there would be an excess supply of foreign exchange. As a result, the rate of exchange falls. This curbs exports and we see that floating exchange rates indeed soften the impact of foreign demand shocks. With fully interest-elastic capital flows, national income even stays put. Under a fixed-rate system by contrast, national income would increase: *IS* and *EE*, if not horizontal, would shift to the right, the market for foreign exchange would be in surplus and the *LM* curve would follow the rightward move. This is fine in a situation of unemployment, but may be undesirable under full employment because of the danger of overheating.

(ii) Next, consider the effects of a fall in the world interest rate. With a positive interest-elasticity of capital movements, this will induce capital inflows, causing a fall in the rate of exchange. Exports are curbed and imports are stimulated by this exchange-rate change and the *IS* curve shifts to the left (the *LM* curve does not move, as capital inflows do not make the money supply grow under full floating; instead, the current account deteriorates). This time around the shock is detrimental to economic activity. In order to undo the effects of the shock an expansive monetary policy would be called for. In a fixed-rate system a fall in the foreign interest rate makes the *EE* curve shift downwards and intersect the *IS* curve (which does not move in this case) at a lower point. The money supply increases, through capital inflows, shifting the *LM* curve to the right. National income increases. Neither exchange-rate system provides insulation, but a shock works out in opposite movements of national income.

(iii) If foreign demand increases, for instance, as a result of a *cyclical upswing* abroad, to such an extent that foreign interest rates increase by more than the domestic rate of interest, the picture changes. Against the downward pressure on the exchange rate resulting from increased exports we see an upward pressure resulting from capital exports. These capital exports take place not only because of higher foreign interest rates, but possibly also because of higher profit expectations associated with higher economic growth abroad (see MacDonald and Swagel 2000 for empirical research). The end result may well be an upward movement of the exchange rate, that is, a depreciation of the domestic currency.[5] Obviously, in this case there is no dampening of the external shock. Cyclical movements are transmitted internationally, not only under fixed exchange rates but also under flexible rates. Exchange-rate changes act as a brake on the cyclical upswing in the country where it occurs first, but as a stimulus in countries in another phase of the business cycle.

(iv) To make things more complicated, there is evidence that a demand shock that is expected to be short-lived works out differently from a shock that is perceived as persisting. In particular, research carried out by the Dutch central bank suggests that it is not so much a cyclical upswing that attracts capital inflows, but a longer-term expected high real growth rate. A higher growth rate in the US than in the rest of the world makes it attractive for non-American firms to take over American firms, which provide them with a distribution network in a fast-growing market and access to new technology. Capital flows then are largely in the form of direct foreign investment, which is assumed to be rather insensitive to non-persisting shocks. High real growth since the early 1990s thus made for a strong dollar, whereas the growth slowdown in 2001 initially did little to weaken it (De Nederlandsche Bank 2002). Only when low growth persisted did exchange rates react (though other factors may have reduced investment flows as well, an example being a drive by non-American firms first to restore capital–asset ratios which had suffered during the 1990s boom, leading to high interest payments on the debt they had incurred in the process).

(v) If, finally, the foreign price level rises, the country in question sees its competitiveness improve and the *IS* curve shifts to the right. As in the case of a foreign demand shock, the current account improves and capital imports increase. The supply of foreign exchange increases and the exchange rate falls, shifting the *IS* curve back. In this case, floating rates again provide protection, whereas in a fixed-rate system overheating of the economy would be a serious threat.

We may conclude that free floating offers (not necessarily full) insulation against isolated foreign demand shocks and foreign price shocks, but not against foreign interest shocks or foreign cyclical and longer-term movements, whereas fixed rates do not offer insulation in any of these cases.

But what about domestic shocks?

(vi) First consider an increase in domestic aggregate spending. This has the same effect as an expansive fiscal impulse. We have seen that with a high interest-elasticity of capital flows floating rates cushion the shock, but fixed rates do not. With a low interest-elasticity of capital flows the effect on national income is magnified under floating rates by a depreciation of the currency, but to a smaller or greater extent neutralised under a fixed-rate system through a fall in the money supply (caused by a balance-of-payments deficit).

(vii) Monetary shocks work like monetary policy. A downward shift in money demand, for instance, has similar effects to an increase in the money supply. If monetary policy is effective under full floating and a high interest-elasticity of capital, a monetary shock will under similar conditions not be cushioned. With a low interest-elasticity of capital flows a monetary shock will have a smaller effect, as a fall in domestic interest rates will not translate into large capital outflows and a large consequent rise in the exchange rate. Under a fixed-rate system a monetary shock will be cushioned more quickly, the higher the interest-elasticity of capital flows. Even with zero interest-elasticity of capital flows a higher money supply or a lower money demand will translate into a deficit in international payments, through higher aggregate spending and higher imports (unless the income elasticity of capital imports is positive and high). The money supply will fall and the effect of the shock will ebb away.

Flexible exchange rates often help to cushion the economy against external shocks. This is fine if shocks are infrequent and lasting, but with frequent or temporary shocks the costs of this cushioning may become very high. If the exchange rate bears the brunt when a shock occurs, the real exchange rate changes. With frequent shocks resulting in erratic movements of the real exchange rate, life becomes very difficult for business firms. Investments that look promising at some point in time may turn out to be unprofitable, because of a real appreciation of the currency, and thus severe foreign competition, a little later. Especially for small, very open economies, a system of fully flexible exchange rates may itself be a source of shocks (Buiter 2000a).

2.3.5 Sticky Real Wages

It should be kept in mind all the time that the results of the analysis in this chapter are predicated on the fixed-price and fixed-wage assumptions of the model. In Appendix 2.2 we will drop this restriction; at this stage it may be useful to study the effects of sticky *real*, rather than sticky or constant *nominal*, wages.

In a floating-rate system an expansionary fiscal policy is, as we have seen, ineffective in the case of fully interest-elastic capital flows. This is because an appreciation of the domestic currency nullifies the effects of fiscal expansion through a deterioration of the current account. However, an appreciation of the domestic currency makes domestic wage earners better off. Real wages increase, as one unit of domestic currency buys more foreign goods than before. If real wages are sticky this implies that nominal wages should fall. A fall in nominal wages reduces the domestic price level. Given the nominal money supply, real balances increase and the *LM* curve shifts to the right (with national income still measured in real terms along the abscissa). Fiscal policy is effective after all, even in the case of perfectly interest-elastic capital flows.

If sticky real wages make fiscal policy less ineffective in the fully floating-rate system, they make monetary policy less effective. If an expansionary monetary policy makes the domestic currency depreciate, foreign goods become more expensive. If real wages are sticky, nominal wages increase in that case. Real balances fall and the *LM* curve shifts back to the left, at least partly undoing the effects of monetary expansion. Higher nominal wages also undo the competitive advantage gained by the depreciation and the *IS* curve too will, after an initial rightward shift, move left again.

2.4   PORTFOLIO ANALYSIS AND INTERNATIONAL CAPITAL MOVEMENTS

In our *IS/LM/EE* model, capital flows were a function of domestic and foreign interest rates and of national income. Essential characteristics of capital flows are left out of account in this approach. The model abstracts from the impact of interest-rate changes on stocks and does not pay attention to questions of risk. The portfolio model, by contrast, considers both flows and stocks and investors decide not only on the basis of expected return, but also of risk. Risk is modelled as the standard deviation of possible returns to an investment with respect to its mathematical expectation. Through the assumption that investors are risk averse and attempt to reduce risk by diversifying their investments, portfolio analysis is able to explain a number of empirical facts that the basic form of the *IS/LM/EE* model is silent about. Coupling the portfolio model to the *IS/LM* model makes the latter more powerful. The difference between the portfolio model covered here and the one in the previous chapter is that in the present chapter wealth may grow (or fall, for that matter).

Assume that wealth holders in a country want to hold both domestic and foreign assets. The fraction of foreign assets in total wealth depends on

(i)   total wealth available for investments;
(ii)   international differences in expected returns, as represented by differences in interest rates;
(iii)   international differences in risk;
(iv)   the correlation between returns on foreign assets and returns on domestic assets, as perceived by economic actors;
(v)   preferences of economic actors as to the combinations of risk and expected return.

We start from an equilibrium situation in the sense that, at the given data of the system, the composition of all individual portfolios is optimal. No adjustments take place and, consequently, capital flows are nil. This means that *there may be international interest-rate differences without capital flows taking place*. Capital starts flowing only if at least one of the data changes. If wealth remains constant, a change in one or more of the data (ii) to (v) will cause an adjustment in existing portfolios. A *stock adjustment* takes place, and the corresponding capital flow is restricted in time.

Continuing capital flows are dependent on continuing changes in investible wealth. In that case, portfolio analysis admits *perverse capital flows*, that is, capital flows from countries with a relatively high expected rate of return on investments, or high real rate of interest, to countries with a relatively low rate of return, or low real rate of interest. This may happen if the country with a high rate of interest is relatively large (possesses large investible wealth) or if its rate of economic growth is high. A low foreign rate of interest results in a small fraction of wealth invested abroad. If wealth is large or grows at a fast pace, capital exports may nevertheless be quite substantial, though. Net capital exports from the high-interest-rate country therefore are a very real possibility. Similarly, net capital outflows from the high-interest-rate country are possible if the perceived risk of investments in the country with the high rate of interest is high. Furthermore, diversification by risk-averse investors, with an eye to spreading risk, makes it possible for *capital flows to arise in the absence of interest-rate differences*, provided the returns of investments in different countries are not fully positively correlated (Grubel 1968).

With investible wealth continuously changing, there will generally be a continuous flow of capital. If, in addition, at least one of the data (ii) to (v) changes, both changes in existing stocks and changes in the volume of the flows will take place. We now analyse what exactly happens in such cases (cf. Argy 1981, pp. 128–9). Foreign assets are held in domestic portfolios to the value of Q in terms of foreign currency or eQ in terms of domestic currency. The share of foreign assets in domestic portfolios depends on the difference between foreign and domestic interest rates:

$$eQ/W = b(i^f - i) \qquad (2.24)$$

with b depending on the factors (iii), (iv) and (v) enumerated above. Note that this approach is similar to that in Chapter 1 (see equation 1.24). In the present model, however, net inflows or outflows of capital may occur and the exchange rate e may be kept constant.

It should be noted that a formulation as in equation 2.24 excludes perfect capital mobility, which of course is appropriate for a portfolio model. With perfect capital mobility, the domestic rate of interest cannot deviate from the international one. Domestic and foreign assets are perfect substitutes, as in the monetary model. The share of foreign assets in portfolios is undetermined, not zero, as would follow from equation 2.24.

In order to study the consequences of changes in the variables $(i^f - i)$ and W, we take total differentials of equation 2.24:

$$e.dQ + Q.de = bW.d(i^f - i) + b(i^f - i).dW \qquad (2.25)$$

Capital inflows follow from sales of assets to non-residents. For the sake of simplicity, we assume that capital flows only result from buying or selling foreign assets, not domestic ones. Net capital inflow K (which may be negative, that is, a capital outflow) then equals minus the increase in the value of domestically held foreign assets:

$$K = -e.dQ = Q.de - bW.d(i^f - i) - b(i^f - i).dW \qquad (2.26)$$

Consider the case of an increase in the domestic rate of interest or a fall in the foreign rate. Investors want to decrease the proportion of their wealth held in foreign assets. With free-floating exchange rates we may expect the exchange rate to fall, or the domestic currency to appreciate, as the interest-rate rise will cause an excess supply of foreign assets. The proceeds of the sale make the supply of foreign exchange increase and the rate of exchange will fall. This in itself will go some way to reduce the proportion of wealth held in foreign assets. In equation 2.26 this effect is represented by the term $Q.de$ (note that de is negative in this case). Of course, with fixed exchange rates $Q.de = 0$. The *stock effect* is denoted as $-bW.d(i^f - i)$. Obviously, this is a short-term effect, for after the rate of interest (either the domestic or the foreign one) has changed, $d(i^f - i) = 0$ again. The interest-rate differential has changed but does not go on changing (if $d(i^f - i) < 0$, as in the present case, we have $-bW.d(i^f - i) > 0$; there will be a capital inflow, that is, a net sale of foreign assets). Such stock effects are neglected in models where capital flows are functions of interest-rate differences only. There is also a *flow effect*, as wealth holders invest a different fraction of new savings abroad after a change in the rate of interest. The value of $(i^f - i)$ has grown; in order to calculate the flow effect we have to deduct the continuing flow at the old rate of interest, $-b(i^f - i)dW$, from the continuing flow at the new rate of interest.

A change in perceived risk differences, correlations or preferences would have a similar result. The only difference is that in our formulas $(i^f - i)$ would be a constant and b would change. An increase in the risk associated with foreign investment, for example, would again result in higher net capital inflows, with in the short term both a stock and a flow effect and in the long term only a flow effect.

To recap: We discern three elements in capital flows (see Figure 2.6):

(1) the *original capital flow* resulting from growth in investible wealth;
(2) after a change in one or more of the data (ii) to (v), this continuing flow is increased or decreased by the *flow effect*;
(3) a change in one or more of the data (ii) to (v) will have in its wake a *temporary capital flow* or *stock effect* as existing portfolios adjust to the new vector of data.

The present model is a *stock-flow model*: both stocks and flows find a place in it. The *IS/LM/EE* model is a *flow model*; it abstracts from existing stocks. Considering that stocks vastly exceed the flow of new investments over periods of a quarter or even a year, researchers have also been content to deploy the other extreme, the *stock model*. In that model, $dW = 0$, as in the very-short-period portfolio model covered in Chapter 1. There is evidence that stock models perform quite well in the case of portfolio investment, whereas flow models fit the case of direct foreign investment better (Boertje and Verbruggen 1988). This is not surprising, as transaction costs, which did not figure in our analysis, will be relatively low in the case of portfolio investment but are often prohibitive in the case of direct foreign investment.

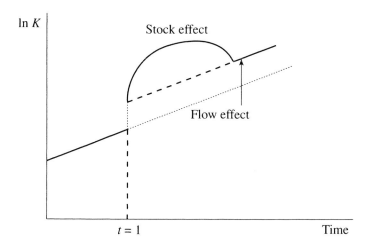

Figure 2.6   Stock and flow effects

2.5   OVERSHOOTING

In the discussion of the Dornbusch model in Chapter 1 we were confronted with the phenomenon of *overshooting*. This resulted from a lagged adjustment of the price level after a change in the money supply. The stock-flow portfolio model provides another case of overshooting. Here, overshooting results from the stock adjustment. If exchange rates are flexible, a change in any of the data (ii) to (v) may lead to a permanent change in the rate of exchange (or even an ongoing exchange-rate movement, depending on the specifications of the model) through the flow effect. The stock effect will make the exchange rate move further in the short term, but as the stock effect ebbs away the exchange rate returns to its new equilibrium rate (or growth path).

Overshooting may also result from a lagged adjustment of the current account after exchange-rate changes. After an exchange-rate change, import and export volumes need some time to adjust, given the relative price changes brought about by the appreciation or depreciation. This case demands fuller discussion. Consider a negative demand shock, for example a shift of demand to foreign products because of the availability of attractive new products (say a new generation of personal computers at low prices). *IS* shifts to the left and a depreciation of the currency is required to prevent a deficit on the current account (with interest-elastic capital flows a further depreciation would be necessary, as the domestic interest rate is likely to fall and the capital account of the balance of payments would tend to deteriorate). If trade volumes react slowly at first, a relatively large depreciation is called for in order to balance receipts and expenditure on the current account of the balance of payments.

As time goes by, imports decrease and exports continue to grow, so that the depreciation has to be partly reversed in order to prevent an excess supply of foreign exchange developing (with interest-elastic capital flows, the rebound should be larger, as the domestic interest rate will rise again and capital outflows will decrease). This process may be protracted if, as seems to have been the case in the United States during the first half of the 1980s, whole industries have disappeared because of a high value of the currency and a depreciation is slow in wooing back those industries, because set-up costs are high (Dornbusch 1987, p. 9). This *hysteresis effect* may necessitate a long period of undervaluation of the currency relative to its long-term equilibrium rate. Anyhow, we see overshooting occurring during the adjustment process to a new equilibrium rate.

If the Marshall–Lerner condition is not immediately fulfilled, the foreign-exchange market would be unstable without capital flows. Stabilising capital flows must come to the rescue in that case. A depreciation that temporarily increases the current-account deficit produces a *J-curve effect*, as the movement of the balance of the current account over time resembles the letter J. This J-curve effect raises the rate of exchange until speculators feel that after some period of time the rate of exchange is set to fall again to some extent.[6] These speculators then sell (owned or borrowed) foreign exchange, in the expectation that they will be able to buy it back at a lower price later. They may also sell foreign exchange in the forward market. The arbitrageurs who buy forward foreign exchange will hedge their positions by borrowing foreign exchange and selling it in the spot market against domestic currency. In either case the spot rate falls.

One may wonder if speculation via currency options would also help to stabilise the foreign-exchange market. Speculators who expect a future fall of the rate of exchange (that is, a future appreciation of the domestic currency) may buy put options on foreign exchange. Increased demand for put options drives their prices up. Some speculators will then find short positions on the forward market more attractive and in this way speculation through the options market will help to lower the spot rate.

With rational expectations and low transaction costs, or efficient markets, capital movements may even prevent any overshooting. Economic agents know the relevant economic model, they know how the data of the model have changed and they therefore know the new equilibrium value of the rate of exchange. Any tendency to overshoot will immediately be counteracted by stabilising speculation.

Leaving the fixprice assumption of the basic *IS/LM* model, it should be recognised that, although a flexible-exchange-rate system may help keep inflationary impulses from abroad at bay, overshooting can contribute to inflation. Overshooting in a downward direction makes imports more expensive in terms of domestic currency. This may give rise to wage demands that would not have been made if the rate of exchange had moved immediately to its new long-term equilibrium value. The price level or even the rate of inflation increases and the long-term equilibrium rate of exchange itself rises, if we make the reasonable assumption that the upward flexibility of wages is larger than their downward flexibility.

A further case of overshooting, resulting from frictions in inter-industry factor movements, will be discussed in Chapter 3.

APPENDIX 2.1   LIMITATIONS AND VARIANTS

A few comments on the model are in order.

(i) We start with a note on *fiscal policy* and *monetary policy* in the *IS/LM* model. Fiscal policy meant a change in $(G - T)$. Pure fiscal policy left the money supply unchanged. This can only mean that the volume of government debt (Treasury bonds) in private-sector portfolios changes, as budget deficits are financed by selling bonds to the non-bank private sector and budget surpluses can only be used to buy bonds from the private sector. The public's portfolios change as a result. At any level of Y the public will be willing to hold a changed volume of government debt with the money supply held constant only if the rate of interest changes as well. In other words, the *IS* curve shifts upwards or downwards. Monetary policy in the guise of open-market sales or purchases (including sterilisation of international payments imbalances) has similar effects, because it too alters the volume of bonds in private-sector portfolios. This *portfolio-balance effect* is neglected in the model presented in this chapter. A way to incorporate the portfolio-balance effect in the model is to add the relation between the volume of government debt and the money supply to the left-hand term in equation 2.2: as the fraction takes on a higher value with the money supply held constant, portfolio equilibrium requires a higher rate of interest (Blinder and Solow 1974).

(ii) Next, the *IS/LM* model is a *short-term model* in the sense that productive capacity is given. Shifts in fiscal policy may influence investments and hence future growth, however, but it is not *a priori* clear in what direction. For instance, higher government expenditure may mean that investments in the infrastructure increase at the expense of private consumption; it may also mean that collective consumption increases at the expense of private investment.

(iii) For the sake of simplicity, *the money multiplier m has been held constant*. It would have been more elegant to make *m* an increasing function of the interest rate, because a rise in the interest rate is equivalent to an increase in the opportunity costs of holding cash balances. The banks will reduce their liquidity ratio, at the cost of more frequent liquidity shortages that force them to borrow on the money market, and *m* increases. No qualitatively different results are to be expected, though.

(iv) *Expectations* generally are assumed to be either static or exhibit unit elasticity: economic actors believe that the various variables will not change within their time horizon, or they adjust expected future values of the various variables in proportion to present changes. Changing expectations can be accommodated within the model, though (as indeed happened in an informal way in Section 2.2.2 above).

(v) Then, there is an inconsistency in the model in so far as *price rigidity* is assumed. As we have hinted at already, a change in the prices of imports resulting from exchange-rate changes can hardly fail to change the domestic price level. This inconsistency can be remedied by distinguishing between the price of domestic production and the domestic price level, the latter a weighted average of the prices of domestic production and import prices.

Some of the defects discussed could be remedied by constructing a model that explicitly includes expectations with regard to the price level (or the inflation rate) and the rate of exchange and in which the price level is a weighted average of the price of domestic production and the price of imports. Such a model would, for the case of fixed-but-adjustable parities, look as follows (Bladen Hovell and Green 1989):

$$y = z(y, i - P^*/P + 1) + go + ex(e/Ph) - im(y, e/Ph) \tag{2.27}$$
$$Ms/P = md(y, i) \tag{2.28}$$
$$Ms = m(C_{-1} + X + H) \tag{2.29}$$
$$X = Ph.ex(e/Ph) - e.im(y, e/Ph) + K(i - i^f - e^*/e + 1) \tag{2.30}$$
$$Ph = Ph(y, e) \qquad Ph_y \geq 0, \ Ph_e > 0 \tag{2.31}$$
$$P = Ph^\alpha.e^{1-\alpha} \tag{2.32}$$

with y = real income,
z = real private expenditure,
P^* = the price level expected for the next period,
P = the actual price level,
$i - P^*/P + 1 = i - (P^* - P)/P$ = the (expected) level of the real rate of interest,
go = real government expenditure,
ex = real exports,
Ph = price level of domestic production,
im = real imports,
md = real money demand,
e^* = the rate of exchange expected for the next period.

Equation 2.31 admits of a non-fully-elastic supply of goods and also reflects the fact that a rise in the rate of exchange makes domestic production more expensive, as domestic production uses foreign inputs. The foreign price level is exogenous (the country in question is small).

With free-floating exchange rates equation 2.29 changes into

$$Ms = m(C_{-1} + H) \tag{2.33}$$

and equation 2.30 into

$$Ph.ex(e/Ph) - e.im(y, e/Ph) + K(i - i^f - e^*/e + 1) \equiv 0 \tag{2.34}$$

To work through this model would be very tedious. It is, however, possible to get a more intuitive idea of how flexible prices work out on the slopes of the various curves. If along the abscissa real production rather than nominal income or production is measured, the curves will run more steeply with flexible prices than with rigid prices. The *IS* curve represents the equilibrium condition in the real sector. With a fall in the rate of interest, private expenditure expands and the equilibrium income level increases as well. As income and production rise, the price of domestic production increases and domestic producers become less competitive (which is represented by a fall in e/Ph). This hinders exports and stimulates imports. Real national product rises, but not as much as under rigid prices (against this, the terms of trade improve).

An increase in nominal income implies monetary equilibrium at a higher rate of interest. With flexible prices, an increase in nominal income is partly a result of a higher price level and real income rises less. The *IS* curve will run steeper as a result.

The slope of a non-horizontal *EE* curve will also increase with price flexibility. Consider the case of an *EE* curve with a positive slope. An increase in the rate of interest induces capital inflows which allow higher nominal imports and a higher nominal national income level. With flexible prices, any increase in nominal national income is accompanied by a smaller increase in real national income and the *EE* curve turns anti-clockwise. In the process, export prices go up as well. With elastic demand, export receipts fall and the *EE* curve rotates still further to the left. With inelastic demand the leftward rotation is reduced, however.

Not only the slope but the situation of the *LM* curve may change as a result of price flexibility, as we have noted in the main text. A rise in the exchange rate for instance makes prices go up and makes the real money supply fall. The *LM* curve shifts to the left (see Minford 1989 for a formal analysis).

Various cases can also be constructed to illustrate the importance of expectations. An expectation of a future rise in the exchange rate, for instance, will induce capital exports and makes the domestic nominal interest rate differ from the foreign one under full interest-elasticity (cf. equation 2.34). These effects force us to modify the conclusions of our analysis of the effects of fiscal and monetary policies in Sections 2.3.2 and 2.3.3 (see Krugman and Obstfeld 2003, ch. 16, for a more extended analysis of temporary versus permanent changes in macroeconomic policies).

Ad Section 2.3.2

A fiscal expansion leads to an appreciation of the domestic currency. If, however, the expansion is thought to be temporary, economic agents will expect a depreciation in the future and interest parity says that the domestic interest rate will exceed the international interest rate. Consequently, the movement to the right of the *IS* curve caused by the fiscal expansion is not fully neutralised by a movement to the left caused by a worsening of the current account. This is because capital imports now start at a higher interest rate and thus at a higher national income. The appreciation will thus be smaller, as will be the deterioration of the current account. A temporary fiscal impulse, unlike a permanent one, has an impact on national income under floating exchange rates with fully interest-elastic capital flows.

Ad Section 2.3.3

A monetary expansion will raise the exchange rate and improve the current account. Both the *LM* curve and the *IS* curve shift to the right. If, however, people expect the money supply to fall again in the future, they will also expect a future fall in the exchange rate (a future appreciation of the domestic currency). Interest parity then requires a fall in the nominal rate of interest. Consequently, the *IS* curve can only move rightwards over a smaller distance, as its point of intersection with the *LM* curve has shifted downwards and to the left along the *LM* curve. The current account will improve less, with lower capital exports, and national income will increase to a smaller degree than with a permanent change in the money supply.

(vi) It is possible to add *wealth effects* to the model. Real expenditure can be modelled as a positive function of wealth. To that end, we could add *M/P* (which represents the *real-balance effect*) as an argument to the private expenditure function z in equation 2.27 and in addition, if bonds figure in the model, the nominal bond supply divided by the price level. An increase in the price level then makes the public poorer and reduces real private expenditure. This again makes the *IS* curve run steeper, if prices rise with the volume of production. Wealth can also be added to the money demand function. Price increases reduce real wealth and with it real money demand, decreasing the slope of the *LM* curve.

Wealth effects may also affect the results of an exchange-rate change. A devaluation, for instance, makes the price level rise. Private wealth is reduced and private expenditure falls. Both z_y and im_y fall. It is not *a priori* clear which way the *IS* curve will shift. The same goes for the *LM* curve: the volume of money demanded on the one hand falls, because of the reduction in wealth, but on the other hand it increases because prices rise. Probably, though, the demand for narrow money is not very sensitive to changes in wealth; wealth will be more important as an argument in the demand function for near money. This would imply that the *LM* curve shifts to the left on balance after a devaluation.

Of course, the rightward shift of the *IS* curve which follows upon a devaluation if the Marshall–Lerner condition is fulfilled will become less pronounced if the domestic price level is sensitive to exchange-rate changes, as the competitive advantage *vis-à-vis* foreign countries provided by a devaluation is partly eroded by the price increases in that case.

(vii) Finally, we introduce the *Laursen–Metzler effect*, also known as the *Harberger–Laursen–Metzler effect*, and the *Niehans paradox*. First the Laursen–Metzler effect. A devaluation may not only reduce real wealth, it also reduces purchasing power, or real income, in terms of a basket of domestic and foreign goods for any level of real income measured in terms of domestic products. This is because the terms of trade worsen, so that foreign goods become more expensive in terms of domestic goods. As spending does not generally fall in proportion to purchasing power, this means that spending (the variable z in our equations) as a function of real income expressed in domestic products increases and the trade balance worsens. An exogenous improvement in the terms of trade by contrast improves the trade balance (Laursen and Metzler 1950; Harberger 1950; see for empirical corroboration Otto 2003).

The Laursen–Metzler effect interacts with the *Niehans paradox*. Niehans (1975) argued that an increase in the money supply need not always result in a higher level of national income under free floating. This is, in his view, because in the short term the Marshall–Lerner condition may not be fulfilled. An increase in the money supply exerts downward pressure on the rate of interest. There is a tendency for capital to flow out and the rate of exchange will rise. However, if the Marshall–Lerner condition is not fulfilled, the current account of the balance of payments will deteriorate and capital will have to flow in. The exchange rate will have to rise to a level that makes it attractive for speculators to move in. The reasoning of Section 2.5 applies. As long as the Marshall–Lerner condition is not satisfied, monetary expansion will cause a contraction.

If a monetary expansion leads to a depreciation and the current account worsens because Marshall–Lerner is not satisfied, domestic spending suffers (the *IS* curve shifts to the left). Still, domestic spending need not decline if the Laursen–Metzler effect is operative (Ford 1990, ch. 4). The depreciation will lower the propensity to save, which means a rightward impulse on the *IS* curve. The Laursen–Metzler effect thus will weaken or even offset the consequences of non-fulfilment of the Marshall–Lerner condition on domestic spending.

Economic models allow of endless variations. It could be argued, for instance, that, if capital flows are not infinitely interest-elastic, the domestic rate of interest may fall after a monetary expansion, stimulating spending. This would work against the Niehans paradox. But if spending reacts with a lag to a fall in the rate of interest, there is still a place for the Niehans paradox, if only temporarily (Levin 1981). Another possibility is a negative reaction of investment to a fall in income which results from non-fulfilment of Marshall–Lerner after a depreciation. This would work against the Laursen–Metzler effect and in favour of the Niehans paradox.

APPENDIX 2.2   DEVALUATION, THE TRADE BALANCE AND THE TERMS OF TRADE

The Marshall–Lerner condition is a special case of a more general condition that must be fulfilled for a devaluation to improve the balance of trade.

This condition is known as the *Metzler–Robinson condition* or, after the British economist C.H. Bickerdike (1876–1961), who was probably the first to formulate it (see Metzler 1948, p. 228), the *Bickerdike condition.*
We start with the trade balance:

$$Tb^f = Ex^f - Im^f = P_{ex}^f.ex - P_{im}^f.im \tag{2.35}$$

with Tb = trade balance,
Ex = value of exports,
Im = value of imports,
P_{ex} = price of exports,
P_{im} = price of imports,
ex = export volume,
im = import volume.
The superscript f refers to prices and values expressed in foreign currency.

Taking the total differential yields

$$\mathrm{d}Tb^f = \mathrm{d}Ex^f - \mathrm{d}Im^f \tag{2.36}$$

or

$$\mathrm{d}Tb^f/Im^f = \mathrm{d}Ex^f/Im^f - \mathrm{d}Im^f/Im^f \tag{2.37}$$

We define

$\varepsilon_{Tb} = (\mathrm{d}Tb^f/Im^f)/(\mathrm{d}e/e)$ = the elasticity of the trade balance (in terms of foreign currency) with respect to the rate of exchange e.
$\varepsilon_{Ex} = (\mathrm{d}Ex^f/Ex^f)/(\mathrm{d}e/e)$ = the elasticity of the supply of foreign exchange, that is, the foreign-currency value of exports, with respect to the rate of exchange.
$\varepsilon_{Im} = (\mathrm{d}Im^f/Im^f)/(\mathrm{d}e/e)$ = the elasticity of the demand for foreign exchange, that is, the foreign-currency value of imports, with respect to the rate of exchange.

Now divide both the left-hand term and the right-hand term of equation 2.37 by $\mathrm{d}e/e$:

$$\varepsilon_{Tb} = (Ex^f/Im^f)\varepsilon_{Ex} - \varepsilon_{Im} \tag{2.38}$$

We trace the demand and supply elasticities of imports and exports underlying this equation. Demand and supply depend, *ceteris paribus*, on prices. Assuming equilibrium in the market for export goods, we have:

$$ex = S_{ex}(P_{ex}^f.e) = D_{ex}(P_{ex}^f) \qquad (2.39)$$

with S = supply and D = demand.
Taking differentials, we obtain

$$dex = (\delta S_{ex}/\delta P_{ex})(e.dP_{ex}^f + P_{ex}^f.de) = (\delta D_{ex}/\delta P_{ex}^f)dP_{ex}^f \qquad (2.40)$$

or

$$dex/ex = (\delta S_{ex}/\delta P_{ex})(1/S_{ex})(e.dP_{ex}^f + P_{ex}^f.de) = (\delta D_{ex}/\delta P_{ex}^f)(1/D_{ex})dP_{ex}^f \qquad (2.41)$$

Dividing by de/e and multiplying both the numerators and the denominators by P^f results in

$$\frac{\dfrac{dex}{ex}}{\dfrac{de}{e}} = \left[\frac{\delta S_{ex}P_{ex}}{\delta P_{ex}S_{ex}}\right]\left(\frac{\dfrac{dP_{ex}^f}{P_{ex}^f}}{\dfrac{de}{e}}+1\right) = \left[\frac{\delta D_{ex}P_{ex}^f}{\delta P_{ex}^f D_{ex}}\right]\frac{\dfrac{dP_{ex}^f}{P_{ex}^f}}{\dfrac{de}{e}} \qquad (2.42)$$

The expression within square brackets on the left-hand side is the price elasticity of export supply, s_{ex}, and the expression within square brackets on the right-hand side the foreign price elasticity of demand for import goods, ε_f. For equation 2.42 we may therefore write

$$\frac{\dfrac{dex}{ex}}{\dfrac{de}{e}} = s_{ex}\left(\frac{\dfrac{dP_{ex}^f}{P_{ex}^f}}{\dfrac{de}{e}}+1\right) = \varepsilon_f\frac{\dfrac{dP_{ex}^f}{P_{ex}^f}}{\dfrac{de}{e}} \qquad (2.43)$$

From equation 2.43 we derive the relative change in export prices in terms of foreign currency with respect to the exchange-rate change:

$$(dP_{ex}^f/P_{ex}^f)/(de/e) = s_{ex}/(\varepsilon_f - s_{ex}) \qquad (2.44)$$

As the supply elasticity is zero or positive and the demand elasticity zero or negative (we abstract from Giffen goods), this expression must have zero or negative value.

For small variations the change in export earnings may be represented as the sum of the change in volume and the change in price:

$$\varepsilon_{Ex} = (dex/ex)/(de/e) + (dP_{ex}{}^f/P_{ex}{}^f)/(de/e) \tag{2.45}$$

Substituting equations 2.43 and 2.44 in 2.45, we obtain

$$\varepsilon_{Ex} = (\varepsilon_f s_{ex})/(\varepsilon_f - s_{ex}) + s_{ex}/(\varepsilon_f - s_{ex}) = (\varepsilon_f + 1)/[(\varepsilon_f/s_{ex}) - 1] \tag{2.46}$$

For the import goods we, again, start off with the equilibrium condition

$$im = S_{im}(P_{im}{}^f) = D_{im}(P_{im}{}^f.e) \tag{2.47}$$

and find in a similar way as in the case of the export goods the elasticity of the demand for foreign exchange with respect to the rate of exchange

$$\varepsilon_{Im} = (s_{im} + 1)/[(s_{im}/\varepsilon_d) - 1] \le 0 \tag{2.48}$$

with s_{im} = the supply elasticity of imports (foreign exports) and ε_d = the domestic price elasticity of import demand.

Note that the elasticity of the demand for foreign exchange is non-positive. In other words, the demand curve for foreign exchange has no positively sloped section. The elasticity of supply, by contrast, may be positive, zero or negative. The supply of foreign exchange may, therefore, fall with a rise in the rate of exchange, that is, the supply curve may slope backwards.

Substituting equations 2.46 and 2.48 in equation 2.38, we obtain for the elasticity of the trade balance (in terms of foreign currency):

$$\varepsilon_{Tb} = (Ex^f/Im^f).\{(\varepsilon_f + 1)/[(\varepsilon_f/s_{ex}) - 1]\}$$
$$- (s_{im} + 1)/[(s_{im}/\varepsilon_d) - 1] \tag{2.49}$$

This is the *Metzler–Robinson* or *Bickerdike* condition. In the case of rigid prices and infinitely elastic supply elasticities (as assumed in the base version of the *IS/LM* model), equation 2.49 simplifies to

$$\varepsilon_{Tb} = (Ex^f/Im^f)(-\varepsilon_f - 1) - \varepsilon_d \tag{2.50}$$

If we start from equilibrium, that is, $Ex^f = Im^f$, we find the *Marshall–Lerner condition*. Note that the demand elasticities are zero or negative. If $\varepsilon_f + \varepsilon_d < -1$, $\varepsilon_{Tb} > 0$ and the current account improves. If $Ex^f/Im^f < 1$, that is, if we have a trade deficit to start with, the Marshall–Lerner condition is a sufficient but not necessary condition for the trade balance to improve.

We now analyse the effects of a devaluation on the *terms of trade*. For small variations we may write the elasticity of the terms of trade with respect to the rate of exchange as

$$\varepsilon_t = (dP_{ex}^{\ f}/P_{ex}^{\ f} - dP_{im}^{\ f}/P_{im}^{\ f})/(de/e) \tag{2.51}$$

The first term in the numerator is already known from equation 2.44. The second one can be derived in a similar way. Equation 2.51 develops into

$$\varepsilon_t = s_{ex}/(\varepsilon_f - s_{ex}) - \varepsilon_d/(s_{im} - \varepsilon_d) = (s_{ex}s_{im} - \varepsilon_f\varepsilon_d)/[(\varepsilon_f - s_{ex})(s_{im} - \varepsilon_d)] \tag{2.52}$$

The denominator in equation 2.52 cannot but be negative. A devaluation then makes the terms of trade improve if the numerator is negative as well, that is, if $\varepsilon_f\varepsilon_d > s_{ex}s_{im}$. The supply elasticities must be comparatively small, so that a change in demand causes a comparatively large price change.

If $\varepsilon_f\varepsilon_d = s_{ex}s_{im}$, the terms of trade do not change. If $\varepsilon_f\varepsilon_d < s_{ex}s_{im}$, the terms of trade worsen. Obviously, this happens when prices are rigid, as in the Marshall–Lerner case.

Note that the demand for and the supply of goods were functions of their prices only. This implies zero cross-price elasticities and no role for changes in income or the money supply. See Takayama (1972, chs 8 and 9) and Tsiang (1989) for analyses in which these restrictions are relaxed.

Source: This appendix is based on Lindert and Kindleberger (1982, Appendix H, which is marred by a number of typographical errors), Robinson (1950) and Takayama (1972, ch. 9).

NOTES

1. A diagrammatic two-country model, with large countries, can be found in Johnson (1972b); see Douven and Peeters (1998) for an algebraic two-country model with endogenous prices and wages.
2. Some authors, such as Minford (1989), reserve the Mundell–Fleming label for the case of fully interest-elastic capital flows; Mundell (1963) indeed restricts his analysis to this case, Mundell (1962) by contrast only covers the finite-elasticity case whereas Fleming (1962) encompasses both. For the early history of the model, see Boughton (2003).
3. In equation 2.5, dX or dH adjusts in such a way that $di = 0$. The implied values of dX or dH can be found from equation 2.5, which after rearranging yields $di/dY = (mdX + mdH)/dY.Md_i - Md_Y/Md_i$.

4. Note that capital exports imply purchases of foreign financial assets and thus foreign payments. Net capital exports therefore mean that the capital account of the balance of payments shows a deficit. In the same way, net capital imports are another term for a surplus on the capital account.

5. Note that we assume here a demand shock and capital flows with a positive income elasticity. Other cases are possible. If foreign production increases thanks to a supply shock, foreign prices will tend to fall relative to domestic prices and the rate of exchange will fall, unless capital flows push it up (cf. Stockman 1998).

6. For empirical studies on J-curve effects, see Doroodian, Jung and Boyd (1999), who found J-curve effects for US agricultural goods but not for manufactured goods over 1977 I–1991 IV; Gupta-Kapoor and Ramakrishnan (1999), whose results for Japan 1975 I–1996 IV support the idea of a J curve; and Wilson (2001), who could hardly find any evidence of a J-curve effect for trade of Singapore, Malaysia and Korea with the US and Japan 1970–96.

3. Dependent-economy models

3.1 THE AUSTRALIAN TWO-SECTOR MODEL

This chapter discusses the Australian two-sector model, which earned itself the 'Australian' sobriquet because the Australian economist Salter (1959) started this kind of analysis. In passing, some attention will be paid to a simpler, less elaborate model, the Scandinavian one. The Australian model is, just like the monetary model, of the neoclassical variety, in the sense that the price mechanism ensures full employment. This sets the model apart from the more Keynesian-oriented *IS/LM/EE* model, in which prices in principle are rigid or sticky or more generally not market-clearing, and full employment is only a special case. There are two sectors in the model: a tradeable-goods sector, producing exportables and importables (import substitutes), and a nontradeable-goods sector. This means that the dichotomy of domestic and foreign goods as found in the *IS/LM/EE* model is replaced by another dichotomy (Table 3.1 lists the differences between the two models). Like the *IS/LM/EE* model, this model is basically a short-term model. It can be used to analyse the impact of various shocks, originating both from abroad and from domestic sources, on the exchange rate and the balance of payments, in particular the current account. As constant full employment is assumed, monetary and fiscal policies have been relegated to the background.

The Australian model presupposes a small country. Like the Scandinavian model, it is, therefore, dubbed a *dependent-economy* model. The prices of tradeables are dictated by the world market. The Law of One Price (LOP) holds for tradeables: at the going rate of exchange they carry the same price at home and abroad. At the high level of aggregation of two-sector models this implies *constant (commodity) terms of trade*. In the model, export goods and import goods carry the same price tag and the terms of trade are not only constant, but unity. Consequently, *the Marshall–Lerner condition is irrelevant* in the two-sector dependent-economy model. Moreover, there is continuous full employment and supply elasticities are therefore finite, whereas Marshall–Lerner presupposes infinite supply elasticities. The domestic price of tradeables is determined by the foreign-currency price in foreign markets and the rate of exchange. The price of nontradeables by contrast is determined by domestic demand and supply. LOP does not apply for nontradeables. As a result, PPP does not apply either.

The price mechanism ensures full employment. Relative price changes of nontradeables and tradeables cause substitution both in production and in consumption (confusingly, in the literature the expression 'terms of trade' is not only used for the relative price of export goods in terms of import goods but also for the relative price of nontradeables in terms of tradeables or its obverse). A relative price increase of nontradeables makes it attractive for producers to increase the production of nontradeables and decrease the production of tradeables. They shift along the economy's transformation curve. Consumers, by contrast, shift from nontradeables to tradeables when the relative price of nontradeables rises. *The distinguishing characteristic of the model is that the nontradeables sector is in continuous equilibrium, while the price mechanism need not equate supply and demand in the tradeables sector.*

Dependent on the world market price and the rate of exchange, there may be excess supply or excess demand in the domestic tradeables sector. Excess supply implies a surplus on the current account of the balance of payments and excess demand implies a current-account deficit. With free floating, a current-account disequilibrium implies an opposite disequilibrium on the capital account; if capital flows are absent, no current-account disequilibrium is possible. In a free-floating system the domestic money supply is not affected by international payments. In a fixed-peg system a current-account disequilibrium need not be matched by an opposite capital-account disequilibrium. Instead, the domestic money supply may change. The monetary authorities are assumed not to sterilise liquidity inflows from or outflows to other countries.

The model is made up of three markets: the market for tradeables, the market for nontradeables and the (Walrasian) money market. The market for nontradeables and the money market are in all circumstances in continuous equilibrium, the market for tradeables is in continuous equilibrium only in the case of free floating without capital flows. In the following sections, we identify the equilibrium conditions for these markets and analyse the adjustment processes that follow upon a shock. First, we look at the fixed-peg system, then at the free-floating system; in both cases we first abstract from capital flows and subsequently assume perfect capital mobility. After all, it would be curious if the market for tradeable goods were perfectly competitive and the market for financial assets were not. We give both a formal representation of the model and a verbal plus diagrammatic explanation of the economic mechanisms underlying the model (the formal models derive from Frenkel and Mussa 1985).

Table 3.1   The differences between the IS/LM/EE *model and the dependent-economy model*

IS/LM/EE	Dependent economy
Dichotomy domestic goods/ foreign goods	Dichotomy tradeables/non-tradeables
Price rigidity and under-employment	Price flexibility and full employment
Variable prices of exports in terms of foreign exchange, finite price elasticity of demand	Prices of exports fixed in terms of foreign currency, Law of One Price
Variable terms of trade → Marshall–Lerner condition relevant	Fixed terms of trade → Marshall–Lerner condition irrelevant

3.2   THE BALANCE OF PAYMENTS IN A FIXED-PEG SYSTEM

3.2.1   Without Capital Movements

In this section the dependent-economy model under a fixed-rate regime is analysed. The equilibrium condition for the nontradeables market is:

$$Nd(z, q) = Ns(q) \qquad \delta Nd/\delta z > 0, \ \delta Nd/\delta q < 0, \ \delta Ns/\delta q > 0 \qquad (3.1)$$

with Nd = demand for nontradeables,
Ns = supply of nontradeables,
z = total real expenditure (in terms of tradeables),
q = the relative price of nontradeables in terms of tradeables.

Domestic real income in terms of tradeables is

$$y = ys(q) = Ts(q) + q.Ns(q), \ \delta ys/\delta q \geq 0 \qquad (3.2)$$

with y = domestic income,
ys = domestic product,
Ts = supply of tradeables.

Note that production capacity is fully utilised; real income in terms of tradeables increases when production shifts from tradeables to nontradeables, because such a shift implies an increase in the price of nontradeables in terms of tradeables. This explains why $\delta ys/\delta q \geq 0$.[1]

The demand for tradeables equals total expenditure less the demand for nontradeables:

$$Td(z, q) = z - q.Nd(z, q), \; \delta Td/\delta z > 0 \qquad (3.3)$$

with Td = the demand for T.

Generally, the demand for tradeables is an increasing function of q. It is, however, possible for the demand for nontradeables to decrease less than proportionally with an increase in q, given z, leaving less to spend on tradeables. We will neglect this special case.

For real expenditure we have

$$z = z(ys(q), i, A/P_T), \; \delta z/\delta y > 0, \; \delta z/\delta i < 0, \; \delta z/\delta(A/P_T) \ge 0 \qquad (3.4)$$

with i = rate of interest,
A = the real value of assets in terms of tradeables.

These assets are made up of the money supply Ms and bonds B. The price of bonds is independent of the rate of interest (Floating Rate Notes or call money). P_T is the price of tradeables; the argument A/P_T captures the real wealth effect. Real balances are defined in this case as Ms/P_T. The reason for using P_T rather than the general price level is a technical one: it makes it easy to connect the current-account imbalance expressed as an excess supply of or excess demand for tradeables with the resulting change in the money supply (see equation 3.10).

Expenditure is not only dependent on current income, but also on the rate of interest and wealth. Given the real bond supply, changes in wealth equal changes in real balances. In a diagram with real balances M/P_T measured on the abscissa and the relative price q of nontradeables in terms of tradeables on the ordinate, the equilibrium condition for the nontradeables market is a line or curve with a positive slope (Figure 3.1). This is because a higher relative price of nontradeables induces a shift in supply from tradeables to nontradeables, but a shift in demand from nontradeables to tradeables. In order to maintain equilibrium and prevent an excess supply of nontradeables, total expenditure has to rise, that is, real balances M/P_T have to increase. The $Ns = Nd$ curve, in other words, represents equation 3.1.

A similar diagram can be constructed for the tradeables market (Figure 3.2). In this case, the slope is negative. As q rises the relative price of tradeables falls; demand shifts to tradeables and supply to nontradeables. To prevent an excess demand for tradeables occurring, total expenditure, or M/P_T, has to fall. As the nontradeables market is in continuous equilibrium, the economy is always on the $Nd = Ns$, or NN, line or curve. By contrast, it need not be on the $Ts = Td$, or TT, line or curve. In a fixed-peg system the tradeables market, and with it the current account, can be in disequilibrium, whether there are non-bank sector capital flows or not. In the absence of non-bank capital flows a current-account deficit results in a decrease of the money supply and a current-account surplus in an increase.

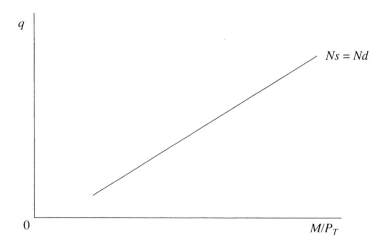

Figure 3.1   The equilibrium condition for the nontradeables market

We can now combine the graphical representations of the equilibrium conditions in the two markets in one diagram and add a section showing the current-account balance as a function of real wealth or real balances. The current account is in surplus to the left of the intersection of *NN* and *TT* and in deficit to the right of it (Figure 3.3). To the left of the intersection, *q* is below the value at which the tradeables market is in equilibrium (remember that the economy is on the *NN* curve). Tradeables are relatively expensive, the surplus of tradeables produced domestically over the volume demanded is sold abroad and the current account is in surplus. To the right of the intersection, *q* is higher than the value at which the tradeables market is in equilibrium. Tradeables are relatively cheap, there is an excess demand that is met by imports and the current account is in deficit. If there are no capital flows, a current-account surplus makes the domestic money supply increase and a deficit makes it fall.

Algebraically the analysis runs as follows. The Walrasian money market is in equilibrium if

$$Md/P_T(ys(q), i, q, A/P_T) = Ms/P_T$$
$$\delta Md/\delta y > 0, \ \delta Md/\delta i < 0, \ \delta Md/\delta q > 0, \ 0 < \delta Md/\delta(A/P_T) < 1 \quad (3.5)$$

The variable q is an argument in the real money-demand function, because a relative price increase of nontradeables makes the volume of money demanded in terms of tradeables increase. An increase in the money supply means an increase in wealth A/P_T and with it also an increase in the demand for money. In addition, it will cause a fall in the rate of interest.

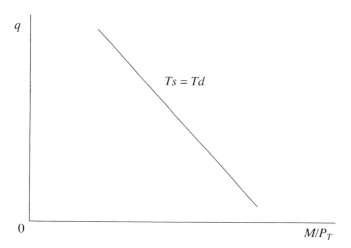

Figure 3.2   The equilibrium condition for the tradeables market

The economy is somewhere on the NN curve. The exact position on the NN curve depends on the money supply. Given P_T and Ms (and also B), it is seen from equation 3.5 that there are three unknowns, namely ys, i and q. As ys is a function of q, two unknowns remain. Substituting equation 3.4 in equation 3.1, we again obtain i and q as the unknowns. From the two equations 3.1 and 3.5 the two unknowns i and q can be solved. Given the money supply, we find a *momentary equilibrium*, that is, an equilibrium that will not be maintained if the tradeables market is not in equilibrium as well. This is because, in the absence of international capital movements, a disequilibrium in the tradeables market means that the money supply changes.

Denote the value of q associated with any momentary equilibrium by $q^\blacklozenge$ and the corresponding rate of interest by $i^\blacklozenge$. We then have

$$q^\blacklozenge = q^\blacklozenge(Ms/P_T, B/P_T) \ \delta q^\blacklozenge/\delta(Ms/P_T) > 0 \qquad (3.6)$$
$$i^\blacklozenge = i^\blacklozenge(Ms/P_T, B/P_T), \ \delta i^\blacklozenge/\delta(Ms/P_T) < 0 \ \delta i^\blacklozenge/\delta(B/P_T) > 0 \qquad (3.7)$$

The excess supply of tradeables, or the current-account surplus CA, at any moment equals

$$CA = Ts(q^\blacklozenge) - Td(z(ys(q^\blacklozenge), i^\blacklozenge, A/P_T), q^\blacklozenge),$$
$$\delta CA/\delta(Ms/P_T) < 0, \ \delta CA/\delta(B/P_T) < 0 \tag{3.8}$$

Given the relative price q and the rate of interest, the current-account surplus diminishes as real assets, and with them expenditure, increase.

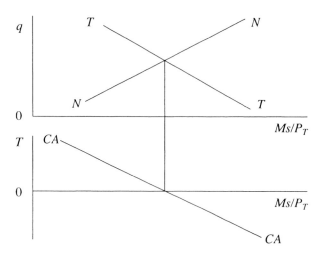

Figure 3.3   Full equilibrium

Naturally the current-account balance also equals the difference between domestic production and domestic expenditure. That relationship follows from equations 3.2 and 3.3, which, given that $Ns = Nd$, show that $Ts - Td = ys - z$. As an alternative to equation 3.8 we therefore have

$$CA = ys(q^\blacklozenge) - z(ys(q^\blacklozenge), i^\blacklozenge, A/P_T) \tag{3.9}$$

In either formulation, the current-account balance in real terms (that is, expressed in tradeables) is a function of $q^\blacklozenge$, $i^\blacklozenge$ and A/P_T, with $q^\blacklozenge$ and $i^\blacklozenge$ in their turn functions of A/P_T, or, with a constant bond supply, functions of Ms/P_T.

International payments imbalances lead to reserve flows that make the domestic money supply change in step. At any moment in time, the rate of change of the domestic money supply is

$$\dot{M}s = P_T.CA(Ms/P_T, B/P_T) \qquad (3.10)$$

Given B and P_T, there is one and only one value of the domestic money supply that is compatible with full equilibrium. At a smaller money supply the current account is in surplus and the money supply increases; at a higher money supply the current account is in deficit and the money supply falls (see Figure 3.3). There is an automatic equilibrating mechanism at work: increases in the money supply will make the system move upwards and to the right along the *NN* curve, decreases will make it move downwards and to the left. The adjustment process goes on until

$$CA(Ms/P_T, B/P_T) = 0 \qquad (3.11)$$

This is where *NN* and *TT* intersect in the diagram. Both the market for nontradeables and the market for tradeables are in equilibrium.

We have postulated equilibrium on the market for nontradeables at all times in our model, but the figure can accommodate imbalances if we drop the assumption of fully flexible prices. A decline in spending brought about by a fall in real balances will move the system to the left, and if relative prices do not adjust swiftly enough, the economy will land somewhere to the left of the *NN* curve. Given the value of q, aggregate spending falls short of the level required for equilibrium in the nontradeables sector, that is, there is under-utilisation of resources.

In order to show how the model works, we analyse the effects of various shocks, starting from full equilibrium, that is, equilibrium in all three markets.

(i) Consider a random increase in the money supply. Expenditure increases both through a wealth effect and a temporary fall in the rate of interest. Such a shock is automatically corrected in this model. Higher spending makes the economy move to the right along *NN* and the current account moves into deficit (if the economy was in full equilibrium to start with, an increase in spending can only mean that domestic absorption exceeds domestic production; the difference has to be made up by net imports). In the process, q rises. The current-account deficit in its turn makes the money supply fall. The economy moves back to the left and q falls again. Given the rate of exchange and P_T, a fall in q can only take place through a fall in P_N. In the real world considerable resistance against an absolute price fall is, of course, likely. The equilibrium in the nontradeables market comes under threat and unemployment becomes a distinct possibility. If then the assumption of fully flexible prices proves too far removed from reality, the adjustment process can be speeded up through a change in the rate of exchange. In the case considered here that would mean a devaluation of the domestic currency. The necessary fall in q is in that case brought about by a rise in P_T, which reduces real balances in the process and in that way helps move the economy quickly back to full equilibrium.

(ii) Now consider an increase in the propensity to spend on nontradeables. The demand function $Nd(z, q)$ changes, with the propensity to spend on tradeables unchanged. In other words, at any level of income and any price relationship more is spent on nontradeables than before and as much on tradeables as before. The government, for example, increases spending on social services, health or education without increasing taxes. Given the supply function, NN will shift upwards, for at any volume of real balances the relative price of nontradeables has to rise in order to fulfil the wishes of economic agents and step up nontradeables production. NN could also be said to shift to the left, for at any value of the relative price q, and thus any given production volume of nontradeables, real balances have to fall in order to neutralise the increased propensity to spend. NN intersects TT at a higher value of q and lower real balances. The CA curve shifts to the left in the process, as a moment's thought will make clear. If the NN curve has moved upwards and the nontradeables sector is in continuous equilibrium, an excess demand for tradeables develops at the level of real balances at which the current account was in equilibrium initially. This is because the relative price of nontradeables, q, has risen and the production of tradeables consequently has fallen, whereas the propensity to spend on tradeables has not changed. Another way of explaining the same phenomenon is that aggregate spending (domestic absorption) has increased, which, at full employment, cannot but result in current-account deficits. The current account turns into deficit and the money supply falls, until a new equilibrium is reached corresponding with the new intersection of NN and TT.

(iii) Next, consider an increase in the propensity to spend on tradeables. At any level of real balances, q has to fall (or, at any level of q, M/P has to fall) in order to enable tradeables producers to increase production. TT shifts downwards and to the left. Again, the CA curve shifts to the left because full equilibrium is only restored when the increased propensity to spend is offset by lower wealth. A current-account deficit appears at the original volume of real balances, real balances fall and this takes the system to the new equilibrium. The relative price q has to fall in the process and, as in case (i), it may be helpful to speed up adjustment by devaluing the currency.

(iv) Finally, another shock worth looking at is a fall in the world market price of tradeables. World demand may have fallen or new sources of supply may have been found. Under fixed exchange rates a fall in the world market price implies a fall in the domestic price of tradeables P_T. At the given nominal money supply the real money supply suddenly becomes larger and the relative price of nontradeables, q, increases. The system jumps upwards to the right along the NN curve. A current account deficit follows. The money supply, and with it aggregate spending, falls and the economy moves downwards again along the NN curve to the intersection between the NN and TT curves. Equilibrium requires a return of q to its initial value, but as P_T has fallen, P_N will have to fall as well. Note that the nominal money supply has fallen, but the real money supply has reverted to its initial value. In case prices are sticky, the pace of the adjustment process can be increased by a devaluation of the domestic currency, which is a fast way to reduce the relative price of nontradeables.

3.2.2   With Capital Movements

We now introduce international capital movements. Like domestic and foreign tradeables, for which LOP holds, domestic and foreign debt are full substitutes. The domestic rate of interest cannot deviate from the foreign one. Any imbalance in the money market will lead to outflows or inflows of capital at the world interest rate and the supply of money adjusts to any change in the demand for money. The balance of payments of the non-bank sector need no longer be identical with the current-account balance. Again, we study the effects of various shocks, starting from full equilibrium. Inflows and outflows of capital have an impact on economic agents' wealth. A change in net wealth may in its turn increase or decrease the propensity to spend. We will analyse these latter effects in Chapter 4.

(i) As in the preceding sub-section, we start with a random increase in the money supply. In the absence of capital flows, the economy automatically returned to the initial equilibrium. In the case of perfect capital mobility, economic actors will, as soon as the domestic interest rate tends to fall, buy foreign debt, again decreasing the domestic money supply and moving the system back to equilibrium. Further adjustments will occur if spending is a function of financial wealth (on this, see Chapter 4).

(ii) Next, let the propensity to spend on nontradeables increase (without the propensity to spend on tradeables decreasing). NN and CA shift to the left. We have seen that, in the absence of international capital flows, equilibrium will be restored at a lower level of the money supply. With fully interest-elastic capital flows, however, the money supply does not fall and capital imports will continue to finance the current-account deficit. There is no unique equilibrium situation. Full equilibrium will be restored, however, if there is a wealth effect for net foreign assets, that is, if increased foreign borrowing makes economic agents cut their spending. This case is analysed in Chapter 4.

(iii) Now let the propensity to spend on tradeables increase. *TT* shifts downward and to the left, as equilibrium requires a higher relative price of nontradeables and thus a lower value of q at any value of Ms/P_T, and the *CA* curve moves to the left. Will full equilibrium automatically be restored? In the case without capital flows a current-account deficit would reduce the money supply and, with lower real balances but still full utilisation of productive capacity, cause the rate of interest to rise. Total expenditure falls and the system moves back to full equilibrium. In the system with perfect capital mobility, by contrast, there is no mechanism that affects spending in the absence of the real wealth effect. With a real financial wealth effect, however, we again have a unique equilibrium, as will be shown in Chapter 4.

(iv) What happens if the world market price of tradeables falls? Capital flows will speed up the movement to equilibrium as sketched for the case without capital flows. In the first instance, real cash balances increase and the interest rate falls. Capital outflows result and contribute to the fall in the nominal money supply required to move the system to equilibrium again.

(v) The next shock is a rise in the world interest rate. This has no direct effect in the case without capital flows, of course. With fully interest-elastic capital flows, the domestic rate of interest cannot but rise by the same amount and expenditure falls. The system moves to the left along *NN* and a surplus on the current account of the balance of payments develops. The central bank and the private sector accumulate foreign financial assets. Further adjustments are analysed in Chapter 4.

(vi) An interesting case is when capital inflows suddenly stop. This happened in foreign-exchange crises such as in Chile in 1982 and during the Asian crisis in 1997 (Corbo and Fischer 1994; Visser and ter Wengel 1999). Capital imports fuelled spending, which in the nontradeables industries led to higher prices (both absolute and relative) and in the tradeables industries to excess demand, that is, a deficit on the current account of the balance of trade. The economy moved upward to the right along the *NN* curve. When capital imports suddenly stopped, the economy had to move to the intersection of the *NN* and *TT* curves, or even to the left of it, because the current account had to shift into surplus in order to generate the foreign exchange needed to pay interest and amortisation on foreign loans. All this called for a fall in q, in order to increase the production of tradeables. With fixed exchange rates, P_T is given and q can only fall through a fall in P_N. What we see in such circumstances is a collapse in real estate prices, but that only goes part of the way to the required change in q.

The shifts in the composition of aggregate production that go with a change in q are likely to cause unemployment in real life, because in the short term there are specific factors of production. Downward stickiness of wages and prices worsens the situation and the economy might well reach a point to the left of the *NN* curve. The neoclassical assumptions of our model sometimes have to be relaxed in order to better analyse real-world situations. Governments can increase the speed of the adjustment in such a situation by a devaluation, which lowers q in one fell swoop. For the current account to turn into surplus and for q to reach a lower value, domestic spending or absorption has to fall. To this end, monetary and budgetary policies have to be restrictive. The 1997 Asian crisis has shown that there is a danger of too tight fiscal and monetary policies being introduced. Aggregate demand is likely to fall even without tight macroeconomic policies. Business firms get caught between falling sales and rising interest rates and if the domestic currency devaluates while they have large uncovered foreign-currency-denominated debts, it may even be difficult to avoid bankruptcy. This would destroy capital and reduce real wealth. The financial sector is also likely to be severely hit, both because of such foreign debts on the liabilities side of the balance sheet and because of a sudden rise in bad debts on the assets side. Bank credit will be harder to get. All this will contribute to a fall in domestic spending. This means that the curves in Figure 3.3 will shift. A fall in the propensity to spend implies that at any value of q a higher value of real balances is required to make demand match supply. Both *NN* and *TT* (and consequently *CA*) will shift to the right. This means that monetary policy, and fiscal policy for that matter (which is one determinant of the economy-wide propensity to spend), should be less restrictive than might be deemed necessary at first sight (remember that restrictive budgetary measures make the curves shift to the right too). It may be noted that the IMF, which included restrictive policies in its rescue packages for Thailand and Korea after the Asian crisis broke out, was soon having second thoughts on fiscal policy (Lane et al. 1999, p. 16; Dawson 2002, p. 227). One may, furthermore, wonder if it is wise policy to try and reduce domestic spending or domestic absorption (the variable z in the present model, or $Z + G$ in the *IS/LM/EE* model) so drastically that a current-account deficit turns around into a sizeable surplus within a very short time, just to be able to repay foreign loans falling due. The question is especially pertinent in the case of countries without large fiscal imbalances, such as South Korea at the time. The alternative is to impose restrictions on international capital flows, a subject that will be discussed in Chapter 5, Section 6.

3.2.3 Applications of the Model in Policy Making

It goes without saying that the Australian two-sector model, predicated on full employment and price flexibility, does not faithfully describe real-world situations. Nevertheless, it appears that useful policy conclusions can be drawn from it. Both the IMF and the World Bank deploy this model for policy analyses. They are fully aware that nontradeable prices are usually characterised by downward rigidity, but that does not in the least remove the need for a fall in the relative price of nontradeables when the current account is in persistent deficit (see the annual reports of the IMF and the World Bank and various studies, such as Aghevli, Khan and Montiel 1991). A devaluation therefore often forms part of an IMF package. In addition, government budget deficits must be reduced. Debt-financed government expenditure not only tends to increase domestic expenditure directly, but also indirectly to the extent that it inflates the money supply. A reduction in government budget deficits helps curb domestic credit expansion, that is, the growth of Ms/P_T or A/P_T from domestic sources. In this view, both fiscal policy and monetary policy have to be restrictive in order for the current account to improve. A devaluation may be needed to bring about the required *expenditure switching*, that is, the shift of spending from tradeables to nontradeables through a change in q, and restrictive fiscal and monetary policies for the required *expenditure reduction*. Without this, total spending on nontradeables would increase, putting upward pressure on q and nullifying the effects of the devaluation through a movement along NN to the right in Figure 3.3. As the Asian crisis has shown, however, aggregate spending may also decline of its own accord, in which case strongly restrictive macroeconomic policies would be unnecessary or even harmful for the economy.

The IMF and the World Bank do not generally aim at bringing the current account of the balance of payments of developing countries into equilibrium. In their view it is perfectly normal for developing countries to run a current-account deficit and finance it with capital imports (see Chapter 5, Section 3 for a rationale). The economic policies followed by the government in question should, however, be sufficiently credible in the eyes of foreign investors to generate the necessary capital inflow.

Another case where the dependent-economy model was used for policy-making purposes was in Sweden in the 1970s, when people representing the Swedish employers' organisation and the trade unions, namely Gösta Edgren, Karl-Olof Faxén and Clas-Erik Odhner, developed a simplified version of the dependent-economy model with an eye to providing rules of thumb for wage policy. The model, which became known as the *Scandinavian two-sector model*, was published in the so-called EFO report (after the initial letters of the authors; Edgren, Faxén and Odhner 1969).

The model is made up of a tradeables sector and a nontradeables sector, but it neglects demand and supply reactions to relative price changes. Relative prices are only affected by technological developments. The basic idea of the EFO model is that the prices of tradeables are determined by the world market. With fixed exchange rates, the room for wage increases in the tradeables sectors is limited by world market price increases plus any productivity increases in the tradeable sectors. If the labour market is sufficiently competitive, or if wage policy is based on some notion of fairness which aims at equal rates of increase in the different sectors, wages in the nontradeables sectors and wages in the tradeables sectors will increase in step.

The EFO report expects productivity improvements in the nontradeables sectors normally to be lower than in the tradeables sectors. Consequently, price increases in the nontradeables sectors will exceed those in the tradeables sectors. If tradeables prices increase by a per cent and productivity in the tradeables sectors improves by b per cent, wages can increase by $(a + b)$ per cent without making the tradeables industry uncompetitive internationally. If productivity in the nontradeables sectors improves by c per cent and wage increases match those in the tradeables industries, nontradeable prices will rise by $(a + b - c)$ per cent. This can indeed be no more than a rule of thumb, because, first, demand and supply reactions in the nontradeables sectors are neglected; second, capital costs are abstracted from; and, third, no account is taken of the complications that may result from intersectoral trade in inputs.

3.2.4 The Balassa–Samuelson Effect

A similar reasoning as was applied in the EFO report can be used to explain why poor countries generally have a relatively low price level and rich countries a relatively high price level, at the going exchange rate, and why poor countries that are catching up will tend to show higher inflation rates (at fixed exchange rates) than countries with slow per capita income growth. Rich countries usually have much higher productivity in the tradeables sector than poor countries, whereas productivity in at least some of the nontradeable sectors differs by a much smaller degree. Examples that spring to mind are haircuts, education, nursing and cleaning. If labour productivity in a European steel factory is, say, ten times as high as in an Indian steel company, steel workers in Europe will earn roughly ten times as much as their Indian colleagues. If hairdressers by contrast have about the same productivity in Europe as in India and wages for hairdressers are comparable with those in tradeables industries such as steel, it follows that haircuts will be about ten times as expensive in Europe as in India. By and large, nontradeables will thus tend to be relatively expensive in the richer countries. As a tribute to the seminal articles by Balassa (1964) and Samuelson (1964) on the subject, the phenomenon is known as the *Balassa–Samuelson effect*.[2]

When a poor country is catching up with richer countries, productivity in its tradeables industries will increase faster than in richer countries with slower growth of per capita income. Under LOP, the prices of tradeables move in step with those in richer countries. Wages, however, rise faster, given those higher productivity increases. Prices in the nontradeables industries, where productivity increases lag behind, will consequently go up at a faster pace in the fast-growth countries than in slow-growth countries. The average price level in such countries will thus increase *vis-à-vis* other countries. In other words, there is *real-exchange-rate appreciation*. It has been found, for instance, that the Balassa–Samuelson effect accounts for more than 1 percentage point of the inflation differential between Greece and a number of other European countries during 1960–96 (Swagel 1999).

Not surprisingly, the Balassa–Samuelson effect is less well established across industrialised countries (Rogoff 1996, p. 662). Still, Alexius and Nilson (2000) found that among 15 OECD countries during 1960–96 high relative productivity growth was associated with an appreciation of the real exchange rate in most cases. The Balassa–Samuelson effect provides a possible explanation.

Of course, a real-exchange-rate appreciation resulting from the Balassa–Samuelson effect may also occur through a nominal-exchange-rate appreciation, instead of through higher inflation. Tille, Stoffels and Gorbachev (2001), for instance, attribute nearly two-thirds of the dollar's appreciation against the euro in the 1990s and three-quarters of its appreciation against the yen to the Balassa–Samuelson effect. Note that this is an alternative explanation to the one given in Chapter 2, Section 2.3.4, which also started from a difference in growth rates between the US and other parts of the world, but explained the rise of the dollar by capital flows (though this explained a smaller part of the rise than Tille, Stoffels and Gorbachev). These explanations do not exclude each other.

A note of caution regarding empirical estimates of the Balassa–Samuelson effect is in order. The model explains the mechanisms at work with the help of simplifying assumptions. In the real world LOP does not apply, wage levels between sectors may diverge and there is no clear dividing line between tradeables and nontradeables. Services such as education and health care, which used to be largely nontradeables, or at least non-traded, assume the character of tradeables more and more, thanks to deregulation, better information on foreign supply and easier travel. Nor does the basic model provide for inter-sector trade. All this does not make the reasoning less valid; it only means that empirical estimates of the effect should be regarded with a degree of suspicion.

3.2.5   An Alternative Diagram

Another diagram that can be used to analyse the Australian two-sector world is the one Salter deployed in his article and which is known as the *Salter diagram*. It is made up of a transformation curve and a set of macroeconomic indifference curves, with the volumes of tradeables and nontradeables measured on the axes.

In Figure 3.4 we start from the situation depicted by *D*. The relative price *q* is represented by the slope of *HH'* which equals the slope of *GG'*. The production point is *B*. Income in terms of nontradeables is *OG* and in terms of tradeables it is *OG'*. Aggregate expenditure in terms of nontradeables is *OH*, in terms of tradeables it is *OH'*. Spending exceeds income. There is a national savings deficit, which equals the current-account deficit *BD = GH*.

The problem faced by the policy makers is how to eliminate the current-account deficit without jeopardising full employment. First reduce aggregate spending, or absorption, at given relative prices. The absorption point shifts along the income–expenditure curve *OZ* towards the origin *O*. We find that a reduction of aggregate expenditure to *OG* at given relative prices is not a satisfying solution. The absorption point is *C*, where there is still an excess demand for tradeables, and in addition an excess supply of nontradeables. A reduction of aggregate expenditure to *OF*, with *E* the absorption point, would eliminate the current-account deficit but cause

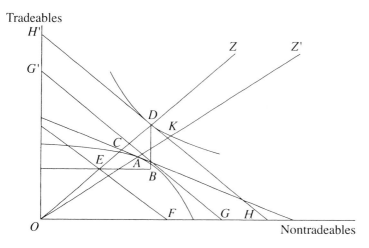

Source: Based on Corden (1978, p. 20).

Figure 3.4   The Salter diagram with a current-account deficit

considerable unemployment. Clearly, one cannot rely on a reduction in aggregate spending alone. In addition, relative prices have to change. Again, not only expenditure-reducing policies but also expenditure-switching policies are called for. It is evident that the relative price of nontradeables *q* has to fall, for at *E*, with the current account and the tradeables market in equilibrium, nontradeables were in excess supply. The tangent to the transformation curve will have to run flatter. At *A* both the tradeables and nontradeables markets are in equilibrium. At that point the transformation curve is tangential to an indifference curve. Expenditure switching alone would not suffice either. It would only move the economy from *D* to *K*.

3.3   FLEXIBLE EXCHANGE RATES

3.3.1   Without Capital Movements

We now turn to the flexible-rate system, first without capital flows. The model slightly differs from the one we studied above. First, the exchange rate is explicitly introduced and second, real cash balances have the usual definition of M/P (there is no longer a link between current-account imbalances, that is, an excess supply of or demand for tradeables, and the money supply and it is therefore no longer expedient to express the real money supply in terms of tradeables). Further, we employ a Cambridge-type money-demand function:

$$Md = kPy^{\alpha}i^{-\beta} \qquad (3.12)$$

In the present model, the interest rate *i* rather than real balances M/P is a pivotal variable. The Cambridge money-demand function serves to link M/P explicitly to *i*. Note that, unlike the money-demand function in equation 3.5, this money-demand function lacks a wealth effect. Taking logarithms, we obtain

$$Md = k + P + \alpha y - \beta i \qquad (3.13)$$

The domestic price level is a weighted average of nontradeable prices P_N and tradeable prices P_T:

$$P = \sigma P_N + (1 - \sigma)P_T \qquad (3.14)$$

For tradeables, LOP applies. Therefore

$$P_T = e + P_T^f \tag{3.15}$$

with the superscript *f* denoting foreign variables.

With an exogenous money supply *Ms*, equilibrium in the (Walrasian) money market is given by

$$Ms = k + \sigma P_N + (1 - \sigma)P_T + \alpha y - \beta i \tag{3.16}$$

or

$$Ms = k + \sigma P_N + e + P_T^f - \sigma P_T + \alpha y - \beta i \tag{3.17}$$

If the foreign income elasticity of money demand is also α, the interest-elasticity of money demand $-\beta$, the weighting variable σ, and the same Cambridge *k* applies, foreign money market equilibrium is given by

$$Ms^f = k + \sigma P_N^f + P_T^f - \sigma P_T^f + \alpha y^f - \beta i^f \tag{3.18}$$

From equation 3.15 it then follows that

$$e = (Ms - Ms^f) + \alpha(y^f - y) - \beta(i^f - i) + \sigma[(P_T - P_N) - (P_T^f - P_N^f)] \tag{3.19}$$

The following may help to form a mental picture of the economics underlying equation 3.19. An increase in the domestic money supply makes the price level increase, *ceteris paribus*. Given LOP, the exchange rate *e* has to rise. An increase in national income will, given the money supply, lower the price level and cause a fall in *e*. A rise in the domestic interest rate makes money demand fall; for money market equilibrium to be restored the price level has to increase, which implies a rise in *e*. All this is as we have also seen in the equilibrium exchange-rate model. What sets the present model apart is that the difference in price structure between countries figures in the exchange-rate equation (the argument between square brackets in equation 3.19). Equation 3.19 shows that a low relative price of tradeables *ceteris paribus* goes hand in hand with a low exchange rate, that is, relatively cheap foreign exchange. This follows from LOP.

We now analyse how the model works in the absence of international capital movements. Under a free-floating system foreign-exchange receipts from abroad always equal payments to non-residents. If (net) capital movements are nil, it follows that the current account is in continuous equilibrium. Unlike the situation in the fixed-exchange-rate case, the economy is always on the *TT* curve. As it cannot deviate from the *NN* curve either, it is always at the intersection of both curves. We first look, with the help of Figure 3.5, at the equilibrium conditions in the three markets in the model and next study the impact of a number of different shocks. *NN* and *TT* represent the loci of equilibrium pairs of *q* and *i* for nontradeables and tradeables respectively. There is no explicit wealth effect on spending in this model and the link between money and spending runs through the rate of interest.

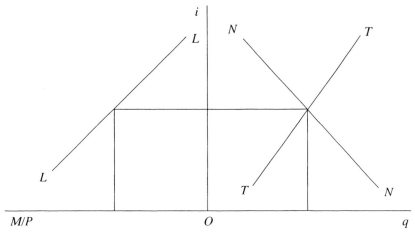

Figure 3.5   The dependent-economy model with free-floating exchange rates

NN has a negative slope, showing that an increase in the relative price *q* of nontradeables induces an excess supply of nontradeables. A lower rate of interest, that is, higher spending, is called for if equilibrium is to be maintained. *TT* has a positive slope. A rise in *q* means a lower relative price of tradeables, which produces an excess demand and calls for a rise in the rate of interest and a consequent fall in aggregate spending for equilibrium to be maintained. The rate of interest is determined on the right-hand side of the diagram at the intersection of *NN* and *TT*. On the left-hand side of the diagram the equilibrium condition for the money market is depicted. On the abscissa real balances are measured. The *LL* curve shows the fall in real balances that, given real income, is necessary for preserving equilibrium upon a rise in the rate of interest. Given the nominal money supply, higher interest rates imply a higher price level. This relationship can be found from equation 3.12: dividing by *P*, we find, with *y* exogenously given and *Md* = *Ms*, a relationship between real balances *M/P* and the rate of interest *i*. After we have found *P*, we can derive the values of P_N and P_T. We know that $q = P_N/P_T$. It follows that $P_N = q.P_T$. Substituting P_N in equation 3.14, we can solve for P_T and then calculate P_N.

The economics underlying this relationship is that a higher rate of interest makes the demand for money fall. An excess supply of money would develop which can only be counteracted by some factor making for an increase in the demand for money. The only factor in the model that could make money demand increase is a rise in prices. Given the money supply, that translates into a fall in real balances. Real income is not a variable in the model, as the economy is always in full employment. Note that a change in the nominal money supply does not make the *LL* curve shift. The relationship between real balances and the rate of interest is not affected by a variation in the supply of money. In order to maintain money-market equilibrium at any rate of interest after, say, a doubling of the money supply, the price level at any rate of interest must double as well. The equilibrium relationship between the rate of interest and real balances is thus independent of the nominal money supply.

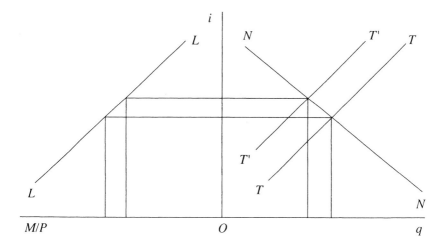

Figure 3.6   A demand shock for tradeables

How does the system react to shocks?

(i) First consider a higher propensity to spend on tradeables, or an exogenous increase in spending through a bond-financed rise in government expenditure that leaves the money supply unchanged. *TT* shifts upwards and to the left: at any value of q, the rate of interest has to rise in order to offset the increased propensity to spend on tradeables and keep demand equal to supply. Alternatively, at any value of the rate of interest q has to fall, that is, the relative price of tradeables has to rise, in order to increase production and meet the increased demand.

A new equilibrium is found at a higher relative price of tradeables (a lower q), which makes tradeables production increase. Also, the rate of interest rises, offsetting the exogenous increase, so that aggregate demand remains in tune with the economy's supply capacity (Figure 3.6). What happens to the rate of exchange? The rate of interest increases and, given the nominal supply of money, the price level increases too. If both the general price level and the relative price of tradeables rise, the absolute price of tradeables cannot but rise as well. From LOP it follows that the currency depreciates, that is, e rises. In equation 3.19 we see $(i^f - i)$ decrease and the expression between square brackets assume a higher value. Therefore, e increases. In this model, a devaluation not only serves to reduce the demand for the good that becomes relatively more expensive, but also to increase its production.

(ii) Next consider an exogenous increase in spending on nontradeables. In this case it is the NN curve that shifts; it moves upwards and to the right (Figure 3.7). Again, the equilibrium rate of interest rises and the price level increases. This time around it is the relative price of nontradeables, q, that increases, as production has to shift from tradeables to nontradeables. Again, we ask ourselves what happens to the rate of exchange. The general price level has risen and the relative price of nontradeables in terms of tradeables, q, has also risen. A moment's reflection will make it clear that the absolute price of tradeables may fall, stay put or rise.

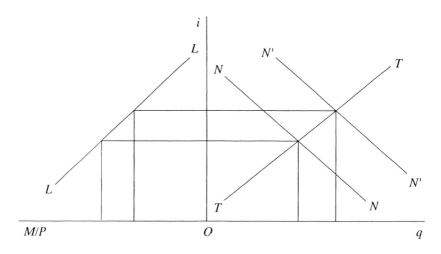

Figure 3.7   A demand shock for nontradeables

In equation 3.19 we see $(i^f - i)$ fall again but the value of the expression between square brackets falls as well, exerting opposite pressures on the rate of exchange. We find the, possibly counterintuitive, result that *increased spending on nontradeables does not necessarily cause a depreciation of the currency*.

(iii) Finally, an increase in the money supply translates into excess demand both in the tradeables and the nontradeables markets, sending tradeables and nontradeables prices upwards until P has risen sufficiently to restore the initial value of M/P at any level of the interest rate. An increase in tradeables prices means a rise in the rate of exchange, that is, a depreciation of the currency.

3.3.2 With Capital Movements

If capital movements are allowed, the tradeables market is no longer confined to equilibrium. Instead, we now have the equilibrium condition that the current-account balance plus the capital account together are in equilibrium. The higher the interest-elasticity of capital flows, the less the increase in the interest rate upon an exogenous increase in spending. With perfectly interest-elastic capital flows the rate of interest will stay put. Equation 3.19 describes the case with capital movements too. Only this time $(i^f - i)$ will change less, or, in the perfectly elastic case, not at all (in that case it is zero and remains zero). We now analyse the effects of various shocks for the case of perfectly interest-elastic capital flows.

(i) An increase in the propensity to spend on tradeables makes the *TT* curve shift upwards and to the left, as in the no-capital-movements case. The rate of interest does not change, however, as it cannot move away from the world interest-rate level. The price level consequently does not change either. The *NN* curve does not shift. Given a constant interest rate, this also means that relative prices do not change; q remains constant (Figure 3.8). As a result, the rate of exchange does not change either. At the value of q determined by the *NN* curve and the world rate of interest, the relative price of T is below its equilibrium level and the tradeables market is characterised by excess demand. An excess demand for tradeables is tantamount to a current-account deficit, which is financed by capital inflows. One might also reason that the interest rate is below the full equilibrium level. Aggregate demand therefore exceeds aggregate supply, which implies a current-account deficit. As in the fixed-rate case, matters do not rest there if a real wealth effect is operative (see Chapter 4).

(ii) A positive demand shock for nontradeables will again shift the *NN* curve upwards and to the right. The rate of interest does not change, but q increases as production shifts from tradeables to nontradeables. An

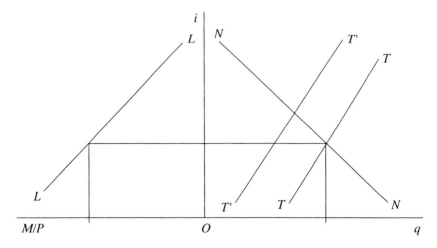

Figure 3.8   A demand shock for tradeables with perfect capital mobility

unchanged rate of interest means that the price level does not change. If, at the same time, the relative price of nontradeables rises, the absolute price of nontradeables has to rise as well and the absolute price of tradeables by necessity falls. The currency appreciates, that is, *e* falls, as can be checked by inspecting equation 3.19 (compare Chapter 2, Section 2.3.2 for the case of a fiscal impulse in the *IS/LM/EE* model, which also resulted in real appreciation). Again, there is an excess demand for tradeables, which

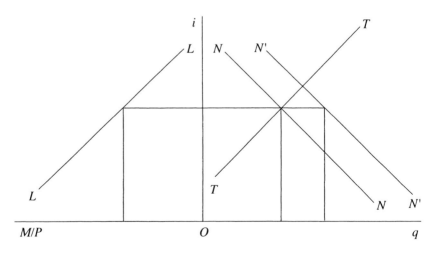

Figure 3.9   A demand shock for nontradeables with perfect capital mobility

translates into net imports (Figure 3.9). Foreign debt accumulates and leads to further adjustment processes (see Chapter 4).

(iii) Finally, consider a rise in the world interest rate. The domestic rate of interest rises in step, an excess supply of money develops and P increases. The economy moves along NN upwards to the left and q falls in the process. With both a higher general price level and a higher relative price of tradeables, the absolute price of tradeables will also be higher. The currency depreciates, q has fallen and is now below the level compatible with tradeables-market equilibrium (Figure 3.10). Tradeables are too expensive relative to the equilibrium situation at the given interest rate and are consequently in excess supply. The mechanism bringing this result about is as follows. The increase in the rate of interest curbs domestic spending. The decline in spending on nontradeables makes the relative price of nontradeables fall and production shifts from nontradeables to tradeables. The current account turns into surplus, that is, tradeables are in excess supply, and net capital exports develop. Seen from another angle, it should be apparent that with full employment a reduction in domestic spending frees resources for export production and makes the current account improve. Once again, see Chapter 4 for further adjustment processes.

The model offers an alternative explanation for the rise of the US dollar over the first half of the 1980s. Within the *IS/LM* framework, the rise of the dollar in 1981 can be explained by a rise in the US interest rate, which induced capital inflows. It could also be explained in a dependent-economy framework as the result of expansionary fiscal policies, in the way of case

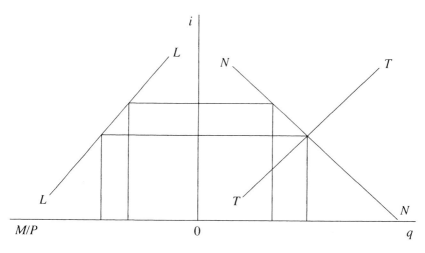

Figure 3.10   An increase in the rate of interest with perfect capital mobility

(ii) above. Hoffmann and Homburg (1990) added a new aspect, which goes some way to explaining the fall of the dollar in 1985, in addition to the earlier rise. Production in one sector can only increase if production in other sectors falls, as factors of production have to shift from one sector to the other. Such substitution processes rely on the expanding sector luring factors of production away from the shrinking one through higher payments. Substitution in production becomes easier as time passes and relative prices can move back in the direction of their initial level. Moreover, for the factors of production that have migrated, a carrot in the form of higher payments becomes less imperative.

It can be argued that the increase in spending in the United States made nontradeable prices increase and helped turn the current account into deficit. As monetary policy was restrictive, the general price level could not increase very much and the dollar had to appreciate for the relative price of nontradeables (the terms of trade in the sense of q) to increase. Both NN and TT shifted upwards, but capital inflows prevented a rise of the interest rate to the level of the new point of intersection and the economy reached a point on NN at a higher q (the interest rate did not stay put, because the United States cannot be seen as a dependent economy; the model can handle this case, provided we still assume that tradeable prices are equal the world over). With the passage of time, a relatively high supply of nontradeables is less and less dependent on a high relative price of nontradeables. In terms of Figure 3.10, it could be said that NN and TT run steeper with the passage of time and the fall in q required for adjustment to a higher rate of interest gets smaller (in terms of Figure 3.4, the transformation curve flattens). P_T rises again and the dollar falls. We have here another case of overshooting. However, as in the IS/LM case, this does not explain the length of the upward movement of the dollar nor the sharp fall afterwards. One would rather have expected a sharp rise, followed by a slow decline.

3.4   ADDING A THIRD GOOD

Additional insights may be gained by splitting up tradeables into importables and exportables. Importables can be produced at home but also imported and exportables can be produced and consumed at home and can also be exported, but not imported. *The commodity terms of trade are no longer necessarily equal to unity.* A small country is, however, still not able to change the terms of trade, whether through a devaluation or otherwise. We remain within the framework of the dependent-economy model, that is, foreign-currency prices of importables and exportables are determined in world markets. The model provides for the analysis of a number of shocks that the two-goods model cannot handle (cf. Aghevli, Khan and Montiel 1991, p. 9; see Corden 1984 for a more thoroughgoing analysis of the various possible cases). We touch upon three such shocks.

(i) First, consider a deterioration in the commodity terms of trade, that is, a relative price fall of exportables. Domestic demand shifts to exportables, leaving fewer goods for export. In addition, each export good now pays for a lower quantity of import goods. The relative price of nontradeables has to decrease in order to bring the current account of the balance of payments back into equilibrium. The shift of demand to exportables caused excess supply in the nontradeables sector. A relative price fall of nontradeables cures this situation and makes production shift to importables and exportables. The import bill is reduced and export receipts increase. If the relative price fall of nontradeables cannot be brought about by an absolute price reduction, a devaluation or, in the flexible-rate case, a depreciation, is called for. Apart from the substitution effects resulting from changed relative prices, there is an income effect: a deterioration of the commodity terms of trade means a reduction in real income. Aggregate real demand falls and equilibrium in the nontradeables market is again restored only if the relative price of nontradeables falls.

(ii) Next, consider the opposite case: exportables face a price increase in world markets. Production of exportables increases and domestic consumption of exportables falls. Export receipts rise and the currency appreciates. Spending on importables and nontradeables increases, calling for a relative price increase of nontradeables which the appreciation at least partly takes care of. The production of importables falls, as its relative price *vis-à-vis* exportables and nontradeables has become lower. If now the production of importables and nontradeables is appreciably more labour intensive than the production of exportables (for example, importables are manufactured goods and exportables are natural resources; whereas nontradeables may be services), serious unemployment may result. This phenomenon is known as *Dutch disease*, a term which refers to the situation in the Netherlands in the 1970s, when natural gas exports kept the guilder high in the face of rising unemployment. With flexible wages and prices further adjustments of course take place. Nominal wages will fall, nontradeables and importables become more attractive to produce and production shifts to these sectors, with the relative price of nontradeables falling again.

(iii) Finally, consider the case of a reduction in import duties. Home-market prices of importables fall. As demand shifts from nontradeables and exportables to importables, while production shifts away from importables, an excess demand for importables and an excess supply of nontradeables and exportables develop. An increased supply of exportables helps pay the higher import bill; a return to equilibrium in the nontradeables market depends on a fall in the relative price of nontradeables, that is, a nominal fall in P_N or a depreciation of the currency. This analysis abstracts from the effects of the reduction in government income resulting from the lowering of import duties and also from the increase in real income that may be expected from the improved allocative efficiency consequent upon freer international trade.

NOTES

1. For a formal derivation take total differentials of equation 3.2:

$$(\delta ys/\delta q)dq = (\delta Ts/\delta q).dq + q.(\delta Ns/\delta q).dq + Ns(q).dq$$

   For small variations of q (that is, a small shift along the economy's transformation curve), $\delta Ts/\delta q \approx -q.(\delta Ns/\delta q)$. It follows that $\delta ys/\delta q = Ns(q)$. Ns being a positive function of q, it also follows that income in terms of tradeables is a positive function of q.
2. The effect was fully explained by Harrod in 1933 (Harrod 1957, ch. 4, in particular p. 61). Kravis and Lipsey (1983, p. 12) note that the Balassa–Samuelson effect is compatible with the standard factor-proportions model with identical production functions: labour in poor countries is cheap because poor countries have much labour relative to capital and the marginal productivity of labour is consequently low. Nontradeables are relatively labour intensive and therefore relatively cheap in poor countries.

4. The long and very long periods

4.1 THE LONG PERIOD

4.1.1 Introduction

In Chapters 2 and 3 we studied models of an open economy where equilibrium was defined as a situation where the market for foreign exchange is in equilibrium, but where the current account of the balance of payments and the capital account separately are not necessarily in equilibrium. If they are not, we can expect further adjustment processes. These are studied in this section, in a somewhat informal and intuitive way.

It must be realised that these are very incomplete analyses. We concentrate on the effects of current-account imbalances on the accumulation of foreign assets or of foreign debt and what this means for aggregate spending, but real capital drops out of the picture. This is a serious omission. In the case of current-account imbalances, the composition of the portfolios changes and relative yields will change as well. Both the rate of investment and the market value of real capital will vary with those yields (see Sarantis 1987 for an empirical model with equity assets, and Stockman and Svensson 1987 for a theoretical model with endogenous investment and production and money as a means of transaction). Depending on wealth effects, that value will in its turn affect spending and money demand. Anything may happen; we no longer arrive at neat conclusions (Dornbusch 1987, pp. 8–9).

We first look at the *IS*/*LM*/*EE* model, next at the portfolio model (which may or may not be grafted onto an *IS*/*LM*/*EE* model) and finally at the dependent-economy model.

4.1.2 The *IS*/*LM*/*EE* model

In the *IS*/*LM*/*EE* model for the short period the economy was in equilibrium if the market for foreign exchange was in equilibrium. The economy was assumed after a shock to move very quickly to the intersection of the *IS* and *LM* curves. If at this intersection an excess demand for or excess supply of foreign exchange developed, adjustment processes started. In the fixed-peg system, the money supply would be affected and the *LM* curve would move until it cut the *IS* curve at the intersection of the *IS* and *EE* curves. In the flexible-rate system, the exchange rate would move, causing shifts of the *IS* curve. Generally, however, the current account and the capital account would show imbalances.

Now, if a country has a deficit on the capital account, its residents buy financial assets from non-residents. Residents' wealth increases and one may expect that at some stage this will increase their propensity to spend. Conversely, if a country has net capital imports and residents sell financial assets, net wealth falls and spending will be negatively affected. In equation 2.1, private expenditure *Z* as a function of *Y* will rise in the former case and fall in the latter. Alternatively, we could add wealth to the function as an argument. Either way, the *IS* curve will shift in the *i–Y* plane: to the right if wealth increases and to the left if wealth falls. Note that if the *IS* curve shifts to the right because of an improvement in the country's competitive position on world markets, the current account moves into surplus and it is the current-account improvement that makes the *IS* curve shift. If fiscal expansion or a higher propensity to spend is the cause of the rightward shift, however, the current account moves into deficit. There would be little point in giving an exhaustive description of all possible cases. To show how the mechanism works we analyse two cases.

(i) Consider a country under a fixed-peg system that starts in a situation with both the current-account and the capital account in equilibrium. The government decides to increase government spending. The *IS* curve shifts to the right and the current account moves into deficit, as national income and thus imports increase. The rate of interest tends to rise, causing net capital imports. The country incurs foreign debt. Net wealth falls, aggregate expenditure declines and the *IS* curve shifts back to the left.

(ii) Next, consider a country under a fully flexible exchange-rate system. International capital flows are fully interest-elastic. An increase in the money supply will, as we have seen in Chapter 2, Section 2.3.3, lead to a depreciation of the currency, which makes the current account move into surplus and shifts the *IS* curve to the right. There are net receipts of foreign exchange on the current account, which are used to buy foreign financial assets. Residents' wealth increases and the *IS* curve shifts further to the right. As in the case of a fiscal expansion, this puts upward pressure on the rate of interest and induces capital inflows that make the currency appreciate. The *IS* curve shifts back again.

It must be realised that there is something artificial in studying a fixed-price *IS/LM/EE* model for the long period. In the long period, one may expect prices and wages to exhibit a fair degree of flexibility. In a situation with under-utilisation of productive resources, prices are likely to fall sooner or later. Given the nominal money supply, real balances increase and the *LM* curve shifts to the right. The country concerned sees its competitive position *vis-à-vis* other countries improve and both the *IS* and *EE* curves shift to the right as well. In the first instance, the current account will improve (that is what made the curves shift to the right). Wealth increases and the *IS* curve will shift further to the right. For the long term, therefore, we must not only take account of shifts in the curves as a result of changes in residents' wealth, but also of shifts resulting from price adjustments.

4.1.3 The Portfolio Model Once Again

In Chapter 1 the portfolio model was studied for the very short period and in Chapter 2 for the short period. The portfolio model can be grafted onto the *IS/LM* model, accommodating a greater variety of cases than the simple specification underlying the basic Mundell–Fleming model. We now extend the analysis to the long period and study portfolio adjustments after two different shocks.

(i) Assume that fear of protectionist measures in the EU prompts Japanese producers to increase the euro-denominated assets in their portfolios. They want to set up plants in euroland, for instance, and first have to build up a portfolio of liquid assets that will later be used to finance direct investment. Their portfolios will thus subsequently be made up of titles to production facilities (the story will be different if they raise the money on European capital markets). Alternatively, we could imagine that Japanese residents show an increased preference for European financial assets because of a change in perceived risk or return characteristics (the variable a_3 in equation 1.23 would increase). Starting from the portfolio model for the very short term, we see the following things happening. First, the Japanese demand curve for, say, euro-denominated bonds Qd in Figure 4.1 will shift upwards. The exchange rate of the euro in terms of yen jumps from OA' to OB', as in Figure 1.3. Next, a current-account surplus develops and capital is exported, that is, the volume of foreign bonds Qs increases. As Qs grows, wealth holders wish to hold the increasing volume at ever lower exchange rates. The economy moves along demand curve Qd' to the right. The exchange rate falls, and with it the current-account surplus. The adjustment process stops at some exchange rate OC' where the current account has regained equilibrium. At that point the capital account is in equilibrium too and the volume of foreign bonds Qs stops changing.

One may wonder whether the exchange rate returns to its initial level. What we saw was a temporary capital inflow into euroland. In the course of time this leads to permanently higher interest or dividend payments to Japan. For the Japanese current account to be in equilibrium, this net investment income must go hand in hand with a deficit in merchandise and service trade. This implies a higher external value of the yen and a lower value of the euro than at the point of departure (neglecting any effects of direct foreign investments on the external trade of euroland). The portfolio stock effect that causes a temporary appreciation is followed by a flow effect that triggers off a more than offsetting depreciation of the euro and appreciation of the yen (see Box 4.1).

The analysis shows clearly how closely the current account of the balance of payments and the capital account are connected. A wish to change the (net) portfolio of foreign assets leads to adjustments of the current account. Empirical research supports the idea that a country sees its RER depreciate when it turns from a net creditor to a net debtor position (cf. Faraque 1995 for the US and Lane and Milesi-Ferretti 2000 for a sample of 64 countries). A depreciated RER serves to generate the trade surpluses required to service the external liabilities.

> These results are subject to some qualifications. First, the fall in the RER consequent upon reaching net debtor status takes place only if the net creditor, say country *A*, has a marginal propensity to spend on its own products which is higher than the net debtor's propensity to spend on *A*-goods. This is of course analogous to the famous transfer problem, with capital income making up the transfer (cf. Keynes 1929 and Ohlin 1929). Second, as Lane and Milesi-Ferretti (2002) argue, a fast-growing debtor country that manages to earn returns on its foreign assets that are higher than the payouts on its foreign liabilities requires a much smaller trade surplus relative to GDP to stabilise its net foreign assets position as a fraction of GDP than slow growers with a more unfavourable net capital earnings flow.

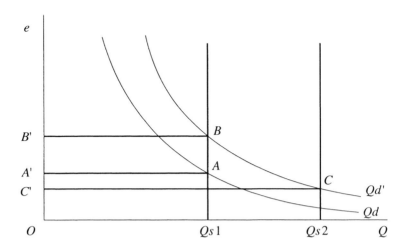

Figure 4.1   Portfolio adjustment and the rate of exchange

(ii) The second shock which we analyse is an increase in the domestic money supply as a result of open-market purchases. The volume of domestic bonds falls and wealth remains constant initially. The rate of interest falls (bond prices are driven up) and investors wish to increase their holdings of foreign titles. The rate of exchange is pushed up. A higher exchange rate will cause a surplus on the current account (provided the Marshall–Lerner condition is met) and a deficit on the capital account. Economic agents increase their holdings of foreign bonds. As their wish for more foreign bonds is being fulfilled, the rate of exchange will fall again. Here investment income will play the same role as in the first case and put additional downward pressure on the exchange rate.

BOX 4.1.   THE CONSEQUENCES OF HIGHER INVESTMENTS BY JAPAN IN THE EUROPEAN UNION

Assume that the Japanese wish to increase their foreign investments.

very short term: the exchange rate of the euro in terms of yen rises.

short term: appreciation of the euro → current account Japan improves + capital exports Japan = additions to Japan's stock of foreign investments.

long term: bigger stock of foreign investments Japan → higher investment income → lower balance on the goods and services account of the balance of payments → higher exchange-rate yen with respect to euro and lower rate euro in terms of yen than originally.

A few remarks are in order. First, the initial upward movement of the exchange rate shown in both cases analysed will be dampened if rational investors foresee the eventual fall in the exchange rate.

Second, we can again introduce wealth effects, as in Section 4.1.2 above. The current-account surplus for Japan increases wealth. We can make the analysis still more complicated if we not only introduce a wealth effect on spending, but also one on money demand. If the demand for money is not only a function of real income, the price level and the rate of interest, but also of wealth, an increase in wealth has the same effect as a fall in the real money supply – the *LM* curve shifts to the left – and will exert upward pressure on the rate of interest. A higher rate of interest will tend to depress the exchange rate (make the domestic currency appreciate) both through capital imports and through a depressing effect on investment and thus on national income and imports. Against this, a wealth effect on spending results in a shift in the *IS* curve. A shift to the right of the *IS* curve leads to a higher national income and thus to higher imports, exerting upward pressure on the rate of exchange. The outcome is uncertain.

Another point is that we have implicitly assumed constant or sticky goods prices. PPP did not hold in the cases covered above and the real exchange rate was not constant. If prices are flexible the adjustment processes will be different. In the second case, for instance, a higher money supply would result in a higher price level and this would reduce the improvement in the competitive position of the country and thus in the current account. Also, the higher price level would prevent a movement back in the direction of the initial exchange rate.

4.1.4   The Dependent-Economy Model for the Long Term

In Chapter 3 we saw that perfectly interest-elastic capital flows may prevent full equilibrium from being restored after a shock. However, it was also argued that, if we add a wealth effect to the model, equilibrating forces are set in motion after all. Foreign borrowing means that liabilities are built up. Foreign liabilities are negative net wealth and lead to reduced spending in a country or group of countries with a given currency. This will tend to reduce the current-account deficit. Similarly, foreign lending means that assets are built up. Foreign assets are net wealth and lead to increased spending and a reduction of the current-account surplus.

First, we look at the fixed-exchange-rate cases from Section 3.2.2. Case (i) concerned a random increase in the money supply. The net holdings of financial assets have increased and a shift from money into foreign assets does not reduce total financial wealth. With a wealth effect on spending, expenditure will increase. Imports increase and a current-account deficit develops. The asset supply will return to the equilibrium level, reducing aggregate spending. We see a shift to the right along the *NN* curve followed by a shift back to the left.

In case (ii) we studied an increase in the propensity to spend on nontradeables. The *NN* and *CA* curves shifted to the left. Capital imports might leave real balances unaltered, with the economy at point *A* on *NN*. Net wealth diminishes, and sooner or later the propensity to spend on both tradeables and nontradeables declines. All curves move to the right (with a lower propensity to spend, higher real balances are required to maintain equilibrium at any given value of q). Full equilibrium will be restored at a higher value of q than initially, which fits in with the increased propensity to spend on nontradeables.

In case (iii) the propensity to spend on tradeables increased. Here the CA and TT curves moved to the left. The fall in financial wealth consequent on capital imports will make all curves shift to the right and full equilibrium is restored at a lower value of q than initially.

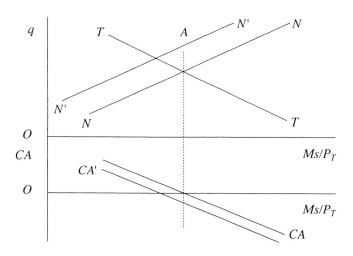

Figure 4.2   A higher propensity to spend on nontradeables in the dependent economy with fixed exchange rates

In case (v) the world interest rate increased and the economy moved leftwards along the NN curve, with capital exports matching a surplus on the current account of the balance of payments. Capital exports translate into an increase in financial wealth. This will result in a higher propensity to spend on both goods. All curves move to the left, as a higher propensity to spend requires lower real balances to restore equilibrium in either market at any value of q. Full equilibrium will be restored at a lower value of real balances.

A complication is that, if the residents of a country have positive net holdings of foreign assets, they will receive a stream of dividend and interest payments. In the case of negative net holdings, they will on balance have to pay dividend and interest. Capital income is included in the current account of the balance of payments. If there are net receipts of capital income, current-account equilibrium requires a deficit on the goods and services account, that is, an excess demand for tradeables. Full equilibrium will then not be found at the intersection of *NN* and *TT*, but at a point on *NN* to the right of and above *TT*. With net payments of capital income an excess supply of tradeables is required and full equilibrium is found at a point on *NN* to the left of and below *TT*. Current-account equilibrium in these circumstances is not found at the intersection of the *NN* and *TT* curves and the *CA* curve accordingly shifts to the right or the left.

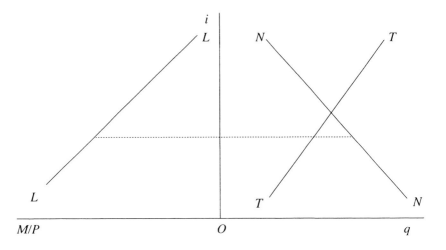

Figure 4.3   The dependent-economy model with free-floating exchange rates and capital inflows

We now turn to the flexible-rate system.

Case (i) analysed in Section 3.3.2 was an increase in the propensity to spend on tradeables. We ended up with a current-account deficit. This is financed by capital imports, which reduces net financial wealth. The propensity to spend falls and both *NN* and *TT* in Figure 4.3 shift downwards until they intersect at the world rate of interest. *q* falls in the process. With no change in the interest rate, real balances *M/P* remain unchanged and as the money supply is held constant the price level *P* stays put as well. *q* falls, and with *P* constant this can only mean that P_T rises. The currency depreciates.

Case (ii) concerned a positive demand shock for nontradeables. This resulted in an excess demand for tradeables, financed by capital imports. The story then unfolds in exactly the same way as in case (i).

Case (iii) was a rise in the world interest rate which led to a current-account surplus. Here, agents accumulate foreign assets and the propensity to spend will increase. *TT* and *NN* shift upwards until they intersect at the new world interest-rate level. The currency had first depreciated. With the rate of interest and the nominal money supply given, the overall price level stays put, but as q rises the price of tradeables must fall. The currency appreciates, but not to the initial level (q may revert to its initial value, but the interest rate is higher and the overall price level remains at its new level; both tradeable and nontradeable prices will thus have risen).

> Net payments or receipts of capital income have similar effects on the final equilibrium in the flexible-rate model as in the fixed-rate model. Net receipts require an excess demand for tradeables and the final equilibrium will be at a point on the *NN* curve to the right of and below the *TT* curve. Net payments require an excess supply of tradeables and full equilibrium will be on *NN* to the left of and above *TT*.

4.2   PURCHASING POWER PARITY

4.2.1   PPP and the Empirical Evidence

One of the building blocks of the monetary model of exchange-rate determination is purchasing power parity. It is essentially a model without frictions, which restricts its applicability in short-term analysis, but one may wonder whether it would still be a useful tool to explain or predict exchange-rate changes over longer periods. However, even if the monetary model were not a good approximation of reality and PPP does not hold in its absolute form, PPP could still hold in its *relative* form. This says that exchange-rate changes reflect differences in inflation rates even if prices at the going exchange rate are not equal. That would be consistent with the dependent-economy model, provided the relative price of tradeables and nontradeables does not change.

If PPP held, if only in its relative form, the real exchange rate would remain more or less constant or return to its original value after a shock. The empirical evidence is a bit confusing. Relative PPP was found to hold, over decades rather than years, in research carried out by Lee (1975) and Manzur (1993). More negative outcomes, however, were found by Adler and Lehmann (1983). Also, quite sharp fluctuations in the Swedish–US and the US–UK real exchange rates seem to have taken place, even considering long periods (1874–1984 and 1869–1989, respectively; Dornbusch 1989). There is overwhelming evidence that PPP is not valid in any strict sense, but that it performs quite well under high money growth and high inflation, and especially during hyperinflations, when monetary disturbances and inflation tend to swamp all other influences on the rate of exchange (see De Grauwe and Grimaldi 2001, who use a sample of 100 countries over a 30-year period, and Frenkel 1978). Indeed, one of the main problems of the post-1973 period has been the extreme variability of real exchange rates

(Frenkel 1981b; De Grauwe 1989, pp. 61–4; though MacDonald 1988b finds that PPP cannot be rejected for the post-1973 period if wholesale prices rather than consumer prices are used). For the early 1920s more positive outcomes have been found, though, not only for exchange rates involving the D-Mark, but also for the sterling–French franc rate, the dollar–franc rate and the dollar–sterling rate (provided we exclude the year 1924, when speculators probably acted in anticipation of a return of sterling to the pre-war rate; see Taylor and McMahon 1988).

Still, there is research indicating that even in the post-1973 period RER moves back to its original value after a shock, that is, relative PPP holds if we consider a sufficiently long time period, say five or ten years (IMF 1995, p. 176; Taylor 1995, p. 20; de Jong 1997; see in particular Culver and Papell 1999; MacDonald 1999; and Kuo and Mikkola 2001 for cointegration and unit root tests and Anker 1999; MacDonald 1999; and Murray and Papell 2002 for a discussion of econometric problems). It has been found that deviations dampen out at a rate of some 15 per cent per year (see Rogoff 1996, pp. 656–8 for a survey of the empirical literature). Also, there is evidence that it was the behaviour of the US dollar during the 1980s in particular that was troubling from the point of view of PPP. The relative movements of other currencies were more in accordance with (relative) PPP and the inclusion of the dollar for other periods was not so damaging for PPP (Lothian 1998; Lothian and Simaan 1998; Papell and Theodorakis 1998; Anker 1999; Choudhry 1999). Consonant with this, D-Mark-based real exchange rates have been found to return to their original levels after a shock, whereas US dollar-based rates moved back in that direction, but not fully (MacDonald 1999). For a group of seven Asian countries it was found that strong PPP with respect to Japan did not always hold for them individually over the period 1977 IV–1998 III, but for the group as a whole PPP was shown to perform quite well in the long run (Azali, Habibullah and Baharumshah 2001). Similarly, Husted and MacDonald (1999) found evidence in favour of the monetary model, including PPP, for a group of nine Asian countries with respect to the Japanese yen, but not for individual countries.

If empirical research has not been devastating for purchasing power parity as a long-term relationship, it remains an approximate relationship at best. There are, in fact, sound reasons why a close relationship is not to be expected.

If PPP does not hold, comparisons of per capita income on the basis of nominal exchange rates give a false picture of real per capita income differences across countries. In order to make comparisons of real per capita income, a real exchange rate has to be calculated from prices of a set of goods and services. In the International Comparison Project (ICP) of the United Nations, which has been running since 1968, such calculations are made. A similar project is run by the University of Pennsylvania, which provides real exchange rates based on the Penn World Table data covering some 150 goods (which is much less than in the ICP, but the Penn World Table covers more countries and a longer time period; see Heston and Summers 1996 for more details). In its annual *World Development Report* the World Bank publishes data on gross national income per capita at the nominal exchange rate plus data based on PPP. Gross income per capita in Indonesia was, for instance, $570 in 2000, against $34,260 in the US. Nominal per capita income thus was 60 times higher in the US than in Indonesia. Real per capita incomes, however, differed by a factor of 12.

4.2.2 Why Does PPP Not Hold?

PPP is based on the quantity theory, according to which prices move in step with the money supply, *ceteris paribus*. The *ceteris paribus* condition is not always fulfilled, however. That is not much of a problem if real growth rates differ between countries (see equations 1.5 and 1.6), but instability of the money-demand function (which manifests itself in volatility of the variable k in equations 1.4, 1.5 and 1.6) is more difficult to handle, and to all appearances money demand has become less stable since, say, 1980 (Rogoff 1999, p. F657). In terms of Irving Fisher's equation of exchange, $MV \equiv Py$ (where M = money supply, V = velocity of circulation, P = price level and y = real GDP), V has become more volatile. Strictly speaking, this does not affect the theoretical validity of the quantity theory, but the proportionality between money and prices is impaired and the theory loses some of its attractiveness for making forecasts or even for tracking history.

Another point is that a necessary, but not sufficient, condition for validity of PPP in its strict form is that LOP holds. If it does not, PPP cannot hold. LOP, or full arbitrage, can be undermined by a variety of factors:

- Natural barriers to trade, which follow from distance and are associated with transaction costs. These hinder arbitrage: price differences between similar refrigerators in, say, Argentina and Chile must be quite large before it pays to hire a truck and ship fridges across the Andes mountains from the cheap country to the expensive one. We can include language and other cultural differences among the natural barriers, because they, too, cause an increase in the costs of transactions: you may have to hire interpreters, lawyers and perhaps even sociologists and cultural anthropologists in order to understand your partner in another country and not make costly mistakes. Distance also implies that dealer networks have to be set up before new markets can be cracked. This again works against fast arbitrage.

- Man-made barriers to trade, such as tariffs and quotas. Even if there are no formal trade barriers, arbitrage can be made difficult because of the hassle involved with administrative procedures (take imports of cars by individuals). The list of possibilities to sour the life of importers is endless. Foreign automobile firms, for instance, complained in 1965 that they could not buy advertising time on Italian government-owned television (Fauri 1996, p. 202 n. 120).
- Imperfect competition, which means that people will be willing to pay different prices for different varieties of a product. A foreign supplier who competes with a domestic one thus need not always adjust his or her prices fully to compensate for, say, exchange-rate changes. In other words, some degree of exchange-rate pass-through is possible.
- Taxes. If indirect taxes differ across countries, tax-inclusive prices will differ even if pre-tax prices are equal.

Empirical research indicates that prices of similar goods in various countries tend to move in the same direction, but are not identical. Arbitrage is not perfect, but it is far from negligible either. Haskel and Wolf (2001) examined the catalogue prices in 25 countries of 119 goods sold by the Swedish household furniture retailer IKEA and found median deviations of relative prices of between 20 per cent and 50 per cent. Note that these are price differences between identical products, and also differences in *relative* prices, which suggests that differences in mark-ups rather than in local costs lie behind these price differences. Price divergences were smaller for countries that are close together, share a common border, speak the same language, are joint members in the EU and have larger markets; in short, where competition is more intense. Moreover, deviations, especially if large initially, tended to diminish over time. This fits in with Vataja's finding that on average two-thirds of any deviations from LOP are eliminated within one year (Vataja 2000). Even in commodity markets, where goods are more homogeneous than in the markets for industrial products, LOP does not generally hold in the short term, though it tends to do so in the longer term (see Protopapadakis and Stoll 1986, who find that 90 per cent of a deviation from the LOP is on average eliminated within ten weeks, the adjustment period varying from one week to 120 weeks, depending on the commodity). Arbitrage, not surprisingly, thus seems to be a function of transaction costs and time.

In line with these results, the weak version of the LOP, which says that exchange-rate changes offset diverging inflation rates between countries' tradeables, does not always stand up (Obstfeld 1985, p. 376). Nor do nominal exchange-rate changes in general immediately lead to compensating price adjustments in the currency of the buyer of a good, thanks to sticky consumer prices (Genberg 1978; Spitäller 1980; Engel and Rogers 2001, who find that this phenomenon explains a much larger part of deviations from PPP across European cities than what they call real-barrier effects, such as distance, city-specific factors and cross-country differences in marketing and distribution systems). In the extreme case of local-currency pricing, pass-through of exchange-rate changes is zero and the real exchange rate moves with the nominal exchange rate. This is more or less what happens initially (Obstfeld 1985, p. 377). Still, research on the real exchange rate between Japan and the US over the 1980–99 period suggests that PPP, if measured on the basis of relative export prices, provides a good description of empirical developments, especially after 1985, when the dollar returned to more normal behaviour (Schnabl 2001). In the same vein, Kong (2000) found evidence of mean-reverting behaviour in the yen/D-Mark RER over 1958–96, when export prices or wholesale prices (where the share of tradeables predominates) are used. Apparently, LOP does not fare too badly on an aggregate level if export or wholesale prices are used.

Even if LOP holds, PPP need not do so. A purely statistical phenomenon is that, if the weights given to various goods in the calculation of the price index differ among countries, divergent price developments of different goods result in divergent price index movements even if LOP holds for all goods and the bundles of goods on which the price is calculated are identical (on the methods to calculate deviations from PPP, see Pilat and Prasada Rao 1996). This does not, however, seem to seriously distort the picture in practice (Davutyan and Pippenger 1985) and even if it did, the problem could be circumvented by concentrating on the relative form of purchasing power parity, provided consumption patterns within countries do not change too much over time.

More important than this index-number problem is the fact that the relative price of tradeables and nontradeables may differ between countries and may diverge or converge over time. Various causes of such a change in relative prices can be thought of:

- The Balassa–Samuelson effect (see Chapter 3, Section 3.2.4).
- Differences in consumer preferences. These may also diverge over time because of different income elasticities of demand (Heitger 1987; Clark et al. 1994).
- Different percentages of government spending in GDP. Government spending is likely to be strongly oriented towards nontradeables (education, social services) and high government spending thus makes for a comparatively high relative price of nontradeables and a relatively high general price level (if government spending is highly

concentrated on, say, imported military hardware, it's the other way round of course).

- International capital flows. These have an impact on exchange rates and consequently on the relative price of tradeables and nontradeables in a country (see Chapter 3).
- Real shocks, such as the relative price increase of oil during the 1973 and 1979 oil crises. These work out differently for exporters and for importers. If oil prices go up, oil exporters will likely see their currencies appreciate, whereas oil importers will see their currencies depreciate (in order to make energy relatively more expensive and shift factors of production from nontradeables to energy). Relative prices diverge and the general price levels do not move in step with exchange rates.

An interesting case is MacDonald's Big Mac, which for all practical purposes is identical in the different markets where it is sold, but nevertheless is sold at widely different prices. Arbitrage is prevented by prohibitive transportation costs. Since 1986, *The Economist* has been publishing an annual comparison of the prices of the Big Mac, using these for a calculation of the deviation of actual exchange rates from PPP exchange rates. In Table 4.1 we reproduce some of the figures for 2003. *The Economist*'s Big Mac standard provides a reasonable approximation of deviations from PPP, that is, it gives a rough indication of which countries are 'cheap' and which are 'expensive' (see Pakko and Pollard 2003, who show that the Big Mac standard is positively, though imperfectly, correlated with the Penn World Table measure). For purposes of testing for LOP one should make corrections for the costs of local services (labour, real estate) included in the selling price of a Big Mac: nontradeables were found by Parsley and Wei (2003) to make up between 55 per cent and 64 per cent of the Big Mac price.

If LOP does not hold, we can distinguish additional causes of RER changes:

- Capital flows, again. If LOP does not hold, these could affect tradeables prices.
- Real shocks. In an *IS/LM* framework, a real shock such as the oil price increases of the 1970s means that a relative fall in the prices of domestic goods *vis-à-vis* foreign goods is called for, in order to redress the current-account deterioration. LOP does not hold in the *IS/LM* model and in the process PPP is violated, not only in its strict form but also in its relative one.
- Sustained current-account imbalances and their associated wealth effects. If a country has a sustained deficit or surplus, its supply of net foreign assets changes. If it has a deficit, it will have to make increasingly higher net interest and dividend payments, that is, it will

have to reach an increasingly higher surplus or lower deficit in goods and services trade in order to obtain the necessary foreign exchange. The country will have to undergo real depreciation. With a surplus, real appreciation will take place.

Table 4.1   The hamburger standard

Country	Big Mac prices (in local currency)	(in dollars)	Implied PPP of the dollar	Actual $ exchange rate 22/04/03	Under- (–)/over- (+) valuation against the dollar (%)
United States	$2.71	2.71	–	–	–
Argentina	peso 4.10	1.40	1.51	2.88	–47
Brazil	Real 4.55	1.44	1.68	3.07	–45
Britain	£1.99	3.08	1.36*	1.58*	16
China	Yuan 9.90	1.20	3.65	8.28	–56
Euro area	€2.71	2.98	1.00‡	1.10‡	10
Indonesia	rp 16100	1.81	5.941	8.740	–32
Japan	¥262	2.18	96.7	120	–19
Singapore	S$3.30	1.85	1.22	1.78	–31
Switzerland	SFr6.30	4.52	2.32	1.37	69

Notes: * Dollars per pound. ‡ Dollars per euro.

Source: *The Economist*, 26 April 2003, p. 66.

4.2.3   A Note on Money, PPP and Causality

In the monetary approach to the rate of exchange it was the exogenous money supply in the trading countries that determined price levels and through these the rate of exchange. PPP *per se* does not imply this direction of causality. It can be interpreted as an equilibrium relationship between the exchange rate and the relation of two price levels (Zis 1988, p. 70). Causality can also be the other way round, as when the money supply in one country is endogenous and the rate of exchange determines the price level. The authorities could in such a case choose any exchange rate. Given the price level in a dominant country, the price level in a dependent economy would adjust so that PPP is fulfilled and the money supply would adjust as well, either through an elastic domestic money supply or through capital imports. This is in effect the fixed-but-adjustable peg variant of the basic flexprice monetary model or global monetarist model which was described in Chapter 1, Section 1.2.

4.3   THE VERY LONG PERIOD

It could be argued that in the very long term the same technology will be available all over the globe and production functions will be identical for similar goods in all countries. We then live in a Heckscher–Ohlin–Samuelson world where goods and services trade serves to equalise factor prices over the various trading countries. As de Roos (1985, pp. 28–9) emphasised, PPP obtains in that case. It might be objected that not all goods will be traded, even in the long term, and that different factor proportions in the nontradeables sectors in the various countries may prevent PPP being established. Factor prices will, however, be equalised, if not by goods trade then by factor migration. Factor proportions in the nontradeables sectors will then be the same everywhere and PPP obtains. It remains possible, though, that PPP will not obtain even then, if measured by producer prices or wholesale prices, if some specialisation in production between countries is retained. In that case the goods bundles produced in different countries differ and price indexes may show divergent behaviour. Again, we have an index-number problem. Specialisation that persists in the very long run presupposes factors of production that are not free to migrate, to wit natural resources, or scale economies, which make it advantageous even for countries with identical factor proportions and tastes to specialise. With identical tastes PPP may obtain in these cases if we deploy consumer prices, even if it does not when deploying the GDP deflator.

4.4   CONCLUSION

In the long term there are factors at work that make the system return to a situation where all markets are in equilibrium and net capital flows have dried up. Within the current account of the balance of payments, however, an imbalance in goods and service trade may be necessary to compensate net flows of investment income. It should be remembered that we only took changes in financial wealth resulting from international payment imbalances into consideration. In a world where countries grow and wealth includes non-financial assets, no such firm conclusion can be drawn and it could well be imagined that trade imbalances and corresponding capital-account imbalances remain intact over time.

For the very long term, when the economy has gone through all possible adjustment processes, PPP can hardly be avoided. Even then, it can only be guaranteed if we deflate nominal GDP by a consumer price index, not by a GDP deflator. The very long term is, however, of little practical value. It only serves as a kind of benchmark, showing the situation where no further adjustment processes can take place.

5. Exchange-rate policy

5.1 INTRODUCTION

With an eye to its international payments, every country has to choose a payments system. Various degrees of flexibility of the rate of exchange are possible and it depends on the objectives of a country's economic policy and on its economic environment which system is preferred. Exchange-rate policy includes, first, the choice of an exchange-rate system and, second, if a fixed-peg or a fixed-but-adjustable peg system is chosen, a decision on the level of the exchange rate. The measures to defend the rate of exchange or to move it in a desired direction fall under the heading of exchange-rate policy as well.

In many cases *price stability* is an important end of exchange-rate policy, provided that large imbalances in international payments can be avoided. In principle, a flexible-rate, or free-floating, system is suitable. Flexible rates can keep foreign inflation at bay and international payments are at all times in equilibrium. In addition, divergent productivity growth rates need not lead to significant price-level adjustments or international payments imbalances if a free-floating system is in force. The price of this flexibility may well be large and/or frequent exchange-rate fluctuations, which are also undesirable, as they make life harder for traders and investors.

If flexible rates are used as a means to prevent foreign inflation from being imported, fixed rates are sometimes seen as a means to curb inflation from domestic sources. This solution may look attractive to smaller countries, especially if they have an important trade partner with a low inflation rate. If the monetary authorities of the country in question have earned themselves a solid reputation, in the sense that people trust them to hold fast to a policy once they start following it, a virtuous circle may be the result. If people believe that the authorities will not waver from the anti-inflationary course, they will gear their own actions to it and refrain, for instance, from making excessive wage demands. This is because they are pretty sure that any unemployment resulting from such excessive wage demands would fail to make the authorities resort to lax monetary policies. Lenders will trust inflation to remain low also and thus will not demand a high nominal interest rate. A firm resolve on the part of the authorities to maintain the exchange rate at some given level can thus be instrumental in enabling them to achieve their objective.

The rate of exchange can also be used as an instrument to improve a country's competitive position in world markets, instead of as a means to keep inflation in check. This would require a low external value of the domestic currency.

The opportunities for attaining various policy ends in different exchange-rate systems, and the constraints imposed by those systems, are further explored in the next section. International capital flows complicate the issue. On the one hand, they can enable a country to maintain some exchange rate even if it runs a deficit on the current account of the balance of payments. On the other hand, they may seriously hamper any particular monetary policy and exchange-rate policy. We analyse balance-of-payments disequilibria and international capital flows on a relatively high level of abstraction in Section 5.3. Countries may follow their own preferred policies without taking account of other countries' possible reactions. The difference which international coordination of policy making makes is the subject of Section 5.4. Section 5.5 analyses the problems which are created if a country chooses to maintain some level of the exchange rate through payment restrictions. Finally, in Section 5.6 we examine the problems that may arise when capital movements have been liberalised and look at ways of dealing with these problems.

5.2   EXCHANGE-RATE SYSTEM AND EXCHANGE-RATE POLICY

5.2.1   Fixed or Flexible Rates?

The authorities may pursue various ends through the choice of an exchange-rate system, as we have seen. Given their aims, the final choice by the authorities will depend on circumstances (cf. Mussa et al. 2000). Some relevant variables are:

- The share of trade with a dominant partner or a few dominant partners on a fixed exchange rate. A high share of trade makes it attractive to adopt a fixed rate *vis-à-vis* that partner or those partners, especially if inflation in that country or those countries is low and if foreign trade is large with respect to national income in the first place. Thus, for a country such as the Netherlands or Belgium it was attractive to link to the D-Mark before the advent of the euro, whereas for the United States there is little reason to link to the euro or the yen.

- The history of domestic inflation. If it has proved difficult, for political reasons, to introduce restrictive monetary and fiscal measures in order to reduce inflation under a floating-rate system, pegging the currency to a foreign currency may provide a politically acceptable way to impose macroeconomic discipline.
- The volatility of capital flows. If a country does not want, or sees no effective way, to control international capital flows, it may see itself forced to adopt some form of flexible exchange rate.
- Symmetry of shocks with other countries. If demand or supply shocks hit countries in a symmetric way, it will be relatively easy to maintain fixed rates (see on this Chapter 6 Section 6.3 on optimum currency areas). Stable exchange rates, or fixed parities, will be less desirable for primary producers, who often face severe external demand shocks and whose terms of trade *vis-à-vis* industrial exporters are volatile. Booming exports would make the money supply balloon and exert sharp upward pressure on prices, whereas a negative export shock would make a serious dent in foreign-exchange reserves and have a deflationary impact. Such shocks on nominal national income and the price level may be severe enough to make a floating-rate system preferred, in particular if the shocks are of longer duration.
- Ease of international borrowing and investing. If international capital flows can be used to neutralise the effects of current-account imbalances, maintaining a fixed exchange rate becomes relatively easy, even under asymmetric shocks. High export incomes could in that case be used to build up a portfolio of foreign assets which can be drawn upon in case of a current-account deficit or domestic economic agents can maintain consumption and investment levels with the help of foreign borrowings (see Section 5.3 below).
- The flexibility of wages and prices. If this flexibility is low, exchange-rate changes should bear the brunt of external shocks; if high, it will be easier to maintain fixed exchange rates.
- Regional cooperation. Depending on the character of regional cooperation arrangements, a fixed exchange rate may be preferred to floating rates in order to minimise administrative difficulties and prevent political quarrels (see Chapter 6 on the European Union's Common Agricultural Policy).

As was emphasised in Chapter 2, flexible exchange rates not only absorb shocks, they themselves are a source of shocks too. Generally, under floating rates the real exchange rate is significantly more volatile than under fixed rates (Stockman 1999). One would expect a substantial negative impact on trade flows, but that is not what is found in empirical research. Dell'Ariccia

(1999) did indeed find a statistically significant negative effect of exchange-rate volatility on trade flows in the European Union. However, it was rather a small effect. Frankel (1995) got similar results in a study covering a much wider set of countries. Stockman (1999) even reports that the behaviour of economic quantities such as output, consumption, investment or trade, does not seem to differ significantly between fixed-rate and floating-rate systems.

In a system with at least some degree of exchange-rate flexibility traders and investors will take account of exchange-rate risk and will often cover that risk with the help of forwards, futures and foreign-exchange options or finance part of their activities with foreign funds. Exchange-rate fluctuations are therefore not likely to lead to insurmountable difficulties, even if cover is not costless and getting cover for long-term foreign-exchange positions may be complicated. If there is, by contrast, a system which gives the illusion that the exchange rate will not move (a fixed-but-adjustable peg, a managed system that succeeds in keeping the exchange rate very stable), traders and investors will not bother to cover their risks and will be taken by surprise if the exchange rate cannot be maintained. Without cover, a sharp depreciation will increase their foreign-currency debt in terms of domestic money and if they have no corresponding foreign-currency-denominated assets, they may easily go bankrupt. This happened during the Chilean crisis in 1982 and the Asian crisis of 1997–98.

5.2.2   Where to Peg Parity?

Under a fixed or a fixed-but-adjustable peg, things may go smoothly, provided (a) domestic inflation does not differ too much from inflation in the country whose currency the domestic currency is pegged to and (b) the current account of the balance of payments is in equilibrium or not too much out of line. If things do not go smoothly, the authorities can use the exchange rate as a policy instrument, either (i) to fight inflation or (ii) to improve the country's competitiveness, but not both at the same time.

(i) In this case the aim is to force domestic producers to keep prices in check through competition from abroad. The exchange rate functions as a *nominal anchor* for the price level. The policy is premised on the idea that LOP is a close approximation of reality. Such a policy can only succeed if domestic expenditure, above all government expenditure, is held in check. There has to be restraint in monetary and fiscal policies. In attaining such restraint, a wage compact can be of great help (Corden 1991, pp. 80–4). If domestic macroeconomic policies are not sufficiently restrictive, the relative price of nontradeables will rise and production will shift to those nontradeables, as long as capital imports or foreign-exchange reserves permit the current account to remain in deficit. The RER will fall and domestic producers of tradeables will fight a losing battle against their foreign competitors. Capital imports result in a mounting volume of foreign debt which may trigger a foreign-exchange crisis. The authorities are then forced to give up the fixed exchange rate and find other ways to keep inflation low.

(ii) If the aim is to improve a country's competitiveness, or to increase exports, the authorities will aim at a high RER, or a high price of tradeables relative to nontradeables. Again, the policy requires not-too-expansive monetary and fiscal policies as a prerequisite for success. In the *IS/LM/EE* model expansive policies make the *IS* and *LM* curves shift rightwards and intersect to the right of the *EE* curve. Sufficiently restrictive macroeconomic policies are required to keep the current account of the balance of payments in surplus. In a dependent-economy setting an analogous reasoning applies. Restrictive macroeconomic policies will keep aggregate domestic spending in check and free resources for the tradeables industries.

The real exchange rate should not be too high. Too high means huge trade surpluses, translating into liquidity inflows from abroad and overheating of the economy, that is, inflationary pressures, unless there are large offsetting capital exports. Some sterilising of these additions to the money supply may be possible, but only some: mopping up excess liquidity involves selling government securities. After some point, these can only be sold at falling prices, that is, higher interest rates, which attract further capital inflows. Another point is that a high RER may cause resentment among other countries, which may charge the country in question with 'unfair competition'.

Instead of linking its currency to another country's currency, a country can stabilise its currency in terms of a basket of foreign currencies. That may be attractive if there is no dominant trade partner. The effects of demand, price and interest shocks coming from abroad are thus spread and weakened. Another case where a basket may be attractive is when a country has a large foreign debt denominated in the currency of a country that is not its main trade partner. If a country, for example, has a high yen-denominated debt but trades mainly with the United States, a fall of the dollar *vis-à-vis* the yen saddles the country with a dilemma: if its currency follows the yen, its debt service (interest payments plus amortisation) expressed in domestic currency does not change, but its competitiveness in its main market will worsen. If it follows the dollar, exports will not be hurt, but debt-service payments expressed in domestic currency (or in dollars) will increase. Such a country may opt for an in-between solution through pegging to a basket.

For poor countries (economically less developed countries or LDCs) this solution has a number of disadvantages. First, there may be substantial opportunity costs in deploying highly qualified people in foreign-exchange dealings. Second, it may become extremely difficult for the public to hedge foreign-exchange risk on the forward market. LDCs do not usually have a forward market for foreign exchange. If the currency is linked to an important foreign currency, there is no need to hedge positions in that currency (provided the link is credible) and positions in other currencies can be hedged through the intermediary of the currency to which one's own currency is linked.

5.2.3   Fighting Inflation: Currency Boards and Crawling Pegs

In order to convince the public that fighting inflation through fixing the exchange rate is policy objective number one, a government can tie its own hands and set up a *currency board* (see Table 5.1). This is a kind of rudimentary central bank whose main task is to stand ready to buy and sell foreign exchange at a fixed price.[1] In principle the liabilities of the currency board that are base money are fully backed by foreign exchange. These liabilities are banknotes, or banknotes and coins, or banknotes and coins and banks' deposits (banks need not always hold deposits at the currency board, as the clearing of interbank payments may be organised in another way than through accounts held with the currency board). There may be variations in the sense that the minimum backing may be a lower percentage than 100 per cent. In Argentina, part of the backing was in the form of dollar-denominated government debt (for a comprehensive survey, see Ghosh, Gulde and Wolf 2000; for the functioning of currency boards, see also Bennett 1994; Baliño, Enoch et al. 1997). It should be noted that countries can take one further, final step to abolish exchange-rate changes, namely adopting a foreign currency as legal tender (official dollarisation) or forming a monetary union. These solutions will be discussed in Chapter 6.

The currency board stands ready to change domestic base money into foreign currency and vice versa and the full or quasi-full backing of the base-money supply serves as a guarantee that it will be able to meet its obligations. The balance sheet of the currency board is mainly made up of foreign-exchange reserves on the assets side and base money on the liabilities side.[2] The currency board thus has little room for manoeuvre in buying and selling domestic government debt. In principle it cannot, therefore, finance government budget deficits – which may even be explicitly prohibited, as in Estonia and Lithuania – nor can it provide credit to the banks or conduct open-market policies, unless external reserves are higher than required to back the base-money supply (interest income on foreign-exchange investments may make external reserves exceed liabilities). It consequently cannot, or only to a limited extent, function as a lender of last resort for the banks.

Here, again, there is no uniformity. The Bulgarian National Bank, though functioning according to currency-board principles, is a lender of last resort. This was deemed necessary because of the fragility of the Bulgarian banking system. Without this arrangement, any rumour of problems in any particular bank might too easily lead to withdrawals from other banks and thus to systemic crises (Dobrev 1999).

In this set-up, base money can only be created through the balance of payments and, in so far as the currency board may hold domestic debt, to a limited extent through purchases of domestic debt. Inflationary finance of government expenditure is not totally excluded, though. The government can borrow abroad, sell the foreign exchange thus obtained to the currency board against domestic money and spend the proceeds. It can also borrow from domestic banks, which after spending increases the domestic money supply but not the base-money supply.

Introducing a currency board can be a useful strategy in cases where the credibility of the government in following an anti-inflationary policy would otherwise be very low, as currency boards require strong fiscal discipline from governments. It serves as a signal that this time around good intentions are backed up by serious measures. The fact that, before the breakdown of the Argentine currency board in 2001, currency boards generally had an excellent track record certainly added to the credibility of such a measure. Credibility immediately translates not only into moderate wage demands but also into low interest rates. In Argentina, for instance, monthly interest rates fell from 12.5 per cent just before the introduction of the currency board in March 1991 to 1.5 per cent in April (IMF 1997b, p. 85). In an inflationary environment debt is predominantly short term and a fall in interest rates helps a great deal to restore balance in the government budget. Credibility is essential.

A currency board is a painful but effective medicine to squeeze inflation out of the economy. There may be unpleasant side-effects. If, for example, people start getting nervous about the ability of the currency board to maintain the exchange rate and rush to exchange domestic currency for foreign exchange, they withdraw deposits from the commercial banks and these run into liquidity problems. As a consequence, the economy may suffer a credit squeeze. The central bank, reduced to a currency board, is hardly in a position to provide liquidity, as it has little room to make advances to the banks or to engage in open-market purchases.

The authorities are, however, not totally helpless in the face of reserve losses. In the first place they could manipulate required cash reserves. If there is a credit squeeze, they can ease reserve requirements (Reinhart and Reinhart 1999). This would offer banks the opportunity to expand credit, or to reduce outstanding credit by a lower amount than they would otherwise do. Alternatively, they could allow the banks to meet part of their liquidity reserve requirements by acquiring foreign-currency-denominated domestic (government) bonds, as was the case in Argentina (Frankel 1999, p. 17 n. 20). Of course, these ways are only open if the foreign-exchange reserves of the currency board have not yet fallen to dangerously low levels.

The currency board could also try to stem an outflow by offering attractive interest rates on balances held by its clients (banks). The banks in their turn would then be able to offer attractive interest rates on time deposits and thus persuade depositors not to switch to foreign deposits. Alternatively, the government could try to persuade residents not to shift their funds abroad by offering government debt at attractive rates. When there are serious doubts about the ability of the authorities to maintain the exchange rate, all attempts will be in vain, but the strategy seems to have worked at times, for example in Hong Kong during the 1997–98 Asian crisis. In Argentina, by contrast, in the aftermath of the December 1994 Mexican peso crisis, the peso came under attack (the so-called *tequila crisis*) and the IMF, World Bank and Inter American Development Bank had to step in in order to prevent the Argentinian financial system collapsing (Carrizosa, Leipziger and Shah 1996; IMF 1996b, p. 112).

If the currency board cannot make advances to the banks, the government still can. Especially if a banking crisis coincides with a foreign-exchange crisis and people exchange domestic for foreign money on a large scale, the government will hardly be in a situation to bail the banks out. Any funds it has set aside for the purpose will be depleted at a fast pace. One way out is to open lines of credit with foreign banks that can be drawn upon in the case of a banking crisis. This is, of course, not free. According to Chang (2000, p. 6), Argentina had private credit lines amounting to $6.1 billion, at a cost of about $18 million a year or 0.3 per cent. This could be seen as an insurance premium against the havoc that would be wrought by large-scale bankruptcies.

If there are high net incoming foreign payments and the base-money supply increases at a fast pace, the currency board could tighten reserve requirements. This may have undesirable side-effects, though. Reserve requirements act as a tax on banks and high reserve requirements weaken the banks' competitive position *vis-à-vis* other financial institutions. These will capture at least a part of the market that the banks are forced to relinquish and thus partly frustrate the restrictive effects of higher reserve requirements. Another way is to lower domestic interest rates.

Apart from fiscal tightness, a currency-board system requires very strict banking supervision, as loss of confidence in banks and runs on the banks may easily lead to bankruptcies, a large fall in the credit supply and a serious decline in economic activity (remember that a currency board has few means to assist problem banks). Furthermore, the so-called *anchor currency* should be carefully chosen. If the link is with a country that is not the main trade partner, competitiveness is impaired if that country's currency appreciates *vis-à-vis* the main trade partners' currencies, as happened with Argentina from 1999.

Table 5.1   Countries with a currency board

Country	Currency board since	Linked to
Bosnia-Herzegovina	1998	DM/euro
Brunei	1967	Singapore dollar
Bulgaria	1997	DM/euro
Djibouti	1949	US $
Cayman Islands	1972	US $
Estonia	1992	DM/euro
Faroe Islands	1940	Danish krone
Hong Kong	1983	US $
Lithuania	1994	US $

Note: A number of dependent territories and small Caribbean countries have been left out.

Sources: Chandavarkar (1996, p. 15); Baliño, Enoch et al. (1997); Enoch and Gulde (1998); Gulde (1999).

If there is a high rate of inflation to start with, a government can opt for a gradual reduction of inflation and a gradual rise in the exchange rate, instead of the cold turkey approach of introducing a currency board. This can be done by introducing a *tablita* or *crawling peg*. A *tablita* involves stepwise, pre-announced exchange-rate adjustments that, if all goes well, get gradually smaller. In this way, it is hoped that inflation expectations, and with them wage and interest-rate demands, will be gradually adjusted downwards. The experience has been that a fall in the rate of inflation tends to lag behind a fall in the rate of depreciation of the currency, leading to RER appreciation and ultimately to a currency crisis. A crawling peg can nevertheless be useful as a first step in an anti-inflation policy.

It should be noted that a crawling peg, as well as being used as a weapon in the fight against inflation, can also be used as a means to stabilise the

RER at a comparatively high level in the face of high domestic inflation, as Brazil successfully did in 1968–79 (Coes 1994, pp. 439–40).

Various attempts to fight inflation through the rate of exchange have miscarried. Chile, which had experienced triple-digit inflation from 1972 to 1976, introduced a *tablita* system in early 1978 and fixed the dollar exchange rate in June 1979. Partly thanks to backward wage indexation, it was not before 1981 that the inflation rate converged to the world inflation rate. In the meantime, there had been severe RER appreciation, made worse by a capital-import-financed boom in the nontradeables industries. The current-account deficit reached 13.7 per cent of GDP in 1981. Capital inflows suddenly stopped in 1982 and in June 1982 the fixed dollar rate had to be abandoned (Visser and Van Herpt 1996).

During the same period, Argentina under Finance Minister José Martínez de Hoz had a similar unsuccessful experience with fighting inflation through the exchange rate. Starting in 1976, the government tried to reduce inflation with the help of fixed-but-adjustable parities. In December 1978 a *tablita* system was introduced, which was intended to end in March 1981. The attempt failed, as the government did not sufficiently reduce its inflationary-financed deficits (it sold its bonds to the commercial banks). Inflation did not end and Argentina priced itself out of the market. To his credit, Martínez succeeded in significantly reducing the primary budget deficit, that is, the deficit less interest payments on outstanding debt. He could not, however, prevent the burden of the interest payments on outstanding debt increasing. It was his misfortune that, in addition, the central bank in 1980 had to bail out the biggest three commercial banks, in fact guaranteeing their liabilities, and that General R.E. Viola, who was to assume office as head of state in March 1981, created considerable uncertainty by refusing to indicate what economic policy, if any, he had in mind (Calvo 1986; Corbo and de Melo 1987).

True, inflation fell from 443 per cent in 1976 to 101 per cent in 1980, but it was still at a high level and people now expected Martínez's policy to fail. They bought dollars to invest abroad (restrictions on international capital movements had been lifted as part of Martínez's economic liberalisation measures). As long as a comparatively high value of the Argentinian peso was maintained in the foreign-exchange market, not only imports and capital exports, but also travel abroad was attractive to the Argentine population. Argentinian tourists in Brazil got the nickname '*deme dos*': everything was dirt cheap for them and they went on a spree, 'just gimme two'.

Later attempts in Argentina to reduce inflation in a more drastic way with the help of a currency board were more successful, for a considerable time. After a near-doubling of the exchange rate compared with the end of 1990 and a near sixfold increase compared with the end of 1989, Economics Minister Domingo Cavallo fixed the Argentine austral at $1 = A10,000 in April 1991 and introduced the new peso on 1 January 1992 at the rate of P1 = A10,000 = $1. The exchange rate was held fixed for about a decade. The reduction in inflation was dramatic: the average consumer price level in 1990 was 2300 per cent above the 1989 level. The rise in 1991 was down to 172 per cent. By 1995 inflation had been completely squashed and between 1995 and 2001 prices were stable or even slightly falling (*International Financial Statistics*, **54** (5), May 2001). The government succeeded in convincing the markets that this time around everything else would be made subordinate to the stabilisation (inflation-reducing) effort. Also, the economy underwent a drastic liberalisation programme, involving the selling off of state enterprises and resulting in remarkable productivity increases during the first years (Cavallo and Mondino 1996). Even so, during the tequila crisis help from outside was needed to prevent the attempt failing. Since then, things have not gone very smoothly. Argentina's competitive position on international markets came under pressure thanks to a large devaluation by Brazil in January 1999 and a strong dollar. On top of that, international capital markets, which had liberally provided Argentina with loans, got more and more concerned about the deteriorating state of Argentina's public finances and funds dried up. A large-scale rescheduling of debt in 2001 gave only a brief respite. Proposals by Cavallo, who was sacked in July 1996 by President Menem but under President De la Rúa was back at the helm from March to December 2001, to replace the dollar link with a mixed dollar-euro link did not help either and in January 2002 the currency board was formally abandoned. The collapse was rather messy. Dollar-denominated private debt was turned into peso-denominated debt at arbitrary rates and bank deposits were frozen (Edwards 2002).

5.2.4 The Walters Critique

If the monetary authorities of a high-inflation country link its currency to another country's currency in order to use the fixed exchange rate *vis-à-vis* that currency as a nominal anchor, they hope in that way to quickly bring down inflation. If economic agents have become wary, possibly because of failed attempts at reducing inflation in the past, it may become difficult to influence inflation expectations. One consequence that we have not yet discussed is that inflation may in fact be fuelled rather than brought down.

If interest rates remain higher than abroad and the financial markets believe that the fixed exchange rate will be maintained within their time horizon, there will be capital imports, which increase the money supply and stimulate spending. Alternatively, if short-term interest rates fall approximately to the level of foreign short-term rates, non-financial firms, which have a longer time horizon than financial firms and may expect inflation to persist, interpret the fall in the nominal short rate of interest as a fall in the real rate, which again stimulates spending. This phenomenon is known as the *Walters critique*, named after the economist Alan Walters (Jager and Pauli 2001).

If inflation does not fall, current-account deficits will develop and sooner or later the financial markets will expect the fixed exchange rate to break down. Capital imports make way for capital exports and the expectation of a breakdown of the fixed-rate system brings the breakdown about. The possibility of the Walters critique scenario happening underlines the importance of inflation expectations and of convincing the market that the authorities will persevere.

5.2.5   Reduced Flexibility

Exchange-rate regimes come in different degrees of fixedness or flexibility. In a world with free and volatile capital flows countries either have to give up their independent monetary policy or their fixed exchange rate. Also, with a fixed exchange rate they may be very vulnerable to speculative capital flows. This situation would call for either a solidly fixed exchange rate or very hard peg or for a freely floating exchange rate. In a monetary union and under official dollarisation a country gives up its own currency, which can therefore no longer come under attack, but a currency board might come close as a means to convince the market that everything will be done to defend the exchange rate (though the Argentinian debacle cannot but affect the credibility of currency boards). A freely floating exchange rate of course precludes a crisis where a depletion of foreign-exchange reserves forces a country to steeply devaluate its currency and/or impose capital controls.

There is a tendency in the literature to consider choosing such a *corner solution* as inevitable with free capital flows (Wagner 2000; see Table 5.2 for developments in the 1990s; note, however, that free and managed floating have been lumped together). Calvo and Reinhart (2002) argue that many countries that claim to float more or less freely, in fact show remarkably high fluctuations in foreign-exchange reserves and interest rates, compared with exchange-rate changes. Changes in reserves point to direct interventions, and interest-rate changes to monetary policy actions with an eye to the exchange rate. These countries may, indeed, have valid arguments for what Calvo and Reinhart call 'fear of floating' and choosing an in-between position. Fixed pegs may be deemed unattractive, for instance, if foreign countries have a higher rate of inflation or if shocks hitting the country in question and other countries are asymmetric. Free-floating rates may, however, lead to volatile exchange rates. The authorities may then opt for a fixed-but-adjustable peg system or for a floating-rate system where they intervene in foreign-exchange markets or manipulate interest rates, with a view to smoothing exchange-rate fluctuations. For another thing, a speculative bubble may occur. Provided the monetary authorities are able to identify such a bubble, they again have an honourable reason to intervene. Instead of a free or *clean float* we get a *managed* or *dirty float*.

Of course, if the monetary authorities intervene in foreign-exchange markets or manipulate interest rates, domestic liquidity creation is affected. In general, if there are shocks in the economy, economic variables will be affected, and if some variables (such as the rate of exchange or the money supply) are held constant, others (such as the money supply and the rate of exchange, respectively) will have to bear the brunt. Nonetheless, countries such as Indonesia were able for many years to keep inflation in check (around the 10 per cent level in the case of Indonesia) through monetary and fiscal policies while manipulating nominal exchange rates in such a way as to keep RER roughly constant (Visser and Van Herpt 1996). Managed floating could be seen as an unmitigated success in the case of Indonesia, until the 1997–98 Asian currency crisis and political turbulence put a spanner in the works. Private-sector short-term foreign debt that could not be rolled over proved an important cause of the debacle and it is important that, with exchange rates that are not solidly fixed, foreign short-term borrowing is subject to restrictions or agents are made to realise that they should seek forward cover.

A managed float can be seen as a halfway house between fixed and fully flexible exchange rates, more flexible than a fixed-but-adjustable peg. Another such solution is the adoption of a band within which exchange rates can move. One advantage of such a band is that macroeconomic policy can at times be directed at domestic policy ends without the danger of immediate repercussions in the form of foreign-exchange crises. The ERM (Exchange Rate Mechanism) that preceded the introduction of the common currency in the EU was a case in point, at least after its mid-1993 reform, when a 15 per cent fluctuation margin on either side of the central rate, or parity, was introduced. The ERM was characterised by so-called *hard buffers*, that is, the central banks of the member countries were bound to intervene if the exchange rate showed signs of leaving the band.

A variant with *soft buffers* has been propagated by Williamson (1985), whose *target-zone* proposal included margins of some 10 per cent either side of the central rate, outside of which rates would be considered 'clearly wrong' (p. 72). Williamson's aim is to prevent the exchange rate deviating too much from, in his words, 'the fundamental equilibrium exchange rate, which is the rate that is expected to generate a current account surplus or deficit equal to the underlying capital flow over the cycle, given that the country is pursuing "internal balance" as best it can and not restricting trade for balance of payments reasons' (Williamson 1985, p. 14). With soft buffers, the authorities aim at keeping the exchange rate within the band on average, but they may allow the exchange rate to move outside the band under exceptional circumstances (Bartolini and Prati 1997). Clearly, it is the real exchange rate that is to be stabilised under such a target-zone system, not the nominal rate. The band, or target zone, consequently has to be adjusted if inflation rates or other fundamentals between countries diverge.

If a shock occurs that makes the exchange rate diverge from the central rate, a band or target zone provides the opportunity to wait and see whether the shock is permanent before taking a decision to adjust the central rate, and with it the band or target zone. In the meantime, speculation is less attractive than in the case of a fixed-but-adjustable peg with a narrow band. In the latter case, the risk involved in speculation is small: if speculators expect a devaluation of a currency and buy foreign exchange but the devaluation fails to materialise, they suffer at best a small loss: the exchange rate can only fall by a small percentage; they also lose interest if they have borrowed money to finance their positions. Speculation is a one-way bet: there are high potential gains and small potential losses. With a wide band, such as the ERM band of 15 per cent on either side of the central rate in operation for the majority of EU currencies before the introduction of the euro, the exchange rate will first adjust under an attack, without the authorities having to step in and use their foreign-exchange reserves. The potential losses for speculators are high, because both the probability that the attack fails and the potential loss suffered in that case are higher than under a small band. After a failed attempt at forcing the authorities to adjust the official exchange rate, say to raise it (to devalue the domestic currency), the market exchange rate may fall appreciably. The potential losses of course are even higher in the case of soft buffers, where the external value of a currency can be driven outside the band but will bounce back if the attack fails, leaving the speculators with hefty losses. Moreover, even if the speculation succeeds and the official exchange rate is adjusted, speculators may end up with a loss.

This is because after a devaluation, when speculative pressure has subsided, the market rate may move from the highest possible position in the old band to the lowest possible one in the new band. If the bands overlap, this will lead to losses for the speculators (see Figure 5.1). The wider the band, the higher the probability of overlap after a devaluation or revaluation. Speculation in this way becomes a *two-way bet*. This will

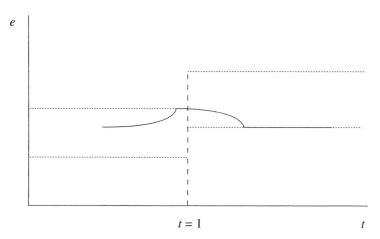

Figure 5.1   Devaluation with overlapping bands

act as a deterrent and help to prevent speculative attacks (European foreign exchange markets were remarkably quiet after the widening of the ERM band in August 1993).

If the width of the target zone is not made public, that in itself may help to prevent speculation. In a system with hard buffers interventions at the weak edge of the band are likely to be interpreted by the market as a sign of weakness, but in a target zone with an undisclosed band width the information which the market can extract from interventions is not so clear-cut and those interventions can, therefore, be more effective (Koedijk et al. 1995). Of course the difference between a target zone with undisclosed buffers and one with soft buffers is very slight indeed, as the authorities can easily move the edges of the band if they are undisclosed.

It may be concluded that a target zone with a wide band, be it with soft or with hard buffers, is superior to a narrow band when it comes to preventing speculative attacks on a currency, at the price of increased exchange-rate variability. If there is a real danger of recurring speculative attacks, this increased variability may well be the more attractive alternative (see Kempa and Nelles 1999 for a technical analysis of target-zone models).

5.2.6 Less-Developed Countries and the Fear of Depreciation and Devaluation

After 1973, when the rich countries moved over to greater exchange-rate flexibility, at first only a small minority of LDCs opted for free floating. It was only after the 1982 debt crisis, when a great number of LDCs had to draw up adjustment programmes with the help of the IMF, that free floating spread more rapidly, not without some prodding by the Fund (Table 5.2 shows developments in the 1990s; but free and managed floating are not shown separately).

The authorities in many LDCs tended to view free floating with suspicion. Quirk et al. (1987, pp. 1, 4) mention some objections against free floating widely subscribed to in LDCs:

- A thin foreign-exchange market, or more generally the underdeveloped state of financial markets, may lead to highly volatile exchange rates and to unstable costs of hedging (if at all possible).
- A small number of big traders may manipulate exchange rates.
- Volatility of the exchange rate may, in the case of depreciations, exert strong upward pressure on the domestic price level.

Devaluations within the fixed-but-adjustable peg system were also associated with inflation. In addition, a devaluation could easily be interpreted as an admittance of failure. In a study of a great number of devaluations, Cooper (1973, pp. 193–4) found that within a year after a devaluation, nearly 30 per cent of the governments concerned fell, as against 14 per cent in a control group without inflation. The corresponding figures for the finance ministers were nearly 60 per cent and 18 per cent, respectively. Incoming governments often saw themselves faced with a crisis situation and settled for a sizeable devaluation. Instead of frequent small exchange-rate changes, infrequent large changes took place, which implied large shocks in the RER. Even worse, governments and central banks resorted to all kinds of impediments to trade and payments or to multiple exchange rates, in a desperate attempt to avoid an official devaluation. It is, of course, much better to adjust exchange rates in time than to make promises that have to be broken and hang on to a level of the exchange rate that is bound to lead to a foreign-exchange crisis.

Even so, there are respectable economic arguments against devaluation. They generally do not look conclusive, though. Residents who have made foreign-exchange borrowings and failed to cover their short position suffer a loss when a devaluation takes place (unless the devaluation was expected at the time the loans were concluded and the devaluation risk was reflected in the interest-rate difference between domestic-currency and foreign-currency loans). Serious bouts of business failures may even result, as happened in the early 1980s in Chile, Argentina and Uruguay and in 1997–98 during the Asian crisis. These were, however, to a large degree the consequence of high real interest rates following from attempts to defend the rate of exchange and of distress borrowing by firms in the tradeables sector trying to survive in the face of a low real exchange rate (Corbo and de Melo 1987, p. 133; World Bank 1990, p. 101). It is better, then, to devalue at an earlier stage.

Another concern was that devaluations would hardly help boost export proceeds in a world where price elasticities were presumably low. This *elasticity pessimism* can be justified in the case of countries that export primary commodities and not much else, as price elasticities of demand in export markets may be low and the (short-run) price elasticity of supply may often be low as well. If, moreover, there is little scope for import substitution and imports amount to a high percentage of GNP, devaluations immediately feed into higher prices without contributing much in the way of improving the trade balance. It is only the reduction in real cash balances that helps to improve the trade balance in this case, but the roundabout route of a devaluation and its implied inflationary impact to bring this about can be avoided by applying a straight monetary contraction. Over the last decades, however, the share of manufactures in LDC exports has steadily grown, so this objection has lost much of its force (as is shown by Coes 1994 for Brazil). Moreover, supply elasticities of primary commodities will be higher in the long run than in the short run. Nevertheless, there are cases in which the elasticity argument against devaluation may carry some weight (see IMF 1994 on Cape Verde).

Devaluation makes the domestic price level rise and resistance against devaluations is often based on a fear of accelerating inflation. If, however, domestic monetary and fiscal policies are sufficiently restrictive, the price level rises less than the exchange rate and real depreciation takes place (empirical evidence can be found in Cooper 1973; Connolly and Taylor 1976; Kamin 1988; see also Kapur et al. 1991 for Ghana in the 1980s and Amitrano, De Grauwe and Tullio 1997 for a rich Western economy, Italy; of course, if macroeconomic policies are insufficiently restrictive, inflation will nullify real depreciation: see Bautista 1982; Edwards 1989 for such cases).

Table 5.2   Exchange-rate regimes, all countries, 1991 and 1999

	1991	1999
All countries		
Hard peg	25	45
Intermediate	98	63
Float	36	77
Number of countries	159	185
Developed countries excepted		
Hard peg	24	34
Intermediate	83	62
Float	30	67
Number of countries	137	163

Notes: Hard peg = currency board or no separate currency (official dollarisation, monetary union); intermediate, or soft pegs = fixed-but-adjustable peg, crawling peg and wide bands; floating = managed float with no specified central rate and independently floating.

Source: Fischer (2001).

If devaluation is accompanied by trade and payments liberalisation, prices will show even less tendency to increase. Trade liberalisation means a lowering of import duties, which directly decreases the domestic price of foreign goods, or a reduction of non-tariff barriers, which brings about the same feat indirectly through an increase in competition and consequently lower profit margins. New technologies become available embodied in import goods, and trade liberalisation often also implies better opportunities to buy foreign technology direct. The devaluations associated with liberalisation provide new opportunities for the exportables industries (see Section 5.5 on payments restrictions), such that economies of scale can be exploited. All this brings the promise of higher productivity and thus a fall in inflation. There should thus be a positive relationship between trade liberalisation and technology improvements (Alam and Morrison 2000 provide evidence using microeconomic data).

However, trade and payments liberalisation will expose the importables industries to the chill winds of foreign competition. Here we discern another source of resistance against devaluation: if it forms part of an effort to open up the economy, producers (including both capital owners and employees) of importables are sure to suffer, unless they significantly increase their productivity, whereas producers of exportables are likely to benefit. The benefits require time and hard work to be reaped, as producers have to make efforts to explore new markets and set up distribution channels, which they will only do if the liberalisation policy is credible (empirical research supports the idea that the benefits need some time to make themselves felt; see Greenaway 1998; Greenaway, Morgan and Wright 2002). Exportables producers thus may first react to devaluation-*cum*-liberalisation with a wait-and-see attitude, whereas importables producers are likely to offer fierce opposition.

Exportables producers should receive support from producers using imported inputs, if these become freely available after liberalisation, and from consumers, who benefit from a wider choice of goods and services. Those consumers, however, are likely to perceive the benefits of liberalisation for each one individually as too small to take action, or they may even fail to see the advantages and instead speak out against liberalisation because of the prospect of higher prices after devaluation. Producers who will suffer from liberalisation will, however, go to great lengths to prevent it being introduced, as it is important for each of them individually to maintain the status quo. Well-organised trade unions in import-competing industries will also make themselves heard. There is no better place to see Olson's Logic of Collective Action at work than the area of trade policy (Olson 1971). Thus, even if trade and payments restrictions have only been introduced to survive a temporary trade or payments shock, sufficient numbers of individuals and business firms may have a vested interest in a low exchange rate-*cum*-protection to prevent a reversal of policy (see Frey 1984, chs 2 and 3; Lanjouw and Wielinga 1994; Pareto 1909, ch. IX, pp. 520–5 on this political-economy approach to protection; see Collier and Gunning 1994 for a critical weighing of the various arguments). If liberal trade and payments arrangements have at last become more popular in the 1990s, it is because of the poor results of protectionist policies, coupled with the conditions attached by the IMF and the World Bank to financial support for countries with economic problems (Drabek and Laird 1998).

5.3 CURRENT-ACCOUNT DISEQUILIBRIA AND CAPITAL-MARKET INTEGRATION

5.3.1 Current-Account Disequilibria and International Capital Flows

The rate of exchange can only be maintained at a certain level if the balance of payments and the current account are not too far away from equilibrium. This formulation does not suffer from an excess of precision, nor was it meant to. One would be hard put to find a sharp criterion. Under a fixed or fixed-but-adjustable parity system and under a dirty float the balance of payments of the non-bank sector can be in disequilibrium for considerable periods of time without cause for concern. It should be noted that a current-account surplus means that spending by residents is less than their income and a deficit means that spending exceeds income (see equation 2.1 in Chapter 2: if we move domestic absorption $Z + G$ to the left-hand side, we see that the balance on the current account equals national income minus domestic absorption). This imbalance may come from different sources (apart from overly lax or tight macroeconomic policies):

- One good reason for current-account disequilibria is that different countries may find themselves in different phases of the business cycle. For a country near the upper turning point of the business cycle a current-account deficit is, *ceteris paribus*, more acceptable (for example, because of higher business spending) than for a country near the lower turning point. This basically bears on short-term imbalances.
- Economic agents in a country with its income fluctuating as a result of volatile export prices may invest abroad in good times and disinvest in bad times in order to let consumption fluctuate less than income. Such *consumption smoothing* again is associated with short-term imbalances (Ghosh and Ostry 1995).
- Demographic developments may cause a current-account deficit or surplus. A country with a relatively young population will have a high savings rate, especially if there is a funded pension system. This easily leads to a current-account surplus (see Bikker 1994 for the Netherlands). This phenomenon could explain imbalances over longer periods.
- A rich country with up-to-date technology and perhaps an ageing population may benefit more from lending money to still-poor countries that expect high yields from investments in new technology than from investing the money in the domestic market. Again, we would expect imbalances over longer periods.

Basically, current-account imbalances and the associated capital flows can be seen as *intertemporal substitution in spending*: spending now is substituted by spending in the future or the other way round.

We can illustrate the potential benefits of (longer-term) imbalances with the help of a two-period model with one good and perfect markets. In the first period, a country has available an endowment of goods that can be either consumed or invested (think of potatoes that either can be consumed or used as seed potatoes). Investments lead to higher income in the second period. In the second period there are no investments, because the world ends after the second period. The country can increase consumption and/or investment in the first period by foreign borrowing. It will then have to spend part of its production in the second period on interest and amortisation. The country also has the option to spend less than its endowment on production and consumption for its own use and lend the surplus to other countries. That will lead to higher consumption in the second period. Of course this is a highly stylised approach. Its function is to show that the current-account balance can be seen as a manifestation of intertemporal substitution and that such intertemporal substitution is potentially welfare improving. In more empirically oriented research one cannot telescope the whole future into 'period $t + 1$' (cf. Cottarelli et al. 1998, ch. 3).

This two-period model is represented by a diagram with an intertemporal production possibility curve and a set of community indifference curves (Figure 5.2). On the horizontal axis we measure quantities of goods in period t, on the vertical axis quantities of goods in period $t + 1$. We start with a closed economy. The intertemporal production possibility curve shows that the less that is consumed in period t, the higher production will be in period $t + 1$. Available resources in period t are *OD*. If total resources *OD* are consumed in period t, nothing is left for investment and available resources in period $t + 1$ are measured on the vertical axis at point O (from Origin, not necessarily zero – even with zero investment some berries will ripen and some fish may be caught). If we move up along the curve, consumption is reduced and the resources not consumed are invested, with the result that more goods will be available in period $t + 1$. In a closed economy, or an economy constrained to current-account equilibrium, an optimum is found at point E, where the highest attainable indifference curve is reached.

If the economy is at E, consumption in period t is *OB*, investment is *BD* and in period $t + 1$ an amount *OI* will be produced and consumed. The marginal productivity of investment is represented by the slope of the line that is tangential to the intertemporal production possibility curve at point E. Given perfect markets, this slope also represents the rate of interest and, as the same line is tangential to an intertemporal community indifference

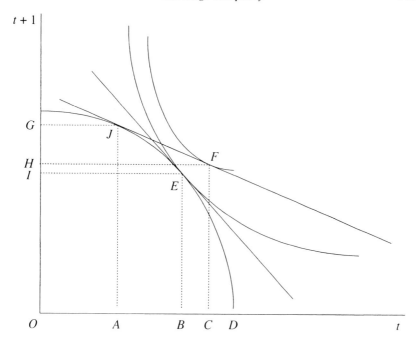

Figure 5.2   Intertemporal substitution with initial capital exports

curve at *E*, marginal time preference as well. Note that at a slope of minus 45 degrees the rate of interest is zero, that is, one unit given up now will give one extra unit at time *t* + 1; a positive real rate of interest is represented by a steeper tangent. More precisely, the slope of the tangent is equal to –(1 + the rate of interest).

If now the rate of interest in world capital markets is lower than the domestic interest rate in the closed economy, the country will benefit from borrowing funds abroad and running a current-account deficit. At a lower rate of interest the consumption point will be, say, *F* and the production point *J*. Consumption in period *t* becomes *OC*, whereas only *OA* consumption goods are produced. Imports, financed by capital imports, amount to *AC* and investment to *AD* (total resources minus domestic production of consumption goods). In period *t* + 1 total production is *OG*, of which *HG* is used to pay interest and repay the loan and *OH* is left for consumption. Borrowing at a rate below the closed-economy domestic rate offers the opportunity to consume more both in period *t* and in period *t* + 1 or at least to reach a higher community indifference curve.

In older, more mature economies it is the other way round. Their production possibility curves will be relatively lower and stretched to the right. They will start out with a relatively low marginal productivity of investment and will reach a higher indifference curve by lending out sums instead of investing themselves. The production point will shift to the right, but consumption will be lower than the production of consumption goods. Goods will be exported, financed by loans. Loan repayments enable the country to reach a higher consumption level in period $t + 1$.

Normally, a country engages in capital imports when it starts its take-off into economic growth, to become a capital exporter in a later period, when it has become relatively rich and other countries start growing. This happened in Britain, a net capital importer in the eighteenth century but a net capital exporter in the nineteenth century, and we have seen the same sequence a century later in the United States. There is, however, no mechanical rule in this respect – witness the US current-account deficits since the early 1980s.

In the two-period model more investment now leads to higher production in the future. The benefits of international capital flows can also be illustrated with the help of the MacDougall diagram, which focuses on international reallocations of existing capital.[3] No net investment is involved and the result of international capital flows, and thus of a temporary current-account imbalance, is simply a change in present production and income levels in the countries involved.

We study a simple neoclassical world, where capital moves from countries with a low marginal productivity of capital to countries with a high marginal productivity of capital. The horizontal axis in Figure 5.3 measures total capital in a two-country world, $O_A C$ is the amount employed in country A and $O_B C$ is employed in country B. The MPC curves depict the marginal productivity of capital with the amounts of the other factors of production given. We start with a situation where the marginal productivity of capital in B exceeds the marginal productivity of capital in A. Total production in A is represented by the area under the MPC_A curve between O_A and C and total production in B by the area under the MPC_B curve between O_B and C. If now SC of capital migrates from A to B, total production in A falls by $SCWT$, whereas total production in B rises by $CSTV$. World production increases by TVW. Capital owners or exporters from country A receive an income on capital invested in B or lent to B equal to the volume of investment times the marginal efficiency of capital (which is the remuneration rate of capital), that is, an amount represented by $SCZT$. Total income of country A's residents thus increases by TWZ and the remainder of the additional production volume, TZV, accrues to residents of country B. Both countries profit. Of course this analysis does not faithfully represent what really happens in the world, as the real world is more messy than a neoclassical model, being full of market imperfections. The model serves, though, to show the potential benefits of international capital flows to both capital exporters and capital importers.

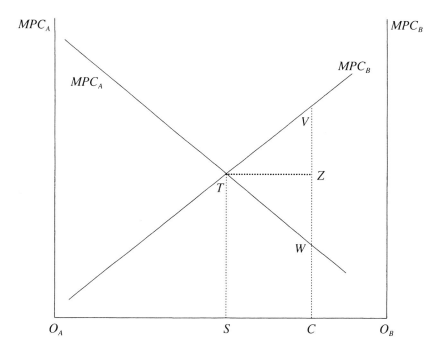

Figure 5.3   Capital reallocation in a two-country world

Empirical research suggests that the model can be useful in interpreting history, though as far as pre-World War I capital exports to North and South America and Australia are concerned, it was not a question of capital flows from regions with a high capital–labour ratio to regions with a low capital–labour ratio, but of movements of both labour and capital from relatively labour-and-capital-rich but resource-poor regions to regions with an abundance of natural resources relative to labour and capital (Taylor and Williamson 1994). Present-day flows to South America and Asia seem to better fit the standard two-factor approach with labour and capital as factors of production. Of course, it is not only capital that moves. If capital flows take the form of direct investment, technologies and skills migrate as well.

5.3.2   Capital–Market Integration

Consumption smoothing and long-term borrowing and lending or direct foreign investment as analysed above presuppose a high degree of capital mobility and, thus, of capital market integration. One could think of different criteria for the measurement of capital market integration. Particularly relevant in the present case is the *Feldstein–Horioka criterion*. Feldstein and Horioka posited that perfect capital mobility implies that domestic saving and domestic investment are uncorrelated: 'saving in each country responds to the worldwide opportunities for investment while investment in that country is financed by the worldwide pool of capital' (Feldstein and Horioka 1980, p. 317). If saving and investment become decoupled, this simply means that international capital flows make imbalances in the current account of the balance of payments possible.

It has been argued that the Feldstein–Horioka criterion is premised on a number of very restrictive conditions. Its validity requires that domestic saving and investment are a function of the world real interest rate so that the domestic real rate of interest must equal the world real rate of interest, that is, there is real interest parity. Also, apart from the interest rate, all determinants of a country's rate of investment should be uncorrelated with its rate of savings. But a country's saving and investment may be correlated, even under perfect international capital mobility:

- A persistent but not permanent productivity shock would increase savings because wages are temporarily high, provided income earners' spending on consumption is a function of *permanent* income, while it would also lead to increased investment because of higher capital productivity (Frankel 1992; Ghosh 1995, p. 107).
- In the long run saving and investment should be correlated (see our two-period model above) because countries cannot borrow without limit.
- Business firms cannot borrow without limit either. Even if this does not act as a serious barrier, firms prefer to finance investment from retained earnings, that is, from savings, as the pecking-order theory of business finance tells us (Myers 2001).
- Governments intervene when current-account imbalances become too large in their eyes (Jansen 1998). They may, for example, change public saving and investment and in that way induce correlation between gross saving and investment even when capital is fully mobile (de Brouwer 1999, p. 57).

The Feldstein–Horioka criterion is extremely strong. Nevertheless, it provides a useful yardstick and it certainly gives an impression of the direction of the integration movement.

There are other, less stringent, criteria for capital market integration. In increasing decree of stringency we could, following Frankel (1992; 1993, ch. 2), mention:

- covered interest parity. It could be said that capital markets are fully integrated if CIP holds and the only risk is exchange-rate risk, which can be covered.
- uncovered interest parity, that is, CIP plus zero exchange-rate risk premium. Clearly, UIP implies a stronger degree of capital market integration than CIP.
- Real interest-rate parity, that is, UIP plus a constant real exchange rate.

Feldstein–Horioka is the most stringent criterion, as it includes real interest-rate parity plus the absence of any correlation between the determinants of savings and the determinants of investment, apart from the real interest rate. Instead of looking at flows, one could also look at stocks. It could be argued that the higher the gross stocks of foreign assets and foreign liabilities as a percentage of GDP, the more capital markets are internationally integrated (Lane and Milesi-Ferretti 2003).

It may be noted that present-time capital market integration is probably not much different from the immediate pre-World War I period if we apply the Feldstein–Horioka criterion: a country such as Canada financed 30 per cent to 50 per cent of its investment with foreign capital in the 1870–1900 period, experiencing capital inflows to the tune of 7.5 per cent of GNP on average. The situation in Australia was similar and the Scandinavian countries were not far behind (Pringle 1989, p. 376). The more successful developing countries have been able recently to finance similar current-account deficits, for example Malaysia (9 per cent of GDP in 1995) and Thailand (over 8 per cent) (IMF 1996a, p. 61). On the export side, it has been estimated that net capital exports from the United Kingdom averaged some 5 per cent of national income between 1870 and 1913, and even roughly 10 per cent in 1912–14, whereas France and Germany exported capital at a rate of 2 per cent to 3 per cent of GNP (Pringle 1989, p. 368). Against this, current-account surpluses in the 1989–96 period fluctuated between 1.2 per cent and 3.1 per cent of GDP in Japan, between 2.3 per cent and 5.2 per cent of GDP in the Netherlands and between –1.0 per cent and 4.8 per cent of GDP in Germany (IMF 1997a, p. 168). Whatever the situation in the past, empirical research has found that the correlation between investment to output ratios and savings to output ratios fell to very low levels over the last decade of the twentieth century (Blanchard and Giavazzi 2002; Calderón and Schmidt-Hebbel 2003).

Unfortunately, net capital flows are *potentially* a blessing, but one cannot always trust markets to function well in the sense that capital imports are used wisely. There are indications, for instance, that capital imports in Mexico during the run-up to the 1994 peso crisis replaced rather than supplemented domestic savings, and thus financed consumption without increasing investment (Singh 1997).

If net capital flows are probably not significantly different as a proportion of GDP than before World War I, gross flows are of course a different matter, thanks mainly to information and communications technology.[4]

It may be noted that surpluses and deficits need not necessarily tend to even out over the years. Even continuous deficits of some fraction of national income need not result in an explosive growth in foreign debt, provided the rate of interest on that debt is lower than the rate of growth of national income (Solomon 1979). Much depends on the creditor country. If the creditor country grows faster than the debtor country, and the debtor stabilises its debt in terms of its national product, the creditor will see its foreign assets fall as a percentage of its national product. Such a situation can continue for long periods (Cooper and Sachs 1986, p. 233; Cooper and Sachs's models provide a profound analysis of the debt problem).

5.4 POLICY COORDINATION

5.4.1 The Benefits of Coordination

So far, we have mainly looked at a country's balance-of-payments and exchange-rate policies in isolation. In the small country case this is unobjectionable, as repercussions on other countries are by definition negligible. The results of policy measures taken by large countries or by country groups will be felt by other countries, though. This may provide a case for international policy coordination. A few cases may serve to illustrate the potential benefits of policy coordination.

Consider a fixed-parity system. The various countries all pursue their own balance-of-payments aims. However, if there are n countries in the system, there are only $n - 1$ independent balance-of-payments targets possible, as worldwide aggregate balance-of-payments deficits must match aggregate surpluses. The same goes for current-account deficits and surpluses. If $n - 1$ countries jointly aim for some given surplus or deficit, they will be thwarted by the n-th country if that country decides to set its own policy ends independently. Let the United States start with a current-account deficit and then try to drastically cut it by means of a reduction of the government budget deficit (through lower expenditure or higher taxes). If other countries, such as Japan and Germany, wish to maintain their surpluses, not all targets can simultaneously be met. These other countries will react by taking measures that may result in a Keynesian deflationary gap and provoke a global depression. This is a counterpart on a global scale of the Keynesian savings paradox, where individual attempts to increase saving end up in lower income for everybody and no increased savings. Two solutions can be thought of:

(i) at least one country accepts any deficit or surplus resulting from the surpluses or deficits aimed at by the other countries;
(ii) countries coordinate policies, in order to make targets compatible (see Cooper 1986 for a fundamental analysis of the issue of policy coordination).

In a floating-rate system similar considerations apply with regard to exchange-rate targets. The exchange rates preferred by the various countries must be compatible or, alternatively, at least one country must passively adjust to the outcome of the other countries' policies. If not, global deflation or inflation may follow. If, for example, all countries in a Mundell–Fleming world with fully interest-elastic capital flows resort to a monetary expansion in order to depreciate their currencies and improve their current accounts, their attempts will come to grief. If they go on trying, in the end only inflation may result.

More generally, if many countries apply the same policy measures the results are bound to differ for each of them from the case where such measures are taken by one country or only a few.

It is also the case that measures that are ineffective when taken by a single country can be quite successful when taken by many countries simultaneously. The income and employment effects of a fiscal expansion under floating rates with full interest-elasticity of capital flows will be undone by a currency appreciation if the measure is taken by one individual country, but not if it is taken by many countries. Similar considerations go for the fixed-rate case. Monetary expansions are effective, even if capital flows are infinitely interest-elastic, if put through by many countries instead of one or a few. This is because the world interest rate will fall. Fiscal expansion on the contrary will be less effective, because the world interest rate will rise.

The results of economic policies followed jointly by many countries differ from the results of the same policies followed by a single country or a few countries. This makes a case for coordination, even if uncoordinated policies are not always incompatible. A related issue is that uncoordinated mixes of monetary and fiscal policies may make exchange rates bob and weave vigorously. To mention one case, the restrictive monetary policy pursued in the early 1980s in the United Kingdom and the United States, combined with an expansionary fiscal policy in the United States, made interest rates soar. Substantial capital inflows followed and sterling and the dollar rose to dizzying heights. These appreciations were at a later stage followed by depreciations. The business world saw itself confronted with large swings in the RER and it was far from clear to what degree these would be permanent or at what point there would be a swing in the opposite direction. The price system was seriously distorted and misallocations of investments were the inevitable result. For instance, products were specially developed for the US market in the expectation that the dollar would remain high, only to prove uncompetitive in the US market after the fall of the dollar after March 1985. Others started factories in the United States before the rise of the dollar and realised they were high-cost producers once the dollar had risen. To pile on the agony, after the closure of such factories the dollar could fall again.

5.4.2   Coordination and Speculative Attacks

Why does it often prove difficult for countries to coordinate their macroeconomic policies? Several factors play a role:

For large countries, domestic problems may dominate the political agenda.
• Their international trade is, *ceteris paribus*, less important expressed as a percentage of GNP or GDP than in small countries. For a large country, stable exchange rates, therefore, are of less significance relative to domestic policy ends (such as economic growth or some price-level objective) than for a small country. International coordination implies fewer degrees of freedom in economic policy, with uncertain benefits. After all, it is very difficult to quantify the expected results of coordination in terms of balance-of-payments disequilibria, trade flows, interest rates and so on (see Grosser 1988 for empirical estimates).

• Small countries generally can be expected to be more interested in policy coordination than big countries, but they lack the necessary clout in the international arena. They may suffer from the policies of big countries without much scope for retaliation. Large countries and large country groups can be expected to prefer looser arrangements.

• Coordination implies that the authorities from the various countries see eye to eye not only on the policy ends, but also on the character of the actual economic situation and on the way to move from the actual to the desired situation, that is, on the relevant model. This is not necessarily always the case. Especially if exchange-rate targets are involved, the authorities may have a tough ride if the market holds different views on the equilibrium exchange rates following from the 'market fundamentals'. The history of the dollar provides ample illustration. In the Plaza Agreement of September 1985 the G5 countries agreed that the dollar should depreciate to the tune of

---

BOX 5.1. FOREIGN-EXCHANGE SPECULATION AND THE SHORT RATE OF INTEREST

If participants in forex markets have a firm expectation of an imminent rise or fall in the exchange rate, short-term interest rates have to rise to stratospheric levels in order to stem speculation. We start from uncovered interest parity:

$$(1 + i) = (1 + i^f).E_t e_{t+1}/e_t$$

Let market participants expect a rise in the price of foreign exchange of 10 per cent in a week's time. $E_t e_{t+1}/e_t$ then has the value 1.1. If the foreign short-term interest rate is, say, 8 per cent per annum, the UIP formula for a one-week horizon becomes

$$(1 + i)^{1/52} = (1.08)^{1/52}.(1.1)$$

Taking logs, we find

$$1/52 \ln(1 + i) = 1/52 \ln(1.08) + \ln(1.1)$$

which yields

$$1 + i = 153.406$$

so that

$$i = 152.406 = 15{,}240.6 \text{ per cent on an annual basis.}$$

Assuming 260 workdays a year and composite interest, this works out at 1.95 per cent interest per day. In Ireland interest rates rose to 25,000 per cent in September 1992, or 2.148 per cent per day, which proved sufficient to stop speculation against the punt at that time.

Source: van der Wal (1992).

10 per cent to 12 per cent over a six-week period and decided to intervene to a limit of $18,000 million. The dollar did indeed fall, but went on falling. The G5 now wished to stop the dollar falling and in February 1987 concluded the Louvre Agreement. The market ignored the agreement, however, and the dollar only stopped falling a number of months later when the Fed raised interest rates, other central banks at the same time lowering theirs (Mussa 1990; James 1996, ch. 13). A prerequisite for policy coordination to have the desired results is that the financial markets deem the authorities credible, in the sense that they are trusted to put their money where their mouth is, and that exchange rates are not out of tune with fundamentals, in the view of most market participants (a complicating factor was that the authorities' mouth was not quite clear: the target zones were not made public). Potential international capital flows are so huge that no amount of intervention can stem exchange-rate movements that the authorities would like to reverse, if the authorities are not deemed credible.

Empirical research suggests that speculative attacks can be expected especially if a period of lax monetary policies is followed by wage and price increases that impair a country's international competitiveness and by high unemployment, which makes it politically difficult for the authorities to introduce monetary and fiscal austerity (Eichengreen, Rose and Wyplosz 1995). However, without such a history doubts about a government's resolution to maintain the exchange rate can also easily be provoked. During the 1997–98 Asian crisis it appears that a combination of real exchange-rate appreciations and increasing current-account deficits, in at least some of the countries involved, with a troubled financial sector (especially in Thailand) made international investors nervous. The preponderance of short-term international debt made it possible to withdraw funds at short notice on a large scale and deepen the crisis, once it broke out (IMF 1998a, ch. IV; 1998b; see also Chapter 3, Section 3.2.2). But the case of South Korea showed that this could happen even in the absence of a large current-account deficit or a large government-budget deficit.[5]

5.4.3   Official Intervention

Coordinated exchange-rate policies such as described above imply that the monetary authorities (the central bank) intervene in foreign-exchange markets, just as with fixed pegs. Interventions make the money supply change. If there is, for example, an excess supply of foreign exchange at the going exchange rate and the central bank wants to prevent the exchange rate falling (the domestic currency appreciating), it will buy foreign exchange. The sellers of foreign exchange receive domestic money. If the foreign exchange was supplied by banks for their own account, the base-money supply will increase. Short-term interest rates will tend to fall. If the banks offered the foreign exchange on behalf of their clients (exporters, capital importers), not only the base-money supply but also the narrow-money supply will increase.

Central banks often *sterilise* the effects of interventions, that is, they resort to open-market sales (as in Table 5.3) or purchases in order to undo the effects of the interventions on the money supply. If the central bank happens to have no open-market portfolio, it can create central bank securities (claims on the central bank) and sell these. While non-sterilised interventions are generally seen as working in the desired direction, there is serious doubt about the efficacy of sterilised interventions. We now compare non-sterilised and sterilised interventions, first under fully interest-elastic capital flows (as in the monetary model) and second with finite elasticity of capital flows (the portfolio model).

Table 5.3 *Foreign-exchange market intervention and sterilisation by the central bank in the case of a surplus in international payments*

Assets	Central bank balance sheet Liabilities	
foreign exchange +	banks +	(intervention)
government debt −	banks −	(sterilisation)

(i) Non-sterilised interventions with fully interest-elastic capital flows
Consider an excess supply of foreign exchange at the going exchange rate, which in the absence of central bank intervention would have led to an appreciation of the domestic currency. The central bank intervenes, buying foreign exchange. Without sterilisation, this will make the money supply increase. Generally, aggregate spending in the economy will increase, putting upward pressure on the domestic price level and boosting the demand for imports and with it demand for foreign exchange. Moreover, there is downward pressure on the domestic interest rate, which immediately feeds into the demand for foreign exchange. The intervention thus is effective in the sense that it helps to relieve the pressure on the exchange rate.

(ii) Sterilised interventions with fully interest-elastic capital flows
Sterilisation makes the money supply M return to its initial volume after an intervention. Open-market sales to mop up the increased volume of money in circulation make the number of domestic bonds in wealth holders' portfolios increase, however. Under fully interest-elastic capital flows the

price of domestic bonds may tend to fall, that is, the domestic rate of interest may tend to rise, but economic agents are indifferent between domestic and foreign bonds and will immediately sell foreign bonds or borrow abroad and non-residents will buy domestic bonds. Every pound, peso or won taken out of circulation by selling domestic bonds is replaced by a pound, peso or won created by capital imports. This happened, for instance, in Colombia in 1991 (Calvo, Leiderman and Reinhart 1995, pp. 378–9). Sterilised intervention is completely ineffective. It is a case of draining the tank with the tap full on, unless expectations are affected. Market participants expect, for instance, a revaluation or appreciation of the country's currency and the domestic interest rate plus the expected profit from an appreciation equalled the foreign rate. If the authorities succeed in convincing the market that they will resist any pressure to revalue or appreciate, speculative capital inflows will stop.

(iii) Non-sterilised interventions with finite elasticity of capital flows

With finite elasticity, that is, in the portfolio model, non-sterilised interventions will again increase spending and put upward pressure on prices. Additional demand for foreign exchange is generated through portfolio adjustments. The increased money supply may increase the demand for both domestic and foreign bonds, pushing up the price of domestic bonds (that is, lowering domestic interest rates). Wealth holders will then demand foreign exchange in order to buy foreign debt. Note that, unlike in the portfolio model for the very short period as analysed in Chapter 1, no actual rise in the exchange rate need occur, as there is an excess supply of foreign exchange to start with in the present case. Without intervention there would have been a fall in the exchange rate (appreciation of the domestic currency).

(iv) Sterilised interventions with finite elasticity of capital flows

Finite interest-elasticity leaves more scope for sterilised intervention than infinite elasticity. If a central bank buys foreign exchange and mops up the unwanted increase in the money supply by open-market sales, the share of domestic debt in wealthholders' portfolios increases. The price of domestic debt falls and the domestic interest rate rises. Unlike with infinite elasticity, the induced capital inflows need not completely nullify the effect of the intervention. This is because foreign and domestic interest rates may differ, reflecting a risk premium.

Interventions would probably have to be on a truly grand scale to be effective via this channel, given the aggregate volume of portfolios in the leading economies. Baillie and Osterberg (1997) could find little evidence of any effect of official (largely sterilised) interventions on the dollar/D-Mark rate or the dollar/yen rate over the 1985–90 period. Numbers played a role: the largest intervention was $1.25 billion, whereas the volume of foreign exchange traded daily was estimated at some $317 billion on average in the spot market alone in April 1989 (in April 1998 this had risen to $568 billion, but in April 2001 the volume was back at $387 billion; BIS 2002, p. 5). It is true that interventions act on the *balance* of all transactions, not on their gross volume. Still, with such large transactions volumes, the odd billion thrown on or taken out of the market may cause no more than a ripple on the surface of foreign-exchange flows. In other words, if there is any effect, it is likely to be short-lived. Other research tends to corroborate this picture (see Aguilar and Nydahl 2000 for the exchange rate of the US dollar and D-Mark against the Swedish krona between 1993 and 1996; see Fatum 2000 on Bundesbank interventions in US dollars, 1985–95), though there is also research that found short-term (less than a month) effects of large (over $1 billion) sterilised interventions (Fatum and Hutchison 2003). Sterilised intervention has furthermore been found effective through the portfolio balance effect and the expectations effect jointly (Sarno and Taylor 2001). Still, it appears that the authorities have mainly to pin their hopes on the expectations effect (also called *signalling effect*, as economic agents may view interventions as a signal about the future stance of policy) in the case of sterilisation. Success is more likely, of course, if the underlying stance of monetary and fiscal policy is deemed consistent with the desired effect of the interventions.

A note on expectations is in order. Implicitly we have assumed that exchange rates were determined by fundamentals. Ramaswamy and Samiei (2000) and Sarno and Taylor (2001, p. 863) suggest the interesting possibility that, if actual exchange rates differ from the fundamentals-based one, sterilised intervention may help to change market participants' decisions. Market participants are not willing to buy or sell a currency that they deem misaligned, fearing that others may hinder a return to an exchange rate that is more in line with the fundamentals. Sterilised intervention may, according to Ramaswamy and Samiei, signal the central bank's assessment of misalignment to the entire market and thus overcome this so-called *collective-action problem* (where one actor does not dare to move because he doesn't know whether others will move too).

If sterilised interventions have a weak effect at best, non-sterilised interventions can be expected to be much more successful, as they make it clear to market participants that the authorities accept the changes in the money supply and the rate of interest necessary to correct foreign-exchange-market imbalances. Symmetrical or coordinated non-sterilised interventions are best in this respect: the authorities in the deficit country sell foreign exchange and decrease their money supply in the process at the same time that the authorities in the surplus country buy foreign exchange and increase their money supply. All this is simply what the 'rules of the game' of the gold(-exchange) standard have always implied.

An attractive aspect of symmetrical or coordinated non-sterilised interventions is that the *world money supply* remains largely unaffected. The money supply falls in one country, rises in another. If the deficit country does not sterilise and the surplus country does, the world money supply falls. If it's the other way round, the world money supply increases. This may have undesirable effects on price developments in world markets. McKinnon (1982; 1984; 1993b, p. 30) saw these mechanisms as the cause of the 1973–79 inflationary period in the world and the monetary contraction in the first half of the 1980s. The first period was characterised by US deficits in international payments, the second period by US surpluses. Generally, if the rest of the world ran a surplus *vis-à-vis* the United States on the official settlements balance, their central banks received dollars which were used to buy US Treasury debt. Dollars that first, thanks to the payments imbalance, were shifted from the bank accounts of US residents to the bank accounts of non-residents, flowed back into the accounts of residents (the sellers of Treasury debt). The US money supply more or less remained constant, or, there was a kind of automatic sterilisation. If the rest of the world ran a deficit, their central banks sold US Treasury debt to US residents and the monetary effect of the US surplus again was automatically sterilised. The rest of the world did, however, sterilise to a much lesser degree, if at all. Thus, as De Grauwe (1989) puts it, 'there seems to be evidence indicating that the movements in and out of the dollar may have triggered cycles of world-wide monetary deflation and expansion' (p. 213). This followed from the special position of the US dollar as the world's key currency, in which other countries' central banks hold their foreign-exchange reserves.

If the authorities are not willing to accept the changes in the price level which will follow the changes in the money supply brought about by non-sterilised intervention, they had better not try and stabilise exchange rates. If the authorities have reason to believe that market fundamentals warrant an unchanged exchange rate at unchanged price levels they can take the risk and engage in sterilised interventions, but only if they can be sure of influencing expectations quickly enough for the market not to increase capital flows. Before the price level is affected, short-term interest rates will bear the brunt of non-sterilised interventions. This is because sales and purchases of foreign exchange by the central bank immediately feed into changes in the balances on the accounts of the commercial banks in the central bank and thus on money-market interest rates. If it is the major lending countries' interest rates that become more volatile as a result of the interventions, borrowing countries, often poor, will be faced with higher volatility of their debt service costs. Lenders may react by asking for a higher risk premium (Reinhart and Reinhart 2002). So higher exchange-rate stability may be bought by higher interest-rate volatility. It's a classic case of 'there's no such thing as a free lunch'.

It should be clear that unsuccessful interventions may be expensive for the central bank. If it tries to prevent a devaluation, it sells foreign exchange at a low price, in part to speculators who later sell the foreign exchange back to the central bank at a higher price. Unsuccessful interventions are also expensive in the case of an excess supply of foreign exchange: the central bank buys foreign exchange at a relatively high price, only to sell it later at a lower price.

What may not be so evident at first sight is that sterilisation may be expensive as well, even if successful. The central bank mops up excess liquidity by selling government bonds, or claims on the bank itself, and invests the foreign exchange bought in foreign Treasury bonds or other liquid foreign assets. The interest rate received on such assets will generally be lower than the interest which was received on the domestic debt held before or than the rate of interest paid on the central bank's own debt. The central bank thus forgoes income or pays more on its newly issued debt than it receives on its newly acquired assets. It has been estimated that the costs of sterilisation in Latin American countries have ranged between 0.25 and 0.80 per cent of GDP (Calvo, Leiderman and Reinhart 1996, p. 134; for Colombia in 1991 the costs have been calculated at 0.5 per cent of GDP; Calvo, Leiderman and Reinhart 1995, p. 379). Note that, if the central bank sells government debt, it will not itself pay interest. It will, however, forgo the interest it first received. This amounts to a loss of income for the government, because interest paid to the central bank will return as part of the profits of the central bank when these are transferred to the Minister of Finance.

Instead of sterilising through open-market operations, the authorities could also manipulate required liquidity ratios or require banks to keep interest-free deposits at the central bank against short-term foreign borrowing. The trouble is that this would place banks in a disadvantaged position *vis-à-vis* other financial institutions and might lead to a shift of lending and borrowing from banks to non-bank financial institutions, thus weakening the effectiveness of monetary policy. A way out would be to require everybody to hold unremunerated deposits against short-term foreign borrowing. This measure is, however, expensive in terms of administrative costs and comes close to a restriction on international capital flows. Still, it may be a useful option in some circumstances (more on this in Section 5.6.4).

It should be realised that the monetary authorities have available alternatives to direct interventions in the foreign-exchange market. Instead of intervening in the spot market, they may operate in the forward market. They may support the external value of their currency by selling foreign exchange forward. Given foreign and domestic interest rates, CIP sees to it that the spot rate is maintained at the level desired by the monetary authorities. Speculators against a currency might otherwise have bought foreign-exchange spot or have bought forward foreign exchange from commercial banks. These would have hedged their position by buying foreign-exchange spot from the central bank and investing the money abroad. In either case official reserves would have fallen. Monetary authorities may feel attracted to offering forward foreign exchange themselves because forward positions do not appear on their balance sheet. Market participants who may become alarmed by a fall in the central bank's foreign exchange reserves are likely to be unaware of the central bank's positions on the forward market. The flip side of the coin, of course, is that unavoidable corrections of untenable policies will be delayed and that a crisis, once it breaks out, may become more serious. A case in point is the 1997 Thai baht crisis, when the Bank of Thailand proved to have built up a forward liability of more than $25 billion (IMF 1998b, pp. 20, 47).

5.4.4   Coordination as a Problem of Public Choice

The significance of policy coordination can also be made clear on a higher level of abstraction, following a line of reasoning that is relevant to a wider area than the balance of payments and the rate of exchange. If a large country, or a large group of countries, follows a given policy, other countries suffer the consequences. There are *external effects* or *spillover effects*. Consider a country that wishes to increase its production, in the framework of a Mundell–Fleming model with infinite interest-elasticity of capital flows under a floating-rate regime. To this end, its monetary policy is expansionary and is aimed at depreciating the currency and improving the current account of the balance of payments. If the policy succeeds, foreign countries suffer; they will see their exports fall. It is a *beggar-my-neighbour* policy. There are negative externalities. Policy coordination in such a situation can be seen as an attempt to *internalise* those externalities. This implies making the decision-making group so large that the external effects are felt by the group members themselves, so that they are no longer external.

If the mutual externalities are of the same order of magnitude, countries will be more willing to enter into coordination agreements than if they differ widely as to their effects on other countries. For the United States there is little reason to bother about the interests of Belgium or Costa Rica; policy measures taken by those countries will hardly make themselves felt. The EU and Japan are other matters, and it can be in the US's interest to achieve some coordination with the EU and Japan sometimes. There is also a more positive way of posing the problem. If the stability of exchange rates or of the price level in itself is seen as a good thing, it can be considered a *public good*. If a large country or a country group sees to it that such stability is maintained, other countries may take advantage of it without themselves contributing to it, if decision making is decentralised. The benefits of stability to the collectivity of countries is greater than the benefits for the country or the country group that makes it its business to provide it. In other words, there are positive externalities, but there is no way to charge the free riders. As a result, with decentralised decision making there tends to be an undersupply of the public good, which would make coordination desirable.

Stability and coordination can easily be provided if there is a *dominant* or *hegemonic* power willing to assume leadership. Indeed, the length and the severity of the Great Depression of the early 1930s were, in the eyes of Kindleberger (1987, p. 11) to a great extent the results of the absence of such leadership, the British no longer being able and the Americans not yet willing to provide it. From the end of World War II until the 1960s, the United States saw to the smooth running of the system (Spiro 1992, ch. 1). The non-system in force since the early 1970s on this view reflects the decline of US dominance and the rise of the EU and Japan as economic powers.

5.5 PAYMENTS RESTRICTIONS

5.5.1 The Costs of Restrictions

So far, we have assumed *full convertibility* or the absence of restrictions to international payments. The monetary authorities of a country may, however, be tempted to try and avoid a devaluation or a depreciation of their currency by means of payments restrictions. As we have seen above, they may act from such motives as fear of losing face or a concern about inflation. Other, more reprehensible, motives may play a role as well. Payments restrictions may have very harmful effects, some of which can be explained with the help of a simple demand-and-supply diagram representing the foreign-exchange market in a country.

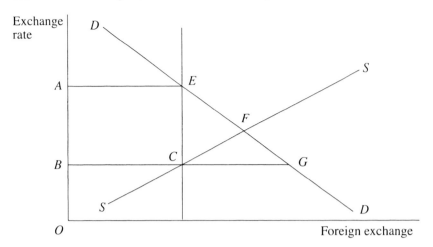

Figure 5.4   Welfare effects of payments restrictions

Under payments restrictions, the amount of foreign exchange demanded for imports of goods and services and export of capital usually exceeds the supply from the export of goods and services and the import of capital. The monetary authorities fix the exchange rate at a level at which there is excess demand.

Let the rate of exchange be fixed at *OB* in Figure 5.4, creating an excess demand *CG*. Foreign exchange must be rationed.

What are the consequences of this restricted access to foreign exchange? First of all, at the exchange rate *OB* there is an excess demand for foreign exchange (*CG*). If there is excess demand in a market, people are willing to pay more than the official price to obtain the good or service in question. Access to cheap foreign exchange is profitable because it can be used to import goods that can be sold at high prices in the domestic market, or the foreign exchange can be sold in the *black market*. Buyers are people who need foreign exchange but did not succeed in securing an allocation or people who need foreign exchange to buy smuggled goods and do not want to leave a paper trail (cf. *The Economist*, 3 August 2002, pp. 59–60 on Nigeria, where this seems to be a favourite pastime). The lucky receivers of an official allocation of foreign exchange have the prospect of earning extra income. In other words, they pay less for the foreign exchange than they are willing to pay: they receive a *rent* to the amount of *BCEA* (over and above the usual consumers' rent made up of the area between the demand curve and *AE*).

We see here two undesirable effects: a black market springs up and there is an income shift to holders of foreign exchange. Why are these effects undesirable? A black market is associated with a growing disrespect for the law and increasing cynicism in society (see Kiguel and O'Connell 1995, p. 23 for an overview of black markets in the 1970s and 1980s and the premiums paid there). As for the redistribution of income, most likely it is the better off, the big industrialists and merchants, who will profit at the expense of small traders and consumers. This redistribution fulfils no useful economic purpose, as it is not a payment for introducing innovations or risk taking or any other useful activity.

On top of this, rents may lead to behaviour that is wasteful from the point of view of society as a whole. The prospect of rent earnings will make people go to considerable lengths to obtain foreign exchange. They will spend time and effort convincing the authorities of the worthy ends for which they need foreign exchange. They will butter up the key figures, create a favourable atmosphere (by treating the authorities to Pavarotti concerts or ocean cruises or promising them cushy jobs after retiring from office) or they will resort to outright bribery. This *rent-seeking behaviour* is costly in that it uses up resources that would otherwise have been available for more worthy ends (see Krueger 1974; Bhagwati 1982, 1983 on rent seeking). Bribing can also work in the opposite direction: the ruling elite may reward its political allies by supplying them with cheap foreign exchange, or it may buy the allegiance of powerful groups in this way. Of course, government officials can also channel part of the rent directly into their own pockets by demanding bribes. Again, this is generally undesirable from the point of view of income distribution and it fulfils no useful economic purpose.

Corruption can be prevented by allocating foreign exchange following some rule instead of by discretion. Such a rule, for instance allocation according to a firm's share in last year's imports, might prevent corruption but does little to redress the income redistribution involved in the rents which the recipients of the foreign exchange earn; nor does it contribute to an allocation that channels foreign exchange to those ends that offer the highest yields to society. It freezes the competitive positions of the firms concerned.

Payment restrictions will often lead to *overinvoicing* by importers and *underinvoicing* by exporters. Importers with access to foreign exchange will ask their suppliers for invoices showing a higher price than they actually pay. The extra amount of foreign exchange allotted to them will be channelled to a foreign bank account or will be sold in the black market. Exporters hand over to the authorities copies of invoices showing lower amounts than they actually receive from their foreign clients. They transfer this lower amount to the authorities and keep the rest, again, in a foreign bank account or sell it in the black market.

Such misinvoicing has been documented for, among other countries, Indonesia before the 1967 liberalisation of the capital account of the balance of payments (Sabirin 1993, pp. 151–2), India and Turkey (see Gupta 1984 for empirical estimates), and more recently, Chile (see Quirk, Evans et al. 1995, p. 39 for estimates over the 1988–93 period). In the process, the supply of foreign exchange made available to the authorities decreases, that is, the supply curve shifts to the left (Agénor 1992). A variant popular in Russia is to set up a business abroad and export goods to it at ridiculously low prices, according to the Russian central bank President, Viktor Gerasjtsjenko, in 1999. He also complained that often payments are made for imports that never take place, with the paying firm vanishing shortly after.

Even if no rent-seeking behaviour or income redistribution were involved, there would be a net loss of utility. This so-called *deadweight loss* is represented in Figure 5.4 by the triangle *CEF*. We can interpret the supply curve as representing the social cost of obtaining foreign exchange: the supply of foreign exchange comes from exporters who have sold goods and services for the production of which resources were used that could also have been used for other ends. The price of a unit of foreign exchange, therefore, can be seen as its cost in terms of what society was willing to give up for it. The demand curve in its turn represents the utility for the users of obtaining foreign exchange. They are willing to forgo the use or consumption of other goods that could have been bought with the money now spent on foreign exchange. With an amount equal to *BC* available, utility in this sense is higher than social cost to the tune of *CE*. If we conduct a thought experiment and start at *F*, where the cost of obtaining an infinitesimal extra amount of foreign exchange equals its utility, and slowly reduce the amount of foreign exchange available, little by little vertical distances between *DD* and *SS* are added and when we have arrived at *C* the total net loss in utility, the excess of utility loss over the reduction in aggregate costs, has increased to *CEF*.

What guise would this loss of utility take in practice? Apart from consumption goods that cannot be bought because of a restricted supply of foreign exchange, one could think of two categories of losses:

(i) Production may suffer. This is because of possibly long waiting periods before foreign exchange is obtained to replace machinery that has broken down or to buy spare parts. This may be very serious, as whole factories may have to close down for protracted periods (see Sabirin 1993, p. 151 on Indonesia).

(ii) As payments restrictions often include restrictions on the purchase of foreign know-how, technological innovation may suffer (Corbo and de Melo 1985). More generally, payments restrictions imply restrictions in international trade and therefore mean a lower accessibility of new goods and new technology (Romer 1994 stresses the importance of this accessibility for economic growth).

A possibly very serious negative effect of payments restrictions which falls outside the compass of the diagram is the *administrative burden* on the business community. Obtaining the required permits or allocations in a regular way may be a costly and time-consuming affair: forms have to be filled in and visits to the capital city may have to be made. Furthermore, foreign investors are likely to be deterred by payments restrictions, as repatriation of interest, dividends and profits may not be free or investors fear that hindrances may be put in the way in the future. If this leads to reduced incoming direct foreign investment, the country misses out on foreign technology and management.

To avoid negative effects, the authorities may opt for an auction system. In that case there is actually only a fixed exchange rate for exports and capital imports, not for imports and capital exports. The rent *BCEA* can be appropriated by the monetary authorities under this system. The deadweight loss cannot be avoided in this way, but the paperwork and waiting involved in obtaining permits can be dispensed with. Nevertheless, suppliers of foreign exchange will seek ways not to sell foreign exchange at artificially low official prices to the central bank. The main advantage of the system would seem to be in providing an additional source of government income.

Finally, it is also possible for the black market rate to be *lower* than the official rate. This can happen if foreign exchange is earned by illegal activities. Dollars earned by drugs exports caused the black-market rate in Colombia to dip below the official rate between 1975 and 1982 (Fonseca 1992, pp. 492, 513). In Greece there was a negative black-market premium for dollars for some periods in the second half of the 1980s, apparently because the Bank of Greece required the commercial banks only to accept foreign currency after proper identification of sellers (Kouretas and Zarangas 2001).

5.5.2 Dual and Multiple Exchange Rates

Many countries have at one time or another attempted to circumvent a number of foreign-exchange problems by switching to a multiple exchange-rate system. At the end of 1997 no fewer than 43 countries were reported to be running such a system (IMF 1999b, p. 46). The basic form is a dual system, with a fixed rate, the *official rate*, for current transactions and a free-floating rate, the *financial rate*, for capital transactions. In the early 1970s such a system was in force in France (1971–73), Italy (1973–74) and the Netherlands (1971–74; with the financial rate only applying to international trade in bonds); the United Kingdom was on this system from 1947 to

1979 and Belgium and Luxembourg from 1951 to March 1990. The Rand Monetary Area was on a dual system from 1974 to 1983. In Latin America multiple exchange rates have been, or were, part of the scene for many years. There was a proliferation of official rates, often three or four, beside floating rates in official markets and often in black markets or unofficial markets in all shades of grey (consult the *Exchange Arrangements and Exchange Restrictions* yearbook of the IMF for information on exchange-rate systems; see also Kiguel and O'Connell 1995 for experiences with dual exchange rates and their abolition in the 1970s and 1980s).

In principle, multiple exchange rates help to insulate the real exchange rate from shocks originating from capital flows, without the need to regulate capital flows. It is an excellent principle, though much is usually lost in the execution. The monetary authorities would have to screen each and every individual foreign-exchange transaction. With the financial rate above the official rate, for instance, exporters can make a profit by receiving part of their foreign-exchange proceeds on the capital account, where there are more pesos in a dollar. This leads to underinvoicing and sham capital imports. With the financial rate below the official rate, non-residents may use the pesos they bought at a low price (in dollars) to acquire financial assets instead of goods, and so on. Nor are shady dealings the exclusive province of private persons and business enterprises. Governments can use a multiple-rate system to confer favours on political allies. It has, for instance, been documented for the Sudan that the government bought the allegiance of certain groups by allocating them foreign exchange at a favourable rate of exchange (Brown 1990, pp. 142, 215). Cheap foreign exchange, together with import permits, offered the opportunity to buy foreign goods cheap and sell them dear. In Iran, Parliament in 2002 outlawed the practice, worth $4 billion a year, of providing privileged companies with foreign exchange at one-quarter of its market rate (*The Economist*, 22 June 2002, p. 45).

If it were possible to fully separate the current account and the capital account, equilibrium on the capital account would be brought about by exchange-rate fluctuations, whereas disequilibria on the current account would have to be met by official reserves, or partly by fluctuations in trade credit (*leads* and *lags*). Trade credit is a close substitute for lending or borrowing at the financial rate, which brings the difficulty of separating the various markets into sharp focus.

A multiple-rate system may be expensive for the authorities; they do not always buy cheap and sell dear. The central bank of Peru is known to have lost some 2 per cent of GDP in 1987 through paying on average a high rate on foreign exchange bought from exporters and asking a low rate from importers (Dornbusch and Tellez Kuenzler 1993, p. 107).

Multiple exchange rates have also been used for other purposes. For example, the central bank could fix a lower exchange rate for exports than for imports. Exporters receive, say, 8 pesos for a dollar while importers pay 12 pesos for a dollar. This is, as Corden (1971, p. 88) argues, tantamount to an import duty of 50 per cent or an export duty of 33.3 per cent. A variant is a low exchange rate (such as 8 pesos per dollar) for traditional exports and essential imports, and a high rate of exchange for non-traditional exports and non-essential imports. This would stimulate non-traditional exports, exporters receiving a large number of pesos for every dollar earned abroad, and curb non-essential imports. In such cases, the rate of exchange is deployed as an instrument of trade policy and industrial policy, that is, as a substitute for (import or other) duties and subsidies. Obviously, this is a second-best or third-best policy (Fleming 1974, p. 8). Multiple-rate systems with different exchange rates for different goods have been set up for other reasons as well. For a number of years, the Argentinian exchange rate for the exports of meat and wheat, the traditional exports, was kept low in order to hinder exports and in that way keep domestic prices low. Consequently, the cost of living for urban labourers remained low, enabling employers to pay relatively low wages (Cooper 1973, p. 169). This had little to do with comparative advantage. Rather, the interests of urban industrialists had won over those of agrarian exporters. After Minister of Finance Martínez de Hoz abolished the discrimination in favour of exports from the urban industrial sector in April 1976, exports of wheat and meat soared.

A final observation on black-market rates, or more generally on the rates in *unofficial* or *parallel markets*, is in order. Depending on punishments (if

Table 5.4   *Average black-market premium in 41 developing countries (per cent)*

Region	1980–89	1990–93	1994–97
Total (41 countries)	82.0	78.2	20.3
East Asia and Pacific	3.6	3.6	3.2
M. East and N. Africa	165.6	351.6	46.5
Idem excluding Algeria and Iran	7.1	8.8	1.4
Latin America and Caribbean	48.7	13.1	4.4
South Asia	40.8	45.1	10.1
Sub-Saharan Africa	116.5	28.6	32.2
Idem excluding Nigeria	112.1	25.8	9.6

Source: World Bank (2001, p. 54).

the parallel market is a real black, or illegal, market) and the probability of getting caught, the parallel rate gives an indication of the equilibrium level of the exchange rate. Parallel rates have been found to be highly correlated with differences in the rate of inflation (Culbertson 1975; Haudeville and Lama 1988; Ding 1998; Diamandis 2003). At higher rates of inflation PPP in its relative or even in its absolute form is closely approached.

5.6   PAYMENTS LIBERALISATION

5.6.1   The Benefits of Payments Liberalisation

If payments restrictions have such negative effects on an economy, payments liberalisation must have positive effects on an economy. In a liberalised environment, it pays to spend time, effort and money on investing in better products, better production technology, better marketing and so on instead of concentrating on rent-seeking activities. Moreover, interruptions of production processes because of a lack of foreign exchange to buy foreign parts will be a thing of the past and there will be fewer efforts to undermine the law.

A liberalised payments system enables a country to participate more fully in international trade and reap the benefits of specialisation in the production of those goods and services for which it has a comparative advantage. The official exchange rate and RER will rise (the currency will depreciate), leading to higher exports. Furthermore, liberalised international payments provide better opportunities for intertemporal substitution, including consumption smoothing. Empirical research indicates that consumption smoothing requires, along with liberalised international payments, a liberalised domestic financial system (de Brouwer 1999, p. 173). Also, there is evidence that financial liberalisation makes for easier and cheaper funding by business firms (Eichengreen 2001).

What will happen to the exchange rate if the foreign-exchange market is liberalised? First, the exchange rate will rise from OB to OA. Next, the system moves from E in the direction of F as exports grow and bring in larger amounts of foreign exchange (see Krueger 1978, p. 176; Donovan 1981; Denoon 1986, p. 5 for the lag between a rise in the exchange rate and export increases). This is another case of overshooting. The extent of overshooting can be even larger if pent-up demand for imports (such as spares) now finds its way to the foreign-exchange market and if a temporarily high demand for foreign exchange occurs with an eye to capital exports for portfolio diversification purposes. The shocks to the system imparted by the exchange-rate changes will often, however, be less severe than the movements of the official exchange rate would at first sight suggest. In many cases there will have been a black market, with an exchange rate way above the official one. If after liberalisation the freed exchange rate first moves in the direction of the former black rate, there is no serious price shock to those who formerly bought foreign exchange in the black market. Nor, it should be added, is there a serious price shock to those who formerly had no choice but to buy imported goods from privileged buyers of foreign exchange (permit holders): they already paid a high price before liberalisation because privileged importers pocketed the rent implied in the low official exchange rate.

The fall of the exchange rate associated with the growth of exports will be helped by the fact that liberalisation removes the incentive for economic agents to hold foreign exchange at foreign banks. Hence, the supply curve of foreign exchange may move to the right. In order to avoid the danger of manipulation by a small number of market participants mentioned in Section 5.2.6 above, in actual practice auction systems are found with the central bank paying the going market price, rather than a fixed price, for the foreign exchange bought (see Quirk et al. 1987 on the functioning of such systems). In lieu of free floating, it is also possible to devalue the currency in a fixed-but-adjustable peg system.

All this suggests that a rise in the official exchange rate or a shift to floating rates need not fuel inflation, provided the government sticks to restrictive macroeconomic policies and wages are not indexed for changes in the official exchange rate. Price hikes will also be restricted by the following forces:

- The disappearance of rents and the freer availability of imported inputs will dampen any tendency of prices to increase.
- Foreign competition forces entrepreneurs to improve product quality and production efficiency, in which they are helped by the greater availability of foreign know-how, both embodied in imported capital goods and in imported technology in the form of licences.
- A higher degree of participation in international trade, that is, more division of labour, involves the closing down of relatively inefficient industries and the expansion of relatively efficient ones, enabling the latter to reap economies of scale. Average costs are lowered in this way.
- The occasional stoppage of production because of the impossibility of importing spare parts is a thing of the past.

All these benefits are reinforced if liberalisation of the foreign-exchange market is supplemented by trade liberalisation. There is abundant empirical evidence that a devaluation coupled with trade and payments liberalisation can be effective in bringing about a real devaluation and an export surge (Edwards 1993, p. 1369; Nsouli et al. 1993; Visser 1996). Nonetheless, it is noteworthy that no unequivocally positive relationship between payments liberalisation, in particular capital-account liberalisation, and economic growth has been found in empirical research. Still, there are indications that liberalisation is likely to have a positive effect if a number of conditions are met, such as: efficient prudential supervision on the financial sector, limited moral hazard associated with depositor protection, transparent auditing and accounting standards, and equitable bankruptcy and insolvency procedures. This is because capital liberalisation, which often goes hand in hand with domestic financial deregulation, may subject the banking sector to shocks that can result in an expensive banking crisis if the sector is not robust. Also, without a well-functioning financial sector, wealth owners may avail themselves of the opportunity to send their capital abroad (Prasad et al. 2003). Therefore, it will generally be wise to liberalise the capital account only after the domestic financial sector has been liberalised (McKinnon 1993a; Wyplosz 2002).

5.6.2   Problems of Capital Liberalisation

A liberalisation process, even if potentially beneficial, is not all sweetness and light.[6] One recurring problem has been that, if a country liberalises on a grand scale and gets its economy going, not only will residents repatriate flight capital but non-residents will also want to invest there. Net capital inflows will result. These are fine if they are a concomitant of capital goods imports and contribute to the building up of productive capacity in a country. All too often, however, capital inflows are governed by considerations of short-term portfolio investment. In a fixed-exchange-rate system they make the money supply balloon and result in inflation; in a floating-rate system they cause overvaluation of the currency. In both cases the real exchange rate falls, that is, the domestic currency appreciates in real terms. Net capital inflows, unless primarily spent on imports, go hand in hand with a booming nontradeables sector (often construction) and squeeze the tradeables sector. Sooner or later the market will come to expect a devaluation or depreciation and capital will flow out until a sizeable rise in the exchange rate becomes inevitable. The nontradeables sector collapses and factors of production become unemployed. The tradeables sector may have become more competitive, but generally it is not able to expand fast enough to employ the factors of production made redundant in the nontradeables sector.

A glaring example of the harm that capital inflows can do is Chile, where they reached no less than 25 per cent of GDP in the first half of 1981

(Corbo 1985, p. 903; see Labán and Larraín 1994 for a comparison between the 1978–81 period and the 1989–92 period, when capital inflows were more successfully restricted). Similar problems beset the Korean financial liberalisation process in the late 1960s (McKinnon 1993a, ch. 10). Relatively low world interest rates contributed to sizeable capital flows to Asian and Latin American countries in the 1990s (Corbo and Hernández 1996; see Fernández-Arias and Montiel 1996 for figures). The repatriation of this capital was instrumental in sparking off the 1994 Mexican peso crisis and the 1997 Asian currency crisis (see Chapter 3, Section 2.2 on the latter).

5.6.3 How to Restrict Capital Imports While Maintaining a Free Capital Market

Capital imports are potentially beneficial, but one can have too much of a good thing. It may be myopia by individual lenders or a herd instinct among bankers that is at the root of too large capital flows, but there may also be policy factors to blame:

- Governments and central banks have provided guarantees in both borrowing and lending countries, either openly or implicitly. One way of doing so is to provide a *de facto* free deposit guarantee to banks, as happened in Chile during the run-up to the 1981–83 financial crisis (Visser and Van Herpt 1996). Another way is to provide swap facilities at the central bank, which means that the central bank shoulders the currency risk: banks borrow abroad and cover their foreign-exchange risk by buying forward foreign exchange from their central bank. If the exchange rate rises at the time the foreign exchange has to be delivered, the central bank suffers a loss. This was the case also in Chile until 1990 (Corbo and Hernández 1996, p. 67), while until 1997 the Thai central bank also provided forward foreign exchange on a large scale, as we have seen above. It was not only that banks took advantage of these guarantees and of the forward cover offered by the central bank. Given the often large wedge between lending and borrowing rates with banks in liberalising countries, it also became attractive for nonfinancial firms to borrow abroad.
- Prudential supervision on banks has been slack in many borrowing countries.
- Governments have sometimes shown little restraint in allowing state entities to borrow abroad, as during the run-up to the 1994 crisis in Mexico (World Bank 1999, p. 79).
- Often, there has been a lack of prudential supervision on lending to LDCs. If lenders had had to take due account of the risks involved in

lending, the capital flows might have been much more modest in size. The rules followed in prudential supervision may also have negative side-effects. In particular, the Basle Capital Accord stipulates that banks' claims on banks outside the OECD with a residual maturity of up to one year carry a risk weight of 20 per cent, whereas claims with a residual maturity of over one year carry a 100 per cent risk weight. Short-term loans thus require a lower amount of own capital than longer-term loans, and thus are made more attractive. As non-renewal of short-term loans is likely to result in a more sudden drying up of capital imports than non-renewal of longer-term loans, this rule may contribute to foreign-exchange crises.

One way to reduce reckless lending and borrowing is thus to introduce effective prudential supervision on banks in both lending and borrowing countries, such as imposing ceilings or capital requirements on foreign-exchange exposure, and to refrain from offering exchange-rate guarantees or forward cover.

There are still other ways available to slow down net capital imports while maintaining free capital markets, even if their effectiveness is often restricted:

- A liberalisation of capital outflows, which may to some extent neutralise high capital imports. Such a measure could consist of a relaxation of rules that restrict the freedom of institutional investors to invest abroad.
- A lowering of domestic short-term interest rates. This would, however, stimulate domestic spending and again contribute to real exchange-rate appreciation.
- A lowering of long-term interest rates through fiscal tightness. If a government reduces its expenditure and with it government borrowing, the demand for credit falls. The rate of interest will fall too, making it less attractive for foreign lenders to supply credit. Fiscal tightening is often politically difficult to realise, but both Malaysia and Thailand succeeded in reducing public consumption by 3.5 per cent of GDP below the 1984–88 level during the 1989–91 period of high capital imports (Calvo, Leiderman and Reinhart 1995, pp. 358–60).
- A shift in aggregate spending from government expenditure to private expenditure, especially if taxes are reduced in step with government expenditure. This could help prevent a fall in RER insofar as private spending is directed to tradeables, or imports to a larger degree than government spending.

- The introduction of some flexibility in exchange rates, such as a widening of the band around some parity. This may increase exchange-rate risk and discourage short-term capital inflows (Corbo and Hernández 1996, p. 69).
- Sterilisation of a surplus in international payments. This is to some extent possible, as we have seen, if capital flows are not fully interest-elastic. A prerequisite for such an attempt is that there is a reasonably well-developed domestic capital market, where there is a potential demand for the financial assets that the central bank would try to sell in order to mop up liquidity. The dangers are obvious: sterilisation makes the domestic interest rate go up, attracting new capital inflows, and the costs for the central bank may be high (because of the negative spread between the interest rate which the central bank receives on its foreign assets and the rate it pays on domestic debt). Uruguay for example, therefore had to abandon this policy after a failed attempt in 1991–92 (Hanson 1995, p. 407).

A longer-term solution is the development of domestic capital markets. Business firms in Asia, in particular Thailand and South Korea, often are to a large degree dependent on short-term bank loans and have a relatively low capital–assets ratio (for empirical data, see Singh 1995; Caprio and Demirgüç-Kunt 1998). They are highly dependent on bank loans, and if there has been a more or less fixed exchange rate for a number of years, they may be lured into contracting foreign-currency debt at attractive interest rates without seeking cover in the forward market. Both a sudden non-renewal of loans and a devaluation of the domestic currency may cause serious difficulties that lead to bankruptcy.

5.6.4 Controls on Foreign Borrowing and Sand in the Wheels (Chile Tax and Tobin Tax)

If the measures discussed above do not have the hoped-for effects, it is also possible to stop short of fully liberalising international capital flows. We have already mentioned the possibility of imposing cash reserve or liquidity requirements on foreign borrowings by banks, but these could be extended to other firms. Ceilings on foreign borrowing, in particular short-term borrowing, would be another option (Fischer 1998; for real-life examples from the 1990s, see Ariyoshi et al. 2000; Reinhart and Smith 2001). Chile, along with Colombia, has made use of *unremunerated reserve requirements* (URR) at the central bank. From 1991 to 1998 the Chilean central bank imposed a one-year URR on foreign loans. Alternatively, firms could pay the Chilean central bank one year's interest (see Ulan 2000, which also describes a similar system functioning in Colombia from 1993 to 1998). As this boiled down to a fixed cost to the investor, it worked against short-term loans. In addition, bonds issued abroad by Chilean companies must have an average maturity of at least four years and there was a URR for external liabilities that did not result in an increase in the stock of capital (IMF 1998b, Annex IV; Nadal-De Simone and Sorsa 1999). Largely because of econometric difficulties no conclusive evidence has been found on the effectiveness of the Chilean URR, also dubbed the *Chile tax* (Nadal-De Simone and Sorsa 1999). Reserve requirements are certainly not enough to preclude currency crises; South Korea, Malaysia and Thailand are known to have used them extensively (Theron 1998, pp. 57–8). This failed to prevent the Asian crisis from breaking out in 1997.

There are indications that restrictions on short-term capital inflows, as in Chile, may help to lengthen the maturity of contracted foreign debt, rather than reducing its magnitude (Quirk, Evans et al. 1995, p. 43; Montiel and Reinhart 1999; de Gregorio, Edwards and Valdés 2000). A shift from short-term capital to long-term capital is generally seen as contributing to less volatility of capital flows. It would make sudden reversals of capital flows less likely (Agénor 2003, pp. 1102–3). It stands to reason that, if capital flows shifted from bank lending to stocks and bonds, attempts to withdraw financial investments would not so easily engender a bank crisis. In the case of short-term bank lending, banks can suddenly decide not to renew credit; if bond and stock holders want to get rid of these assets they have to find a buyer. Insofar as residents are unwilling to buy, it boils down to a transaction between non-residents and no foreign-exchange flow is involved. The improvement in the current account of the balance of payments required to cope with the drying up of capital imports will be less drastic. Foreign direct investments are even more attractive in this respect.

Attempts to limit capital inflows have met with modest success at best. High interest-elasticities are one explanation, attempts by economic agents to circumvent regulations another. If a central bank, for instance, imposes reserve requirements or a ceiling on foreign borrowing by banks, this may work for some time. As intermediation by the commercial banks becomes more expensive as a result of such measures, however, non-bank financial institutions will spring up to circumvent them, as we have seen above (Section 5.4.3). When Germany imposed a Chile-like tax like *Bardepot*, or non-interest-bearing deposit at the central bank against foreign credit taken up by residents, in 1972, capital imports were directed to other financial instruments (Bakker 2003, p. 28). In addition, all the misinvoicing, red tape and black markets described in Section 5.5.1 may reappear. A small country with an able and efficient government bureaucracy such as Chile will be better placed in this respect than others. The reason, indeed, why Indonesia started liberalising its capital account of the balance of payments in 1970, ahead of current-account liberalisation, seems to have been the realisation by the authorities that monitoring and controlling capital flows would be an uphill struggle (Cole and Slade 1992). Formal liberalisation in the EU was also hastened by the increasing awareness of the authorities that control of capital flows was well-nigh impossible (Bakker 1996).

If the Chile tax is meant as a flexible weapon for short-term use, some want to throw sand in the wheels of international finance, that is, to hinder international capital flows on a permanent basis. The discussion has centred on the *Tobin tax* proposal. Tobin (1974, pp. 88–9) proposed to introduce a generally applied tax on international financial transactions. This would, in his mind, be helpful in preserving some national monetary autonomy. Others have recommended a Tobin tax because it would reduce speculative activities. If foreign-exchange transactions carry a tax of, say, one-half of 1 per cent, that would translate into 4 per cent on an annual basis for a three-month foreign-exchange investment (Eichengreen, Tobin and Wyplosz 1992). The impact of the tax would be greater the shorter the investment period and in that way national monetary authorities would have some leeway to conduct a national monetary policy that would not immediately be frustrated by international capital flows. The Tobin tax would enable short-term interest rates to differ between countries. By the same token, a Tobin tax would hinder speculative activity.

There are, however, various reasons to doubt whether the Tobin tax would serve a useful purpose:

- If market participants expect a substantial change in a currency's parity, a one-half per cent tax only increases the costs of speculation marginally and will often not be sufficient to deter such speculation (Davidson 1997). Whereas a Chile tax can be made to measure, a Tobin tax is of the one-size-fits-all variety. If a tax is to stem speculative activities, a low level will suffice most of the time, but steep increases may be called for at other times.
- Preventing speculative activities may be positively harmful. The word speculation may have a negative connotation, but it can nevertheless be stabilising (see Chapter 2, Section 5). This would be hindered by a Tobin tax.
- One wonders whether, and if so how, covering foreign-exchange risk in forward and futures markets could be made exempt from a Tobin tax. The perfectly respectable activity of hedging foreign-exchange risk would be punished under a Tobin tax, it seems, even if forwards

were made exempt, as the banks that provide forward cover hedge their risks by a spot transaction.

- Foreign-exchange swaps, involving a spot transaction jointly with a future opposite transaction, are increasingly part of normal money-market transactions to manage interest-rate risk. A Tobin tax would seriously hamper this function of the foreign-exchange market (Grahl and Lysandrou 2003).
- As for current transactions, it would be impossible to separate them from capital transactions and the Tobin tax would have to fall on both. International trade might suffer more than speculative activity.
- It has been estimated that 80 per cent of daily flows on foreign-exchange markets represent hedging activities by dealers. They may themselves hold a fraction of a currency offered by speculators and pass on the rest to other dealers, who in their turn keep a fraction and pass on the remaining part. Through this so-called 'hot-potato trading', foreign-exchange risk is spread over a perhaps large number of dealers. If a Tobin tax is imposed, this passing-on among dealers is disproportionately taxed and risk spreading is discouraged. This may well lead to greater exchange-rate variability, as stressed by De Grauwe (2000).
- A Tobin tax would be difficult to put into practice. First, it would require all financial centres in the world to participate, as market activity would otherwise move to a non-participating financial centre. Second, if a tax is levied on foreign-exchange transactions, people will switch to close substitutes for money and, for instance, engage in Treasury bill swaps (Garber and Taylor 1995). More and more financial activities would have to be made subject to the Tobin tax and derivative markets in particular might be harmed (Spahn 1996; see ul Haq, Kaul and Grunberg 1996 and the review of that collection in Grieve Smith 1997 for further analyses of the Tobin tax).

It may be noted in passing that a Tobin tax has also been advocated as a means of bringing in funds to finance global developmental or ecological programmes by the UN (Arestis and Sawyer 1997). It would seem that better alternatives are available. A tax on harmful emissions or on the use of non-renewable resources would seem preferable, as such a tax would have positive instead of negative side-effects. Moreover, given that the majority of daily transactions is inter-dealer trade or done for managing interest-rate risk, both of which would be seriously hurt by a Tobin tax, the yield from such a tax might be significantly lower than expected by its proponents. One of these, Dean Baker (2000), would expect currency trading, in his estimate some $200 trillion annually, to fall by one-third consequent upon the introduction of a 0.1 per cent tax. A worldwide Tobin tax of $133 billion would result if the tax were universally adopted. To put this amount into perspective, official development aid by the 21 OECD countries that form the Development Assistance Committee amounted to $53.7 billion in 2000 (Reisen 2002). The Tobin tax thus looks very attractive at first sight, but the sums that the proponents of the tax dream about appear highly optimistic, the more so as the costs of perception are entirely neglected. Experience with taxes on stock-market transactions in Sweden between October 1983 and December 1991 certainly suggests that such taxes have a dramatic impact on trading volume and on the liquidity of markets. Also, market participants find or create substitutes for the taxed transactions. The revenues of such a tax are thus disappointing and the efficiency of the markets in managing risks is reduced, whereas price volatility increases (Habermeier and Kirilenko 2002).

5.6.5   Temporary Controls on Capital Outflows

Measures to limit capital imports have met with limited success at best. Some kinds of measures, moreover, have undesirable side-effects. But even if they work, they can hardly prevent large-scale outflows of capital if market sentiments suddenly change. It is a moot question whether, in the event of such a *currency crisis*, stringent capital controls aimed at limiting outflows could be useful (for a description of measures taken in Malaysia 1997–2000, Thailand 1997–98 and Spain 1992, see Ariyoshi et al. 2000, ch. VI). If imposed for a restricted period, say a couple of months, they might be less harmful than less stringent but permanent hindrances such as a Tobin tax. This might prevent the countries involved being forced to suddenly and substantially improve the current account of their balance of payments, as described in Chapter 3, Section 2.2. To give an idea of the magnitudes involved, during the 1997–98 Asian crisis Korea's current-account balance shifted from a deficit of 4.4 per cent of GDP in 1996 and 1.7 per cent in 1997 to a surplus of 12.8 per cent in 1998 (IMF 2000, p. 234). Such a huge shift in such a short time can only be brought about by severe deflationary measures that cause high unemployment and bring much human suffering in their wake. Short-term stringent controls on outflows might then be the less unattractive measure.

5.6.6   The Role of the IMF

The IMF's *Articles of Agreement* so far allow countries to introduce capital restrictions. They stipulate that one of the purposes of the Fund is 'To assist in the establishment of a multilateral system of payments in respect of current transactions between members and in the elimination of foreign exchange restrictions which hamper the growth of world trade' (Article I sub (iv), IMF 1993, p. 2). They are silent about the capital account.

As the liberalisation movement gathered pace in the 1980s and 1990s, the IMF actively furthered capital-account liberalisation and during the 1997 annual meeting of the IMF and the World Bank in Hong Kong it was decided to amend the Articles of Agreement and include the absence of capital restrictions as well. In the wake of the Asian currency crisis, however, this plan was put on hold.

Highly integrated capital markets can clearly be beneficial, but it has become all too clear in the past few decades that liberalisation may bring serious problems in its wake. Not only will liberalised capital flows reduce the degrees of freedom of the authorities with regard to monetary policy, it has also been the experience of countries liberalising their financial markets that the banking system may come under pressure. In the ideal situation, these problems force governments to do their utmost to make their policies credible and, in particular, to put efficient banking supervision into place and ensure macroeconomic stability, that is, low inflation and a sustainable budget deficit (Dixon 1997). Nevertheless, panics may arise every now and then that threaten to develop into a crisis and endanger the international financial markets.

Walter Bagehot stressed in 1873 in his classic *Lombard Street* that in the event of a panic the central bank should act quickly and make funds liberally available: 'it is ready lending which cures panics' (Bagehot 1920, p. 298). As Charles Kindleberger (1978, ch. 11) never tired of emphasising, all financial systems need a lender of last resort, including the world financial system. As we have seen, after the 1994 Mexican peso crisis, the IMF took up this role and pumped billions of dollars into Argentina, jointly with the World Bank and the Inter American Development Bank. In the 1997–98 Asian crisis, programmes involving tens of billions of dollars were put together for Indonesia, the Philippines, Thailand and South Korea.

In a regular IMF programme, however, the money is not immediately made available and the Fund does not act as a lender of last resort. The money is paid in several tranches, and then only under the condition that the countries involved meet a number of performance criteria. It has been the experience that signing an agreement with the IMF and introducing adjustment measures are not enough to stop speculative attacks. In 1999 the IMF, therefore, introduced the Contingent Credit Lines (CCL; see IMF 1999a, 2001), a facility under which money was promised to member countries in order to prevent contagion from financial and foreign-exchange crises in other countries. CCL took the form of stand-by agreements, and the fact that the money was immediately available in case of need was expected to help prevent speculative attacks. Member countries were only eligible for this facility if they met a number of standards as to their economic policies. In this way, *ex ante* conditionality was imposed, rather than *ex post* conditionality, as under the traditional IMF programmes. CCL was never used, though, and when the programme expired in 2003 it was not renewed.

As with any lender of last resort, one recurrent theme in the discussion is the danger of moral hazard. This refers to the behaviour of lenders and borrowers, who may become more reckless if they feel they can be more or less sure that the IMF will come to the rescue if things go wrong. The moral-hazard problem does not seem really serious in the sense that it causes losses from non-repayment of IMF loans (Jeanne and Zettelmeyer 2001). Nonetheless, the IMF is looking for ways to make private creditors shoulder the burden of foreign-exchange crises and to make them more careful in their foreign lending. After all, the volume of funds which the IMF can dispose of is limited. Unlike central banks, it cannot create base money and it cannot consequently function as a fully fledged lender of last resort (Bird 1999). Furthermore, even if moral hazard does not cause appreciable losses to the IMF and its creditor member states, it is still in the interests of taxpayers in borrowing countries for excessive borrowing to be prevented.

If a currency crisis leads to insolvency of governments, the problem is how to restructure government debt, or sovereign debt. The IMF is in favour of Collective Action Clauses (CACs) in bond contracts, which ensure that a qualified majority of lenders can decide on a restructuring of terms and a solution of a crisis cannot be stymied by a dissenting minority. CACs are common in sovereign bonds that are governed by English law, but most emerging market sovereign bonds are governed under New York law and do not include CACs (a detailed discussion of CACs can be found in IMF 2003a).

Opinions among IMF directors differ on another approach, a Sovereign Debt Restructuring Mechanism (SDRM). An SDRM would be more far-reaching than a CAC, as it would allow collective action not only for bonds but for all debt instruments, and a single agreement would be sufficient to decide on restructuring multiple debt instruments (IMF 2003b, ch. 3). An SDRM would prevent individual bond holders from demanding full repayment if others agree to a rescheduling and a reduction of debt, as they are entitled to do under New York law, under which many international bonds are issued. SDRMs, promoted by the IMF's first Deputy Managing Director Anne Krueger, resemble the American 'chapter 11' procedure, which gives heavily indebted business firms a breathing space, during which debt restructuring takes place.

5.7   CONCLUSIONS

Governments cannot avoid choosing some foreign-exchange policy. All policy options have their pros and cons. If price stability is the overriding objective one might opt for the extreme solution of a currency board, but usually governments will not be willing to tie their hands so rigorously. Moreover, it can be a risky strategy. If countries decide on a fixed-but-adjustable peg system, it can be useful to maintain a wide rather than a narrow band, possibly with soft borders. This may help to make speculative attacks a two-way bet. International cooperation may help to avoid unintended consequences from various countries pursuing incompatible policy ends.

Exchange-rate policies or balance-of-payments policies have become more complicated over the past few decades because of the explosive development of international capital movements. These are potentially conducive to attaining higher income levels, but they may become so large as to frustrate a country's monetary policy. In addition, they may be very volatile. Measures to reduce the negative effects of international capital flows while avoiding the serious disadvantages of payments restrictions are not easy to find and implement.

Our analysis of payments restrictions has shown that government controls may lead to dubious dealings, and may even be introduced with dubious dealings as their aim. The world is a wicked place, but it is satisfying that some at least of mankind's less laudable activities can be analysed with the help of simple microeconomic methods. To end on a positive note, there are institutionalised attempts to redress and prevent crises in foreign-exchange markets, even if IMF interventions cannot always be considered an unqualified success.

NOTES

1. The first currency board was established by the British in Mauritius in 1849, and the use of currency boards eventually spread to 70 British colonies. For a complete list of pre-1990 currency boards, see Ghosh, Gulde and Wolf (2000, pp. 330–3).
2. In Hong Kong, banknotes are issued by three commercial banks. Only these three banks have access to the Currency Board (called the Exchange Fund). When they sell foreign exchange, they receive Certificates of Indebtedness in return, and they are required to hold these certificates as backing for their banknote issue. They have the right to buy foreign

exchange against Certificates of Indebtedness, in which case the banknote circulation falls.

3. Named after G.A.D. MacDougall, who developed this approach in MacDougall (1958). It may be remarked in this context that, if the Heckscher–Ohlin trade model applies, factor payments will be equalised and trade is a substitute for the international migration of production factors.

4. Just to give an impression of the cost reductions that have taken place: the cost of an international telephone call fell sixfold between 1940 and 1970 and tenfold between 1970 and 1990 (World Bank 1995, p. 51), and in 1975 it cost $10,000 to send a megabyte of data from New York to Tokyo, as against about $5 some 22 years later (Steinherr 1998, p. 12).

5. Formal *currency-crisis models* reflect this development. So-called *first-generation models* focus on expansionary monetary and fiscal policies that lead to a fall in foreign-exchange reserves, which alerts economic agents and sparks off a speculative attack on the currency. *Second-generation models* emphasise the fact that a change in investors' sentiments can set off a speculative attack irrespective of the stance of macroeconomic policy and foreign-exchange reserves. In addition, *third-generation models* can be distinguished that concentrate on the financial intermediaries' balance sheets and their vulnerability to insolvency (Hallwood and MacDonald 2000, ch. 14 and Sarno and Taylor 2002, ch. 8 provide surveys of currency-crisis models).

6. For the special experience of transition countries, see McKinnon (1993a) and Bakker and Chapple (2003).

6.   Monetary unions

6.1   WHAT IS A MONETARY UNION AND WHAT IS THE USE OF IT?

A *monetary union* is an area without payments restrictions within which exchange rates are permanently fixed. A special case of a monetary union is a *currency union*, that is, an area where the different currencies of member countries have been replaced by one common currency. Synonyms for a currency union are *full monetary union* and a *common-currency area*.

Why do countries enter into monetary union?

•   First, uncertainty in economic life can be reduced if economic agents do not have to take account of the possibility of exchange-rate changes. This is a benefit which is hard to quantify but is likely to be of major importance. It will make business people more eager to enter foreign markets and thus may help to integrate markets and contribute to a higher level of competition and dynamic scale economies. National markets in the union will become more integrated.

•   Second, if a monetary union has earned itself a reputation for maintaining low rates of inflation, it may be advantageous for a country to join the union in order to enhance the credibility of its monetary policy. This will, among other things, contribute to lower inflation expectations and thus to a lowering of interest rates and wage demands. A country may indeed decide to join a monetary union just in order to give the Minister of Finance the necessary support against his or her colleagues from the spending ministries and prevent the government from following irresponsible fiscal policies. If there is, therefore, a hegemonic country with a low inflation rate or a hard core of countries with low inflation to begin with, the forming of a monetary union may help to introduce credible non-inflationary monetary policies in other countries, too.

•   Third, a monetary union may serve to make an economic union function more smoothly. An economic union does not require monetary union, but without monetary union real exchange rates may easily change, both because of differing inflation rates across countries at given nominal exchange rates and because of nominal exchange-rate adjustments in discrete steps. Groups that believe they suffer in the process will put pressure on governments to restrict imports or give compensation for damage caused by a disadvantageous real exchange rate, pressure that will only increase if these groups accuse foreign governments of purposely bringing about a real-exchange-rate devaluation (Eichengreen 1996). All this is a thing of the past in a monetary union.

If these three points are generally valid for a monetary union, the following points are only valid for a common-currency area.

• First, money is used to facilitate transactions. Transaction costs are lower if a group of countries shares a common currency than if different countries use different currencies. If the various national currencies remain in use, economic agents still face the necessity of changing one currency into another. Estimates by the European Commission put the savings from a switch to a common currency at 0.3 per cent to 0.4 per cent of EU GNP (European Commission 1995, Introduction, para. 5). Seen from another angle, these transaction costs represent income for the banks (estimated at about 5 per cent of EU banks' revenue). The savings on transaction costs for society as a whole of switching to a common currency are made in the form of people and office space first employed in currency transactions and now available for other ends.

• Money is not only used as a means of payment, but also as a unit of account. In a currency union there is only one unit of account, which makes it easier to compare prices in different countries. A currency union thus leads to greater transparency of markets and a reduction in the costs of processing information (for example, accounting).

• Settlement of intra-union payments by international reserves is a thing of the past in a currency union. International reserves are pooled and less is needed, or alternatively, fluctuations in international payments can be more easily accommodated. Reserves can be invested in assets with a lower degree of liquidity which earn a higher yield, or the central bank could reduce its capital and free resources which the government can use for other ends.

• With a common currency, the functioning of financial markets improves. Large transactions will be less likely to cause a price shock in a large union market than in a relatively small national market. Put differently, the liquidity of financial assets (that is, the probability of being able to sell these at short notice without serious loss) is higher in a currency union. Then, it becomes much easier and cheaper to float large issues of new debt or equity. In the case of the Economic and Monetary Union (EMU) in Europe, not only has the depth of the market (liquidity) increased, but also its breadth: new market segments have emerged, which allow for much better diversification (Danthine, Giavazzi and von Thadden 2000).

• The European Commission highlights another advantage of currency union: the EU being the world's leading trading bloc, the European currency, the *euro*, will play an important role as international money, on a par with the US dollar. In particular, European business firms will be able to impose the euro on their trading partners as the invoice currency, thus avoiding exchange-rate uncertainty (European Commission 1995, Introduction, para. 6). One suspects that there are political motives behind the desire for the common European currency to emulate the dollar as an international currency. Such a role is not necessarily a blessing for European economic agents, as it could lead to increased foreign demand for the euro and thus to an appreciation, making life for exporters more difficult. On the other hand, it could bring in seigniorage income (see below).

•   Perhaps more importantly, a monetary union is likely to spur both the monetary authorities and the commercial banks into developing more efficient international payment mechanisms. In order to help create a smoothly functioning European money market, the start of the euro on 1 January 1999 went hand in hand with the start of the TARGET payments system (Trans European Automated Real Time Gross Settlement Express Transfer), which connects the settlement systems of the EU central banks. The commercial banks' EBA (Euro Banking Association) developed the EURO1 payments system, which makes use of TARGET for final settlement at the European Central Bank. The decision of the European Commission that from 1 July 2003 fees are allowed to be no higher for europayments than for domestic payments, also forces the banks to find ways to make the payments mechanism more efficient.

A monetary union that stops short of full monetary union is unlikely to profit fully from the integration of national financial markets. If there are separate national currencies, a watertight guarantee that exchange rates are irrevocably fixed cannot be given and economic agents will not see the various national currencies as perfect substitutes. In addition, unrestricted capital movements within the union may play havoc with the fixed rates; there is always a possibility that doubts arise as to the irrevocability of the fixed exchange rates and once they scent blood, the speculators move in for the kill. So, in the absence of capital controls, a monetary union without a common currency may be subject to speculative attacks whereas with capital controls it would be a caricature of itself.

Empirical research by Rose and van Wincoop (2001) suggests that the benefits of currency union for international (intra-union) trade could be surprisingly high. They applied a gravity model to trade between almost 200 countries, covering 98 per cent of all international trade, and found that not having a common currency is equivalent to an import tariff of 26 per cent. An earlier study by Rose (2000) came to the widely criticised conclusion that monetary union might lead to a tripling of trade between union members, but a respecification of his model in Rose and van Wincoop reduced this to the still high figure of a 58 per cent increase in the case of EMU (critiques in Pakko and Wall 2001; Persson 2001; for the pitfalls of the gravity model, see Porojan 2001). Micco, Stein and Ordoñez (2003) put the effect for euroland countries (till 2002) in the range between 4 and 16 per cent.

6.2   DISADVANTAGES OF MONETARY UNION

6.2.1   Nationalism and Macroeconomic Policies

If monetary unions brought only benefits, the fact that the world is not one big monetary union or even currency union could only be ascribed to the stupidity of our rulers. Such apparently was the view of John Stuart Mill, who wrote that 'So much of barbarism, however, still remains in the transactions of the most civilised nations, that almost all independent countries choose to assert their nationality by having, to their own inconvenience and that of their neighbours, a peculiar currency of their own' (Mill 1917, p. 615). However, that can hardly be the whole story; there can be real disadvantages to monetary union.

Why would a country decline to enter into monetary union with other countries? Several reasons can be thought of:

•   A national currency is still seen as an important element of a country's national identity by its citizens. The nationalistic sentiments that Mill wrote so disparagingly about more than a century and a half ago may not yet be dead. Resistance against the adoption of a common currency comes down to resistance against any but the lightest forms of transfer of power from national to supranational bodies. This is a factor that plays against currency unions, not against monetary unions where partners retain their own currency.

•   Countries may be loath to lose monetary autonomy. In a monetary union, with a common currency or completely fixed exchange rates and capital flows, individual countries cannot independently manipulate interest rates or the money supply. This is also the case, of course, in a fixed-but-adjustable peg system with highly elastic capital flows, but such a system at least provides the opportunity to loosen monetary policy at the cost of a parity change.

•   Countries may hesitate to say farewell to the exchange rate as a policy instrument. Generally speaking, exchange rates have to be adjusted if inflation rates between countries diverge for longer periods, but also if diverging real rather than monetary developments call for a change in the real exchange rate. A country may, for instance, experience faster productivity growth than other countries, or develop new energy sources that bring in additional export revenues or save on imports. In such cases an appreciation of the currency is called for if the current account of the balance of payments is not to be in permanent surplus; the only alternative is higher inflation. Further, demand may shift from one region to another, again necessitating price increases in one country or price decreases in another country if exchange-rate adjustments are ruled out. Apart from these movements in economic fundamentals, changes in macroeconomic policies by other countries will have an impact. As we saw in Chapter 2, Section 2.3.4, a flexible-rate system generally provides better insulation against such shocks than a fixed-rate system. In a monetary union the exchange rate can no longer absorb shocks. Wage and price flexibility will have to take over the role of the exchange rate in this respect. We will see below, in the section on optimal currency areas, that factor mobility may help too. But if economic agents are accustomed to low downward flexibility of wages and prices and to low labour mobility, it is not always easy to get them to accept flexibility and mobility.

• Countries may resent the loss of seigniorage income that they suffer if joining a monetary union implies accepting a lower inflation rate. This calls for further explanation, which is provided in the next subsection.

6.2.2 Seigniorage

Joining a monetary union has been cited as a means to enhance the credibility of non-inflationary policies. Some governments may, however, deplore the lowering of inflation rates that could be a prerequisite of joining a monetary union. They may value inflation because it can be used as a tax. It is a form of *seigniorage*. Seigniorage is income for the government from creating money, in particular base money: notes and coin plus the balances held by the banks with the central bank. In the first instance the creation of base money inflates the profits of the central bank, but these profits accrue to the Ministry of Finance.

Base money is created if the balances held by the banks with the central bank grow and they provide seigniorage income if those balances carry a zero interest rate or an interest rate below the market rate (note that the European Central Bank (ECB) pays a market rate of interest on required reserves and a lower rate on its deposit facilities). If, for example, the government finances its expenditures by borrowing from the central bank and spends the sums borrowed, we see an increase in the entry Advances to Government, Government Bonds or Treasury Paper on the Assets side of the central bank's balance sheet, and an increase in the entry Banks' Balances on the Liabilities side (see Table 6.1). The government bonds carry the market interest rate, whereas the central bank's liabilities to the commercial banks carry a zero interest rate or a rate below the going market rate. Base money is also created if the banks sell assets, such as foreign exchange or Treasury bonds, to the central bank or borrow from the central bank in order to increase their balances held with the central bank (either from free choice or in order to meet cash reserve requirements). The central bank receives an income from those assets (see Table 6.2). Profits from the central bank accrue to the government.

Table 6.1 Creation of base money through government borrowing from the central bank

Central bank balance sheet			
Assets		*Liabilities*	
advances to government	+	Treasury	+
		Treasury	–
		banks	+

Table 6.2 Creation of base money through sales of assets to the central bank

Central bank balance sheet			
Assets		*Liabilities*	
foreign exchange	+	banks	+
government bonds	+		
advances to banks	+		

Notes and coin, too, are base money. If the public wishes to hold more banknotes, the commercial banks buy banknotes for their clients from the central bank. Their balances with the central bank fall and the banknote circulation increases. Notes in circulation are a liability of the central bank that carry no interest. For coins the reasoning is similar, albeit that in this case the government pockets the seigniorage directly, and not via its claim on the profits of the central bank, as the banks buy the coins from the Treasury (the Treasury's account with the central bank is credited).

There are different ways to calculate seigniorage. In empirical studies seigniorage is often defined as the increase in the base-money supply minus the interest paid on the balances held by the banks with the central bank. Another way to calculate seigniorage is to take the difference between the market rate of interest and the interest actually paid by the central bank to the holders of base money (Gros and Vandille 1995). The two methods imply a different distribution of seigniorage over time.

In order to calculate seigniorage, one has to deduct the costs of producing banknotes and coins, and also the costs of checking the quality of banknotes (for example, some four million notes pass through the machines of the Dutch central bank for inspection every day). The costs of production, of course, do not only concern an expansion of the note and coin circulation, but also the replacement of worn-out notes and coin, including the destruction of worn-out notes (which is quite a complicated and expensive process, because of the heavy metals contained in the special ink used for printing banknotes).

Something similar to the creation of base money happens if the government forces financial institutions to invest in low-interest government debt. The difference between the interest paid by the government and the market rate of interest provides an income to the government akin to seigniorage. This privileged position of government debt used to be common in Southern European countries. At the end of 1986, for instance, more than 80 per cent of Spanish government debt was in the hands of financial institutions, largely the banks, including the central bank (Boonstra 1990). It is to be noted that since 1 January 1994 public authorities in the EU are not allowed to borrow directly from their central banks or other bodies governed by public law (such as government employees' pension funds) or to force financial institutions to buy government debt. Central banks are free, however, to buy government debt in the secondary market.

In an economy with zero real growth, stable prices and constant required reserves, seigniorage under the first method of calculation would be zero. With inflation, however, even with zero real growth the base-money supply increases and seigniorage accrues to the government. Nominal income growth generally goes hand in hand with an increase in real balances and thus with seigniorage under the first method of calculation. Seigniorage is also created by an increase in the reserve requirements imposed on the commercial banks (at below-market rates of interest).

Seigniorage provides income for the government which can be spent on goods and services. Its mirror image is a fall in private-sector spending which frees production capacity for government demand. If economic actors increase their base-money balances, part of their income is diverted from buying goods and services. It can be seen as a form of *forced saving*.

The forced character of these savings may cause resentment if seigniorage is created by inflation. The government then in a sense taxes existing balances M/P by creating additional money and causing inflation. Economic actors have to save part of their income to supplement nominal cash balances just to maintain their real balances. Inflation thus has similar results to a tax; it is therefore labelled *inflation tax*. It is a tax in which Parliament has no say, or, in the words of Milton Friedman, it is 'taxation without representation' (Friedman 1974, p. 13). Friedman's terminology was meant to give inflation a negative connotation in the eyes of his American readers, as one of the main causes of the American War of Independence (1776–83) was the fact that Westminster decided on trade taxes without the American colonists themselves having any say in it.

It should not be assumed that the inflation tax revenue is a monotonously increasing function of the rate of inflation. As inflation rates go up, people hold smaller real cash balances. Inflation implies a loss of purchasing power from holding cash balances and economic agents, in particular business firms, will spend more time and effort on cash management in order to be able to reduce their average real cash holdings. The volume of real balances can be seen as the tax base and the rate of inflation as the tax rate. As the rate of inflation reaches higher levels, at some rate the decrease in the tax base will just offset the increase in the tax rate. In a growing economy, maximum seigniorage from the creation of new money is reached at a lower rate of inflation than in a stationary economy, because inflation also reduces the increase in real balances associated with real growth in the economy.

Starting from the Cambridge money-demand function

$$M = kPy$$

and differentiating with respect to time, we obtain

$$dM/dt = kP(dy/dt) + ky(dP/dt)$$

and, after dividing by P,

$$dM/(P.dt) = ky(dy/dt)(1/y) + ky(dP/dt)(1/P)$$

or

$$(dM/dt)/P = ky(g + \pi), k = k(\pi), k_\pi < 0$$

where M stands for M_0 or base money (currency and deposits held with the central bank),
k = the Cambridge k,
P = the price level,
y = real national income,
$(dM/dt)/P$ = seigniorage (first calculation method),
g = the growth rate of real national income and
π = the rate of inflation.

Seigniorage can also be expressed as a fraction of national income:

$$(dM/dt).(1/Py) = k(g + \pi)$$

At, say, 3 per cent real growth, coupled with an inflation rate of 10 per cent and $k = 0.2$ (remember we are dealing with base money, not the total money supply), seigniorage would amount to 2.6 per cent of national income.

A maximum is found for

$$d[k(g + \pi)]/d\pi = 0$$
$$g(\delta k/\delta \pi) + k + \pi(\delta k/\delta \pi) = 0$$
$$(g + \pi)(\delta k/\delta \pi) = -k$$
$$\delta k/k = -\delta \pi/(g + \pi)$$

which reduces for $g = 0$ to

$$(\delta k/k)/(\delta \pi/\pi) = -1$$

which means that seigniorage is at its maximum when the elasticity of the demand for real balances (of base money) with regard to the rate of inflation is minus unity.

When discussing seigniorage, it should be kept in mind that inflation is often fluctuating, the more so if inflation is high (Choudhury 1991). High and fluctuating inflation cannot but be detrimental to the economy, as it impairs the functioning of the price mechanism.[1] Money cannot satisfactorily fulfil its role as a unit of account under high and fluctuating inflation, and long-term investment in productive capacity usually suffers. With high inflation, economic agents may switch to other currencies and such currency substitution reduces seigniorage income. More often than not, inflation is simply the result of weak government rather than a consciously engineered policy objective. However, if inflation has its costs, conventional taxes also have their costs in terms of collection costs and distortions. In theory an optimum is found, starting from some given amount of total tax revenues, when the marginal costs of the various taxes are equalised.

A moderate inflation, say below 10 per cent, may be irritating but cannot be said to be disastrous and the associated seigniorage may be very attractive to some governments. Anyhow, there are many cases where seigniorage has been an important part of government income. According to calculations by Click (1998), average seigniorage income (defined as changes in the monetary base) over the 1971–90 period was 0.54 per cent of GDP in the Netherlands and 0.66 per cent in Germany, but no less than 10.3 per cent in Chile and 14.842 per cent in Israel (see also Ramírez-Rojas 1986; Gros 1990; 'One Market, One Money' 1990, p. 122; Cody 1991; Dijkstra 1995). Figures fluctuate wildly and diverge between authors, but it seems clear that seigniorage revenues can be substantial.[2] It should be recognised that a loss of seigniorage income as a result of lower inflation can work out beneficially in the sense that it may force governments to organise tax collection better.

This is what Greece did (IMF 1999c, p. 59), with the help of experts from the US Internal Revenue Service.

Full European Monetary Union was estimated to cause a fall of seigniorage to below 1 per cent of national income for the Southern European countries ('One Market, One Money' 1990, p. 122). A loss of some 2.5–3 per cent of GDP has indeed been found (Lange and Nolte 1998). Against this, a union central bank such as the ECB earns seigniorage from the increase in the demand for real balances. Seigniorage will also be earned if non-union countries decide to hold their international reserves in the union currency (unless they hold their reserves in assets that pay a market interest rate) and if non-union residents hold the union's currency in the form of notes and coin. To get an idea of the order of magnitude involved, if the assets that the Federal Reserve System acquired against the $300 billion of US banknotes estimated to be held by foreigners in 1999 (mentioned in Chapter 1, Section 1.4.3) earned, say, 3.5 per cent, these holdings would have brought in more than $10 billion of seigniorage income.

6.3 OPTIMUM CURRENCY AREAS

Obviously, there are sound arguments in favour of monetary union and sound arguments against. Arguments for monetary union are arguments for permanently fixed exchange rates and by the same token arguments against floating rates or even fixed-but-adjustable rates. There is an extensive literature studying the criteria which can be used to establish the optimum area within which to fix exchange rates (summarised by Ishiyama 1975 and Maes 1992). This *optimum currency area* literature focuses on the means to maintain both external balance and internal balance after an asymmetric shock, that is, a shock that hits one country more than another. External balance means balance-of-payments equilibrium (seen as equilibrium in international payments without interventions by the central bank) and internal balance means full, but not overfull, employment. It should be realised that if a group of regions or countries does not fulfil the criteria for a currency area, it does not follow that they should adopt free floating. A fixed-but-adjustable peg or some form of managed floating may be preferable.

6.3.1 Mundell: Factor Mobility

In 1961, Mundell (1961) started the discussion on optimum currency areas by analysing how countries could best adjust to a demand shift, or, in today's parlance, an *asymmetric demand shock*. Suppose that, starting from full employment and balance-of-payments equilibrium, demand shifts from country B's products to country A's products (because country A has developed a new, cheaper and faster, generation of PCs, for instance). Given downward wage and price stickiness, an appreciation of A's currency with respect to B's currency would be called for in order to prevent unemployment in B and inflation in A. Now let a demand shift occur between regions within a closed economy with a common currency. The authorities would be faced with the dilemma of expanding the money supply to combat unemployment in the depressed region at the cost of fuelling inflation in the prosperous region or contracting the money supply in order to curb inflation in the prosperous region at the cost of compounding unemployment in the depressed region. Giving each region its own currency without fixing the exchange rate would solve the problem.

This dilemma would not be found in areas with high factor mobility. Prosperous regions attract factors of production from depressed regions, curing both unemployment and inflation. An optimum currency area, therefore, is an area within which factor mobility is high. Such optimum currency areas do not necessarily coincide with national boundaries.

Factor mobility, in particular labour mobility, is never perfect. Is Mundell's argument then a plea for a proliferation of currency areas? That would only be the case if there were no disadvantages or costs in having a great number of areas with their own currency and floating exchange rates. First, Mundell mentions the role of money as a unit of account, which is less adequately fulfilled the larger the number of different monies. Second, with a large number of currencies, the foreign-exchange market for any currency is likely to become very thin. Speculators could unduly influence exchange rates in such markets. Finally, the smaller the currency area, the higher the proportion of imported goods in consumption. A devaluation in a very small currency area seriously eats into real wages, given nominal wages, and will be more likely to give rise to compensating wage demands than in a large currency area where imports are relatively less important. The fall in real wages which was the *raison d'être* of exchange-rate flexibility thus may fail to come about, in the view of Mundell.

If shocks are frequent and strong, within an optimum currency area substantial migration of factors would be implied. It is one thing for capital to be mobile, but high mobility of labour is quite another matter. It may carry high costs in terms of social and psychic disruption and also in terms of the cost of building new homes and the required infrastructure in prosperous areas on the one hand and the deterioration of living conditions in depressed areas on the other hand. There may be much logic in Mundell's approach, but it is not always to be hoped that his criterion is fulfilled. There is another way out for currency areas: wage and price flexibility.

6.3.2   McKinnon: Openness of the Economy

McKinnon (1969), commenting on Mundell, proposed the openness of an economy, defined as the ratio of tradeable to nontradeable goods in domestic production and consumption, as a criterion. His model depicts a dependent-economy world where downward price stickiness may exist, whereas Mundell's model was more in the *IS/LM* mould.

McKinnon first considered the case of a high share of tradeables. Suppose that the price of nontradeables is fixed. In order for the current account of the balance of payments to improve, the domestic currency is devalued. Domestic demand for tradeables falls and production increases. Possibly monetary and/or fiscal policy has to be restrictive in addition, in order to suppress excess demand in the nontradeables sector. However, in a very open economy the implied variations in the domestic price level would be substantial, because of a fast-increasing marginal rate of transformation for tradeables if the production of nontradeables is already low to start with. An increase in the production of tradeables would require a substantial rise in their relative, and in this case also absolute, price. It is highly unlikely that trade unions would not react by demanding compensating wage increases.

The more open, therefore, the economy, the weaker the impact of a nominal exchange-rate change on real competitiveness. As the economy becomes more open the suppression of excess demand or current-account deficits becomes increasingly more dependent on restrictive macroeconomic policies, as devaluations or depreciations tend to lead to higher price levels without a substantial reduction in the trade deficit. Complete openness would in McKinnon's analysis boil down to a one-product world, where current-account equilibrium can only be restored through income variations, unaccompanied by relative price changes. Expenditure switching does not work in such a world; expenditure reduction is needed.

McKinnon next considered the case of a large share of nontradeables in domestic consumption and production. Fixing the domestic price of nontradeables and changing relative prices through the exchange rate is now less harmful to price-level stability, whereas restrictive macroeconomic policies would create more unemployment in the nontradeables sector, which is now much larger than in the first case.

It follows that in McKinnon's world monetary union would be attractive if the countries concerned are very open *vis-à-vis* each other. Obviously, under fixed exchange rates, the desired price stability can only be reached if prices in the outside world are stable as well. In the case of external price shocks, in a very open economy flexible rates are preferable if great store is set by price stability.

6.3.3   Kenen: Product Diversification

In Kenen's (1969) view, the logic of Mundell's approach requires that regions are defined by their activities. Demand will shift from one region to another if it shifts from one product to another. Perfect interregional labour mobility then equals perfect occupational mobility. Given the absence of such high mobility, Kenen proposed to use the degree of product diversification as a criterion for the desirability of fixed exchange rates. Suppose foreign demand for one good falls (again an asymmetric demand shock). If the country in question produces and exports a large variety of goods, the resulting unemployment is less serious than in a less diversified economy and it is hardly necessary to change the exchange rate.

This conclusion is strengthened by the argument that shocks will tend to average out over time. With a diversified economy, one can expect both positive and negative shocks (not only demand shocks but *supply shocks*, such as bad harvests, technological developments or OPEC oil price hikes, may be involved). Consequently, it is less-diversified and presumably smaller economies that can profit from flexible exchange rates. This may at first sight seem to contradict McKinnon's findings, insofar as less diversified economies tend to have a higher share of tradeables in domestic consumption. However, the criteria could be seen as different dimensions. Given the share of tradeables in total consumption, fixed rates become more attractive as product diversification increases and given the degree of product diversification, fixed rates become more attractive as the economy becomes more open.

6.3.4   Scitovsky and Ingram: Financial Integration

Scitovsky (1962, pp. 85–97; 1967) and Ingram (1969, 1973) point to the significance of financial integration as a requirement for a currency area, in addition to labour mobility. With a high degree of financial integration, economic agents that need external finance (deficit units) in one region can easily sell financial assets to economic agents that have means available for financial investment (surplus units) in other regions. Ingram argues that depressed regions can thus finance investments and government budget deficits without having to generate the required savings beforehand themselves (remember the Feldstein–Horioka criterion). The upshot is that in the case of a negative demand shock that creates unemployment and a current-account deficit there is no need for an exchange-rate change to minimise the damage.

Scitovsky pays attention to other cases, in particular current-account deficits not caused by negative demand shocks but by high economic activity.

A high degree of financial integration will make it easy to generate a capital inflow that offsets the current-account deficit. Labour migration and a shift in government spending to depressed regions would, in addition, be required to prevent serious unemployment developing there.

On a more general level it can be said that financial integration helps to absorb *asymmetric shocks*, that is, shocks that hit one country but not others, or that do not hit all countries in a currency area with the same intensity. It does not really seem necessary to require a high degree of financial integration as a prerequisite for a monetary union, as monetary union can itself be expected to contribute to financial integration.

6.3.5 Fleming: Similarity in Inflation Rates

Fleming (1971) emphasised that only countries with roughly similar inflation rates can maintain fixed exchange rates *vis-à-vis* each other. It stands to reason that a fixed-rate system cannot survive protracted periods of strongly diverging inflation rates, even if similarity of inflation rates offers no guarantee of current-account equilibrium (because of different growth rates, different development of natural resources and so on). However, to the extent that inflation rates can be manipulated, similarity of inflation rates cannot be used as a criterion to decide which countries can best form a monetary union. It is rather the other way round; countries that wish to form a monetary union have to take measures to make their inflation rates converge.

If the members of a monetary union adopt a common currency, the supply of which is controlled by a central bank having price stability as (almost) its sole objective, one may wonder why the rate of inflation in terms of any pre-union national currency should matter at all (De Grauwe 1996). After a currency union has been formed, and consequently a common monetary policy has been adopted, it would take trade unions that are both very strong and very myopic to drive wages up and raise inflation in one region or country much above the union average. The credibility of the proposed low-inflation policy will be higher, though, if there is pre-union convergence to low inflation rates. This will contribute to low interest rates (and thus make it easier to keep government budget deficits low) and help prevent speculative attacks in foreign-exchange markets.

6.3.6 Some Comments and an Application to European Monetary Union

It seems that no single criterion is available for assessing the desirability of a monetary union. The various criteria emphasise different aspects. It should be noted that in much of the above analysis stickiness of wages and prices was assumed. Wage and price flexibility would, in the cases analysed by Mundell, McKinnon or Kenen, make exchange-rate changes superfluous. Flexibility would not only imply flexibility of the general wage or price level with respect to the degree of unemployment, but first of all flexibility in *relative* wages and prices. High labour mobility could also solve the problems caused by demand shifts, but it may cause problems in its own right, as we have seen.

It seems useful to distinguish between *nominal* and *real* flexibility. Nominal flexibility of wages and prices is a good substitute for exchange-rate flexibility. If nominal wages and prices are sticky, but real wages are not, the exchange rate, a nominal price, can be used to bring about real adjustments (that is, a change in relative prices). Real-wage inflexibility would make things pretty hopeless. Exchange-rate changes would only lead to wage and price adjustments, leaving relative prices unaffected.

From the *IS/LM/EE* model we know that, with sticky prices, a fixed-exchange-rate system is not well placed to absorb external shocks. Conversely, the greater wage and price flexibility are, the easier it is to maintain fixed exchange rates. Further, within the context of Mundell's approach, it is obvious that if shocks hit a group of countries in a more or less similar way, that is, if they are *symmetric*, the case for a currency union is stronger. There is less need for those countries to change relative prices in such a case; they should rather float collectively *vis-à-vis* third countries. Countries with a similar industrial structure are better candidates for monetary union than strongly different countries. Developed industrial countries are better placed in this respect than a combination of countries with a diversified industrial structure on the one hand and countries specialising in a limited number of primary commodities on the other.

Interestingly, economic union could make the case for monetary union less strong, seen from this perspective. De Grauwe (1992, p. 32) observes that car production in the EU is much less regionally concentrated than in the United States. He argues that the EU, as it moves to further integration, may see more regional concentration of industries. This would make the EU more susceptible to asymmetric shocks. Indeed, there is evidence of increasing specialisation in some EU countries between 1968 and 1990. Some industries with high scale economies, where a common market leads to a smaller number of firms, and a high intermediate-goods content, which makes clustering of those firms with suppliers attractive, have become more concentrated. Examples are shoemaking, boilers, textile machines, shipbuilding and ready-made clothes (Amiti 1999). If shocks are industry-specific and uncorrelated, monetary union can thus make macroeconomic policy making (demand management) after a shock harder (see also Kenen's criterion). Against this, business cycles seem to have become more synchronised in the EU over the years, as trade and financial integration has proceeded (IMF 1997b, p. 72; Demertzis, Hughes Hallett and Rummel 2000; Dalsgaard, Elmeskov and Park 2002; Ducker and Wesche 2003). Symmetric demand shocks seem to dominate asymmetric shocks, especially within a 'core' made up of Germany, France, the Netherlands, Belgium, Austria, Denmark and Luxembourg.[3]

One may note that in the case of a high degree of financial integration asymmetric shocks can, if they are of a temporary nature, be cushioned to a certain extent by financial flows (enabling consumption smoothing) and do not require substantial adjustments of relative prices. Exchange-rate changes would be of little help, as they need time before taking effect. Still, macroeconomic policies would run up against the diverging needs of individual countries.

It seems safe to conclude that a monetary union is likely to bring more benefits the more intensive is intra-union trade, and that the loss of the exchange rate as a policy instrument is less harmful, if

- labour mobility is high or wages and prices are flexible, and/or
- the industrial structure in all member countries is diversified.

In the EU of the 15 intra-union trade is quite high. The industrial structure is diversified and quite similar in most of the member states, with Ireland, Portugal and perhaps even more so Greece the exceptions. Labour mobility, however, seems to be lower than, for instance, in North America. The enlargement of the EU with Central and Eastern European countries alters the picture insofar as they are more dependent on agriculture than the older members. The correlation of GDP growth between the five Central European candidate-members and the euro area in the second half of the 1990s was correspondingly low, but industrial production was highly correlated. This fits in with the high intensity of intra-industry trade. Moreover, over 60 per cent of the international trade of these countries was with the EU (Doornbosch and Brzeski 2002). Asymmetric shocks look like a minor danger.

Depending on one's view of the social costs involved in high labour mobility, low labour mobility can be seen either as a good or a bad thing, but if it exists, a larger burden of adjustment is placed on wage and price flexibility (if indeed adjustment is necessary, that is, if shocks are asymmetric and do not even out over time). It is to be expected that labour mobility in Europe will remain lower than in the United States, which can boast of a more uniform culture, has one dominating language and only one other widely spoken language (Spanish), does not have to contend with different labour laws or different pension systems and has a footloose tradition.

Even so, Eichengreen (1990, p. 165) notes that the tendency for US regional labour-market conditions to converge is surprisingly weak. In the interest of cushioning shocks, low labour mobility combined with the loss of the exchange-rate instrument makes downward wage and price flexibility all the more important in the European Monetary Union. Interestingly, there are indications that wages in Germany and the Netherlands are more sensitive to business-cycle movements than in the United States (Pauli 2002). Other aspects of flexibility in labour markets should not be neglected either, such as frictions in the housing market (sales taxes), the availability of retraining facilities and opportunities for part-time work (for a discussion of labour market flexibility in Europe, see Scheerlinck and Pans 2000).

The case of Germany after unification suggests that the adoption of a common currency may make the call for 'equal pay for equal work' louder, more so than the removal of impediments to labour migration in an economic union without common currency. Full monetary union, therefore, may be detrimental to wage and price flexibility, just when it is most needed. If, however, the authorities take an uncompromising stand and make it abundantly clear that they will not resort to increased spending in order to relieve unemployment, rational economic agents will revise their strategies and accept higher wage and price flexibility. Privatisation of government-owned business firms will help people accept the discipline of the market. In private firms there is a more direct, and more obvious, relation between high wage demands and redundancies. One should not, in this respect, judge the desirability or the potential dangers of monetary union simply on the basis of past developments. If the economic environment changes, economic agents are likely to adapt their behaviour, as the Lucas critique stresses.[4]

6.4 POTENTIAL PROBLEMS OF MONETARY UNION

6.4.1 Spread and Backwash Effects

It was argued above that economic union may cause concentration of industries in specific regions. One cannot be sure that regions that see business firms migrate will be able to attract others in numbers large enough to keep labour and capital employed. As there are no formal restrictions on movements of factors of production in an economic union, some regions may be confronted with a serious net outflow of labour and capital. This view was propounded by Myrdal (1963) even before the EEC came into being in 1958. Myrdal contrasted the neoclassical view of a smoothly operating, equilibrating economic system with the vicious circles he himself discerned in the actual world. He saw, in a world where factors of production can move about unhampered, a tendency for capital and the most productive and enterprising members of the labour force to cluster in certain localities or regions, abandoning other regions to stagnation.

A case in point are the southern regions in Italy, the phenomenon is, therefore, sometimes called the *Mezzogiorno problem*. Growth in one region may in this way have negative effects, *backwash effects* as Myrdal called them, on other regions. From a more neoclassical point of view, which assumes that economic forces tend to move the system to equilibrium rather than disequilibrium, one would predict that growth in one region would stimulate economic activity in other regions. There would be *spread effects*, in Myrdal's terminology.

Generally speaking, a clustering of economic activities in a limited number of regions depends on the size of the economies of scale that can be exploited on the one hand and on transportation costs on the other hand. No *a priori* conclusions seem possible. Nevertheless, monetary union significantly contributes to the transformation of separate national markets into an integrated union-wide market and may be expected to increase the mobility of the factors of production. Backwash effects may easily get the upper hand. For the EU the available evidence (looking at GDP growth and employment rates) does not, however, suggest that this will always be a serious problem. Apparently, relatively low wages in the poorer and less developed regions, possibly helped by investment grants from the union, offset possible disadvantages for industrial firms compared with other locations, ensuring satisfactory profit levels. As for labour, the availability of jobs at relatively low but rising real wage levels proves sufficient to prevent large-scale migration. From this point of view there thus need not be *real convergence* as a prerequisite for monetary union, that is, countries need not strive for a similar economic structure or similar per capita income levels on the way to monetary union (we also distinguish *nominal convergence*, that is, the convergence of such variables as inflation and interest rates).

6.4.2 Fiscal Policy

Even in the case where member states in an economic and monetary union have formally kept their fiscal autonomy, the mobility of capital and labour, in particular highly educated labour, may in actual practice limit this autonomy. People and capital will tend to migrate to countries where they are lightly taxed. This raises the spectre of *tax competition*, that is, of countries lowering taxes in order to keep or attract mobile production factors. Countries are able to maintain different tax levels only insofar as factor mobility is low. Even with high factor mobility, it is not impossible for high tax rates to be maintained, especially if the group paying high taxes is also the direct beneficiary of government spending. Business firms may, for instance, be willing to invest in a country where they pay relatively high taxes if they can in return profit from a well-developed material infrastructure (roads, railways) or from government-financed vocational training. Nevertheless, higher factor mobility will increase the need for fiscal harmonisation if tax competition is to be avoided. Such harmonisation may involve agreements on minimal tax rates, but also on the tax structure and the social security system. This need not necessarily occur beforehand. Harmonisation of fiscal systems with an eye to trade between member states in an economic union is another matter. Such harmonisation took place, for instance, with the substitution of a VAT (Value Added Tax) system for the previous turnover tax system in the EEC member countries before the economic union started functioning in 1958. Economic union, not monetary union, is involved here.

Fiscal harmonisation, as discussed above, refers to the microeconomic aspects of fiscal measures. The aim is not to distort the allocation of economic resources. There are also macroeconomic aspects involved. First, fiscal policy is one determinant of aggregate spending. Second, fiscal policy has an impact on financial markets and may affect interest rates and the availability of credit to borrowers other than the government.

As for the first aspect, member states' economies in an economic and monetary union may be expected to become increasingly open and interlinked. The effects of the fiscal policy of any member state will thus more and more spill over to other member states. This will work as an incentive to harmonise fiscal policy. Another issue is that in a monetary union governments have lost the exchange rate as an instrument of macroeconomic policy. An asymmetric shock can no longer be met by an exchange-rate change. Wage and price flexibility will often not be high enough to prevent unemployment and even if they are high enough, real per capita income may still fluctuate violently. Within individual countries, there are mechanisms, such as unemployment benefits and increased government spending, that provide for income transfers in such cases. On a union-wide scale, such mechanisms are likely to be relatively undeveloped as long as the union is not a fully fledged political union (such as the United States or Canada). One may expect constant pressure from the poorer members in an economic and monetary union to increase the funds available at union level for such transfers.

Another point is that in a currency union a supranational central bank is responsible for monetary policy. If the union central bank is to have sufficient grip on the money supply, individual countries should not be given the opportunity to throw a spanner in the works. The opportunities for monetary financing of a government budget deficit should therefore be restricted, for example by prohibiting direct central bank credit to governments (as is the case in EMU). The question then arises to what extent the fiscal policies of the member countries can remain independent. Individual countries would remain able to borrow in union capital markets, so they would still be able to run budget deficits. However, they would no longer have recourse to the central bank for monetising their debt should they accumulate so much debt that they have difficulty in servicing it, that is, where capital markets refuse to lend additional sums to them, or demand exorbitant interest rates. But could capital markets be trusted to cut off lending to irresponsible governments at an early stage? There is some evidence from US states and Canadian provinces that higher debt leads to higher borrowing costs (Masson and Taylor 1992, p. 53), but recurring debt crises in the world certainly do not suggest that market discipline can always be counted on to prevent excessive debt growth. Consequently, on this ground at least, a case can be made for imposing rules on budget deficits in a monetary union. Attempts by the European Union to tackle this problem will be discussed below (Section 6.5.4).

6.5   EUROPEAN MONETARY UNION

6.5.1   Why European Monetary Union?

Perhaps the most important prerequisite to make a monetary union a success is the political will to form such a union. Economic unions imply giving up some national sovereignty (for instance in trade policy or tax policy). Monetary union is economic union taken one step further. The EEC was set up with the aim of integrating Germany into Western Europe so as not to repeat the mistakes made at Versailles in 1919, so eloquently, but in vain, denounced by Keynes (1919); also, it was in its first guise as the *European Coal and Steel Community* (ECSC) developed as an instrument to secure access by the French steel industry to the coal supplies of the Ruhr area (Loth 1990, pp. 60, 82). The loss of sovereignty, even if it is given up reluctantly, was intended right from the start. The founding fathers, the French businessman and civil servant Jean Monnet, who in 1919 at the age of 30 had become the Vice-Secretary-General of the League of Nations, and the French Foreign Minister Robert Schuman, saw the ECSC as a first step in the federation of Europe. In the same vein, the later *neo-functionalist* approach, with Ernst Haas as its most prominent representative, expected that cooperation in supranational institutions such as the ECSC would lead to a transfer of loyalties among national elites from the national to the supranational level and thus give the integration process a snowball effect (Cram 2001; Haas 1972).

As for monetary integration, one important reason for putting it on the agenda in the 1960s was that exchange-rate changes threatened to undermine the Common Agricultural Policy (CAP). Common price levels for agricultural products across the EEC would have meant full adjustment of agricultural product prices for exchange-rate changes. French devaluations would in this way inflate the cost of living in France, German revaluations would eat into German farmers' real income (Lutz 1970). To shield national agricultural markets from these effects of exchange-rate changes, artificial 'green' exchange rates were introduced, which did not follow the exchange-rate rearrangements, or did so to a lesser degree. The difference between the 'green' exchange rate and the official one was made up by levies and restitutions at the border. In our case, this implied a levy on French agricultural exports (to be paid to the European Agricultural Guarantee and Guidance Fund by German importers) and a subsidy (from the same Fund) on German agricultural exports (Hill 1984; Szász 1988, p. 130; Aldcroft and Oliver 1998, pp. 143–6). These payments were known as *Monetary Compensatory Amounts*. This arrangement (which was in force until 1993, though 'green rates' lingered on until 1999) conflicted with the idea of a common market for agricultural products. The European Commission was spurred into action and this led to the report of the *Werner Committee* in 1970, proposing a plan to form an economic and monetary union. It came to nought, though, because of divergent views on the need to proceed with political integration alongside monetary integration and because of the upheavals following the first oil crisis in 1973–74 (Gros and Thygesen 1992, ch. 1). Also, all energy was concentrated on the enlargement of the Community.

Nevertheless, the prospect of stability of exchange rates remained alluring. Under flexible rates, whenever people started to get nervous about the dollar, they fled to the D-Mark, causing an appreciation and making life harder for the German tradeables industries. The French have traditionally been proponents of fixed rates and the French President Valéry Giscard d'Estaing and the German Chancellor Helmut Schmidt took the initiative to reinstate a system of fixed-but-adjustable parities, the European Monetary System (EMS), which started in 1979 (Gros and Thygesen 1992, ch. 2).

However, the French complained about the asymmetry between surplus and deficit countries in the case of balance-of-payment imbalances; it was the deficit countries that had to take measures to correct the imbalance, not the surplus countries. More generally, the French felt that they had lost their monetary autonomy and had no choice but to follow German monetary policies. With a common central bank they would not have to leave monetary policy to the Germans but would themselves be at the helm too (Szász 1999, ch. 11). Moreover, there were occasional speculative attacks on some of the EMS currencies and the French Finance Minister Edouard Balladur and the German Foreign Minister Dietrich Genscher agreed that a common currency with a common central bank would be the only way to ensure monetary stability. At the Hanover European Council in June 1988 a committee, chaired by the President of the European Commission Jacques Delors, was appointed and charged with the task of developing a blueprint for a European Monetary Union. The report by this committee, the *Delors Report*, was presented in 1989 (Delors Report 1989) and formed the basis of EMU, created by the 1991 Maastricht Treaty.

The German Chancellor Helmut Kohl played an active role in getting EMU accepted. Kohl wanted to take advantage of the more open political climate in the Soviet Union after Gorbachev had become the Soviet leader and bring about disarmament and détente. His need of Western, in particular French, support and his wish to anchor Germany firmly in Western Europe led him to cooperate with the French on monetary union. This support was needed all the more after the fall of the Berlin wall on 9 November 1989, when Kohl, working for an early reunification (which took place less than one year later, on 3 October 1990), had to allay fears in other countries of a new, strong Germany. Monetary union was a way to embed Germany even more firmly in Western Europe and prevent it from becoming a destabilising factor in the future, as it had been in the past (Szász 1999). At the European summit at Strasbourg in December 1989 the French President, Mitterrand, thus had little difficulty in persuading Chancellor Kohl to accept EMU in exchange for his support for Kohl's reunification plans. Political factors have been decisive in decision making about European Monetary Union; the Bundesbank always showed a characteristic lack of enthusiasm.

6.5.2 The Treaty on European Union (Maastricht Treaty)

If it is agreed that monetary union is desirable and that real convergence is not a strict prerequisite, the next question is how to go about forming a monetary union. The Delors Report envisaged three stages and in the 1991 Maastricht summit further agreements were reached on the third stage, monetary union, and on the criteria for admittance.

In Stage I, the Community should become a single financial area in which all monetary and financial instruments circulate freely.

In Stage II, a European System of Central Banks (ESCB) would be set up, replacing a number of existing Community institutions (the European Monetary Cooperation Fund, the Committee of Central Bank Governors, the subcommittees for monetary policy analysis, foreign-exchange policy and banking supervision, and the permanent secretariat). Exchange-rate realignments would not be excluded, but would be made only in exceptional circumstances. The ESCB should begin the transition from the coordination of independent national monetary policies to the formulation and implementation of a common monetary policy to be executed by the ESCB in Stage III. A certain amount of exchange reserves would be pooled, to be used for exchange market interventions. In the Maastricht Treaty the ESCB as a fledgling central bank was replaced by the European Monetary Institute (EMI), whereas the ESCB as the fully fledged central bank of Stage III was defined as composed of the European Central Bank (ECB) plus the national central banks (Article 106). The EMI administered the then existing European Monetary System and prepared the ground for the ECB by coordinating national monetary policies and creating the instruments and procedures for the ECB.

In Stage III, exchange rates would become irrevocably fixed and national currencies would preferably be replaced by a common currency, the ECU (European Currency Unit). Unlike the ecu in use before monetary union, the common currency was to be a currency in its own right and not a basket currency. At the European summit in Madrid in December 1995 the new common currency was baptised the *euro.* Monetary policy in the Community became the sole responsibility of the ESCB, which would also decide on foreign-exchange interventions in accordance with Community exchange-rate policy. Official reserves would be pooled and managed by the ESCB.

The Treaty on European Union, unofficially called the Maastricht Treaty, contains five convergence criteria, that is, criteria that must be fulfilled for a country to be allowed in:[5]

(i)   its inflation rate, observed over a period of one year before examination, is not more than 1.5 per cent higher than the average of the three lowest inflation rates in the EMS;

(ii)   its long-term interest rate observed over a period of one year is not more than 2 per cent higher than the average in the three low-inflation countries;

(iii)   it has not experienced a devaluation during the two years preceding the entry into the union;

(iv)   its government budget deficit is not higher than 3 per cent of its GDP at market prices; countries also qualify if the deficit is higher but has declined substantially and continuously and reached a level close to this value or if the excess over the reference value is only exceptional and temporary and the ratio remains close to the reference value;

(v) its government gross debt is not higher than 60 per cent of its GDP at market prices; countries also qualify if that level is exceeded but the ratio is diminishing sufficiently and approaching the reference value at a satisfactory pace.

(Note that 'government' means general government, that is, central government, regional or local government and social security funds, to the exclusion of commercial operations; debt is gross debt; *Protocol on the Excessive Deficit Procedure*, Article 2).

The first stage started on 1 July 1990, when remaining capital restrictions were lifted. The second stage began on 1 January 1994 and on 1 January 1999 the third stage commenced. The participating countries were Germany, France, Italy, Belgium, the Netherlands, Luxembourg, Ireland, Finland, Austria, Spain and Portugal, with Greece joining two years later. The Maastricht Treaty had opt-out clauses for Denmark and the United Kingdom attached to it and Sweden simply stayed out.

6.5.3 The Independence of the European Central Bank

The primary objective of the ECB is price stability. It was felt that, in order to shield the ECB from political pressure to make monetary policy serve other ends, the ECB should be given a high degree of independence. To guarantee this independence, the members of the Executive Board are appointed for a period of eight years and their term is not renewable. They thus have no reason to follow the wishes of politicians with an eye to the renewal of their term, though the prospect of a cushy job at the end of their term could still be held out by politicians. Governors of the national central banks must have terms of at least five years. Complete independence would mean that the ECB could not be forced to intervene in foreign-exchange markets and in that way increase or decrease the Union's money supply. However, decisions on the exchange-rate system, and within any system decisions on the central rates (parities), or, in the case of a floating rate, decisions on the 'general orientations for exchange rate policy', may be taken by the European Council (Article 109).

Central bankers fear further political interference with ECB monetary policy if the fight against inflation results in under-employment. It is stated twice (both in Article 105 of the Treaty and in Article 2 of *Protocol on the Statute of the European System of Central Banks and of the European Central Bank*) that 'the primary objective of the ESCB shall be to maintain price stability. Without prejudice to the objective of price stability, it shall support the general economic policies in the Community'. This formulation may act as an invitation to politicians to try and use Community monetary policy to pursue short-term ends, at the cost of higher inflation. Conflicts are thus not excluded.

With regard to the objective of price stability itself, relative wage and price changes will meet with less resistance if there is low inflation than if there is no inflation. Low inflation would allow such changes to be brought about without nominal wages having to fall, or fall much. The pre-ECB Committee of Central Bank Governors of the EU interpreted price stability as an inflation rate of between 0 per cent and 2 per cent (Hoogduin and Korteweg 1993, p. 66) and this has been adopted as the policy target of the ECB.

One may wonder whether independence of the central bank is really so important. The idea is that politicians have a short time horizon and have difficulty in resisting the temptation to follow expansionary policies when elections come up. They may instruct the central bank to lower interest rates and increase the growth of the money supply. In the first instance real income and production would surely increase, but later only higher inflation would result. This is because the relationship between the rate of unemployment and the rate of inflation is negative in the short term, whereas in the long term the rate of unemployment is independent of the rate of inflation. In other words, the short-term Phillips curve has a negative slope, but the long-term Phillips curve is vertical, or may even have a positive slope. Governments therefore, so runs the argument, have a tendency to renege on promises to keep inflation low.

In countries with a large volume of government debt, governments might also engineer a surprise inflation in order to reduce the real value of outstanding government debt. However, rational economic agents learn fast and will demand high interest rates if a government has earned itself a poor reputation. Promises to do better next time will not be believed and a country may be faced with a situation where a government earnestly tries to keep inflation low, by means of restrictive fiscal and monetary policies, yet economic agents remain suspicious and demand high real interest rates. Interest payments on government debt remain high, making it more difficult to reduce the deficit. Delegation of monetary policy to an independent central bank is seen as a solution to this problem (Begg 1997).

It has generally been found in empirical research that independence goes hand in hand with low inflation (see Eijffinger and de Haan 1996 for an extensive survey), but that does not necessarily mean that independence of the central bank in itself ensures low inflation. One may expect the central bank to be made independent, or rather, to be explicitly charged with committing itself to price stability, if there is a political will to fight inflation to start with. Without this political will, a central bank may face an uphill battle. Governments can thwart attempts by the central bank to restrict money growth even if they are not allowed to borrow directly from the central bank. They may sell debt to commercial banks or borrow abroad and indirectly increase the money supply by fixing exchange rates at a high level, thus forcing the central bank to buy foreign exchange against domestic money.

It should be remarked that independence of a central bank is hardly ever meant to include complete independence in all respects. There is *organisational independence*, which means that the ECB and the national central banks are legal entities and are expressly forbidden, as are individual members of their decision-making bodies, to seek or take instructions from other bodies (*Protocol*, Article 7). There is also *financial independence*: the ECB and the national central banks are not paid from other institutions' budgets. On the other hand, there is no *goal independence*. The goal which the ECB has to pursue is enshrined in the Maastricht Treaty. There is not even full *instrument independence*, as the *Protocol on the Statute of the European System of Central Banks and of the European Central Bank* included in the Maastricht Treaty enumerates the policy instruments at the ECB's disposal: open-market operations, credit operations and minimum reserve requirements (Articles 18 and 19). Other instruments may be introduced, under the condition of a two-thirds majority in the Governing Council. Instruments such as direct credit controls are not allowed. Indeed, these would conflict with Article 3a of the Treaty, which stipulates that monetary policy shall be 'in accordance with the principle of an open market economy with free competition'. The point at issue is *policy independence*, the freedom of the ECB to follow its own course in fulfilling its task to keep the price level stable. Politicians will from time to time exert pressure on the ECB to use, for example, short-term interest rates with an eye to increasing employment rather than keeping prices stable. This of course would amount to a violation of the Maastricht Treaty.

6.5.4 The Fiscal Norms

The Maastricht Treaty contains two fiscal convergence criteria (iv and v). It is said that these were adopted because Germany was afraid of fiscal laxity that might endanger the anti-inflationary policies of the ECB. Why should fiscal laxity make the task of the ECB more difficult?

First, governments may create large deficits. These would lead to high spending levels and possibly to substantial inflation. They may also lead to high interest rates and to pressure on the ECB to relax monetary policy in order to keep interest rates low.

Second, high budget deficits in a country may produce spill-over effects. High deficits make for high interest rates. With integrated capital markets, upward pressure on interest rates is not bottled up in one country, but spreads to other countries as well. There is a moral-hazard risk, as governments may feel less inhibited to create high deficits because the resultant costs are partly shifted to other countries.

Third, with fiscal laxity, pressure may be brought on the ECB to buy up government bonds that have lost the trust of investors. If debt is downgraded and bond prices fall, commercial banks holding large volumes of such bonds may face bankruptcy, endangering the stability of the banking system. Systemic threats to the insurance and pension fund sectors may also result. If then the ECB gives in and buys up such debt, moral-hazard risks will loom large again (Eichengreen and Wyplosz 1998; Beetsma and Uhlig 1999).

The fiscal criteria have come under attack for not being based on sound economic reasoning (Buiter, Corsetti and Roubini 1993).[6] It has been argued, for instance, that net debt would have been more relevant than gross debt, and that the harm that large budget deficits can do is much reduced if there is little opportunity for inflationary financing, as under the statute of the ECB (De Grauwe 1994). Meanwhile, some observers feared that member countries' attempts to reduce their fiscal deficits and debt/GDP ratios would result in recession. Further, governments may see themselves forced to privatise government firms or have infrastructural works (roads, tunnels, railways) financed by private capital, not on its own merits but simply in order to avoid excessive deficits. More serious, perhaps, is that the fiscal criteria would effectively rule out Keynesian fiscal expansion policies in the case of a severe depression (see below how this problem was solved). Conversely it could be argued that in the political arena uncomplicated rules of thumb are an asset. This argument can also be used against Buiter and Grafe's view that potentially fast-growing countries, in particular new members that have low per capita incomes and can be expected to catch up with the older EU members, can absorb larger debt ratios, as they will grow out of their debt (Buiter and Grafe 2002).

EU member countries have to fulfil the convergence criteria before being allowed into the EMU. Once they are in, the first three criteria cease to play a role. The fiscal ceilings continue to apply, though. The Maastricht Treaty contains provisions in the event that member countries forget about fiscal discipline once they are past the post. The Treaty allows for the imposition of financial sanctions if a member country has an 'excessive deficit' and does not heed the advice that the Council of Economics and Finance Ministers of the EU, ECOFIN, gives in such a case. The then Finance Minister of Germany, Theo Waigel, moved by German fears that fiscal laxity might endanger the anti-inflationary policies of the ECB, proposed in November 1995 that a Stability Pact with further regulations should be drawn up (cf. Bofinger 2003). After taking account of French objections, the Stability Pact became the *Stability and Growth Pact* (SGP), which was concluded at the Council of Amsterdam in 1997 and entered into force on 1 January 1999.[7]

Under the Pact, member countries aim at a medium-term fiscal deficit close to zero, or even at a surplus. This leaves room for some fiscal expansion under the 3 per cent ceiling during a cyclical downturn. Under exceptional circumstances the 3 per cent limit may be exceeded, according to the Maastricht Treaty. The Pact specifies that a 2 per cent fall in GDP provides such an exception, but ECOFIN may also accept a lower deficit, though 'as a rule' it should apply a limit of at least 0.75 per cent. A fiscal deficit of over 3 per cent in such a year would not be seen as 'excessive'.

If the ECOFIN Council finds excessive deficits, on the basis of data for the previous year submitted by national authorities in March each year, it will inform the government in question in May. If no adequate measures are taken, sanctions should be imposed by the end of the year. These take the form of non-remunerated deposits of between 0.2 per cent and 0.5 per cent of GDP, depending on the size of the deficit. If the excessive deficit is corrected within two years, the deposit is returned, otherwise not. A country has to make additional deposits if the excessive deficits are repeated year after year.

The SGP has had a bumpy ride. The ECOFIN Council decided on 5 November 2002 that an excessive deficit existed in Portugal (it amounted to 4.1 per cent in 2001) and recommended measures to reduce the deficit. France and Italy, however, openly flouted the Pact and when Germany in 2003 also refused to abide by the Pact and stymied efforts by the European Commission to have ECOFIN discipline Germany and France under the excessive deficit procedure, the Pact was for all practical purposes dead and buried. With a strong euro against the US dollar and low inflation, financial markets hardly noticed. Inflation expectations were apparently not adjusted upwards and interest rates remained low. One solution might be to give more emphasis to the debt ratio rather than the deficit and to replace the gross debt ratio by a net debt ratio. This would give countries more leeway to run up deficits in a cyclical downswing if their debt ratio is low, that is, without endangering the government's solvency. While the economic harm done by the foundering of the SGP may not be very serious, the political damage for the EU could be substantial. Large countries are apparently free to ignore the '*pacta sunt servanda*' adage, that is, the requirement, fundamental to international law, that treaties are to be respected.

6.5.5   Conversion Costs

A conversion to a common currency is quite costly. First, economic agents have to accustom themselves to gathering information and making calculations in a new unit of account. Second, provisions have to be made for existing contracts expressed in the now obsolete national currencies. Third, vending machines, telephone booths, ticket machines, cash dispensers and point-of-sale terminals have to be converted or replaced and computer systems have to be adapted. The costs for the financial sector alone have been estimated at 8 to 10 billion euro (Expert Group 1995, p. 4). In addition, 56 billion euro coins and 14.5 billion euro banknotes had to be available on 1 January 2002 (ECB 1999; De Nederlandsche Bank 2000, p. 15).

The euro in the form of bank deposits was introduced in 1999, first to be used on the capital markets and in wholesale payments. The banks and the public were free to go on using domestic money for bank money payments before the domestic currencies fully made way for the euro early in 2002. Given the huge scale of the operation, it was remarkably free of hitches.

6.5.6   Monetary Policy

In a monetary union there is one common monetary policy. We have already mentioned the difficulties that present themselves in the case of asymmetric macroeconomic shocks. Quite apart from these difficulties, there is another problem: monetary-policy measures may work out differently in one country than in another. This is because the *transmission mechanism* of monetary-policy measures may differ between countries (cf. Angeloni and Ehrmann 2003). Generally, differences in the financial infrastructure will be responsible. Monetary-policy measures first of all influence the commercial banks' liquidity and short-term interest rates. In countries where business firms are highly dependent on bank loans there will be a greater impact on spending by business firms than in countries where business firms are more dependent on capital markets. The structure of output may also play a role, as spending on goods with a long useful life is more interest-sensitive than spending on goods with a shorter useful life. This factor, of course, is also relevant across regions within a country.

6.5.7   EMU and New Entrants

The enlargement of the European Union will bring in many new member states with a far lower average income per capita than the existing 15 members. New members are expected to join EMU. Opt-out clauses as in the cases of Denmark and the United Kingdom, or *derogation*, will not be provided. If all goes well, new member states will undergo relatively fast per capita income growth and reduce the income gap with the richer EU member states. There is a concern that we will consequently see the Balassa–Samuelson effect at work, that is, that there will be real-exchange-rate appreciation in the sense that nontradeables prices in the new entrants will rise faster *vis-à-vis* tradeables prices than in the 'old' member states. Buiter (2000b) and Buiter and Grafe (2001) fear that the Balassa–Samuelson effect will make it difficult to meet the inflation and the exchange-rate criteria for EMU membership simultaneously. In their view, keeping inflation at the same level as the existing members would imply nominal exchange-rate appreciation and keeping the nominal exchange rate steady would imply higher inflation. If, however, the Balassa–Samuelson effect accounted for an inflation differential of about 1 per cent at steady exchange rates, as was found to be the case for Greece (see Chapter 3, Section 3.2.4), the convergence criteria are not impossible to fulfil. Keeping inflation at the same level as in euroland for a period of two years would imply an exchange-rate appreciation that could be accommodated within the ERM-II exchange-rate mechanism that the EMU members introduced for non-members along the lines of the earlier ERM after the introduction of the euro (see Chapter 5, Section 5.2.5). Even the band width of 2.25 per cent either side of the central rate announced by the European Commission in May 2003, with only occasional swings to the old maximum of 15 per cent allowed, would not make this impossible. With a stronger Balassa–Samuelson effect new candidates might consider keeping inflation at euroland level and revaluing their currencies. According to Article 109j of the Maastricht Treaty (Article 121 in the 1997 Amsterdam Treaty) no devaluation should occur in the two years preceding accession, but a revaluation is not precluded.

Once a country has joined EMU, nominal revaluations are no longer possible. With a common currency, the Balassa–Samuelson effect cannot but lead to higher inflation. In order to keep inflation below the 2 per cent ceiling which the ECB imposed, the 'old' members would then have to reduce their inflation rate below 2 per cent, which might be painful. The Balassa–Samuelson effect may thus cause more trouble after the new candidates have joined EMU than during the run-up to entry, unless the ECB relaxes its self-imposed 2 per cent ceiling.

6.5.8 The Euro as an International Currency

The EU is a force to be reckoned with in the world economy. It ties with the United States in terms of GDP and exports and, even before EMU, EU currencies were widely used in world trade and payments. With monetary union, it was to be expected that the euro would make further inroads into the US dollar's hegemonic position. To the extent that the euro replaced the US dollar in economic agents' portfolios, this would entail loss of seigniorage for the United States and a gain for the EU. On the other hand, a high demand for the euro in foreign-exchange markets might result in a high external value. A relatively low RER would follow, with high terms of trade but also a difficult competitive position in world markets. However, it has also been argued that the transformation of the various national European capital markets into one integrated, highly liquid capital market may lead to high euro borrowing. If the volume of loans contracted in euros is high and a large part of it is changed into other currencies, downward pressure on the euro will follow (McCauley and White 1997). The transformation of the financial markets has come about surprisingly quickly (Danthine, Giavazzi and von Thadden 2000; Eichengreen 2000) and it seems that, at least over the first two and a half years of the euro's existence, this has contributed more to capital outflows than to inflows, which could explain part of the fall of the euro with respect to the dollar during this period (see also Chapter 1, Section 1.4.3).

The euro certainly made its presence felt on international capital markets after its introduction in 1999 (see Table 6.3). Still, the euro has so far failed to make inroads into the dominant position of the US dollar on the world's foreign-exchange markets. The euro has lost more ground in forex spot trading, compared with its predecessor currencies, than could have been expected from the elimination of trading between those predecessor currencies (see Table 6.4). Indeed, it has been found that transaction costs, that is, the spread between bid and ask prices quoted by forex dealers, have increased, compared with the transaction costs of the D-Mark. This makes the euro less attractive than the D-Mark as a medium of exchange (Hau, Killeen and Moore 2002). But if the euro has not yet dethroned the dollar in its role as an international means of transaction, or *vehicle currency*, it nevertheless plays a prominent role as a currency used for borrowing and investing, that is, as a store of value. Also, the euro is increasingly adopted as a unit of account or *invoice currency*, for instance on international commodity markets. This may or may not lead to more payments in euros. For official international purposes, the euro does fulfil the role of money to a lesser extent. As regards its role as a unit of account, a number of countries peg their currencies to the euro (mostly European countries and former French colonies in Africa). The euro functions as a store of value in the official sphere in that it forms part of official reserves. The euro is still far behind the US dollar on this score. This also goes for the euro's role as a medium of exchange, or *intervention currency* (see Pollard 2001).

One may wonder whether it would really be a good thing if the euro vied with the dollar as an international currency. It remains to be seen whether a world monetary system with two dominant currencies would not lead to higher exchange-rate instability. Shifts in the perceived relative solidity of the dollar and the euro might lead to huge capital movements and to sizeable swings in exchange rates as private economic agents and perhaps also central banks shifted funds from one currency into another.

Table 6.3   Relative economic size and relative use of currencies: United States, Japan and euro area

	USA	Japan	Euro area
in per cent			
Share of world GDP, 1999 (on PPP basis)	21.9	7.6	15.8
Share of world exports, 1999			
(except intra-euro area)	15.3	9.3	19.4
Relative use of currency in world trade,[1] 1995	52.0	4.7	24.8
Relative use of currency in new issues of			
international debt securities, 1998	54.1	5.6	24.6
International debt securities, 2000	44.0	8.3	33.9
Foreign exchange transactions, April 1998	87.4	20.8	52.2[2]
Share of currency in foreign-exchange			
reserves, 1999	66.2	5.1	12.5

Notes:
[1] Per cent of world exports invoiced in, respectively, US dollars, Japanese yen and D-Mark plus French franc, plus Italian lira, plus Netherlands guilder.
[2] Including Danish krone and ecu; the total adds up to more than 100 per cent as two currencies are involved in each transaction (totalling over all currencies in the world would give 200 per cent).

Source: Pollard (2001).

Table 6.4   Relative use of currencies: United States, Japan and euro area, 1998 and 2001

	USA	Japan	Euro area
in per cent			
Spot foreign-exchange transactions, April 1998	84.3	26.5	46.7
Spot foreign-exchange transactions, April 2001	84.4	26.0	43.0
Foreign-exchange swap transactions, April 1998	96.6	16.9	46.5
Foreign-exchange swap transactions, April 2001	95.0	20.2	33.7

Note: Trade between predecessor currencies of the euro in 1998 was subtracted from totals before shares were calculated.

Source: Detken and Hartmann (2002).

6.6   OFFICIAL DOLLARISATION

In a full monetary union individual countries give up their own national currencies and replace these with a common currency. Such an arrangement might be called a *symmetric* monetary union. One could also identify *asymmetric* monetary unions, where a country gives up its own currency and simply adopts the currency of another country. The dollar being the main international currency, this phenomenon is known as *dollarisation*. To distinguish this case from the competing currency situation where foreign exchange circulates alongside the national currency, we call the adoption of the dollar, or more generally a foreign currency, as legal tender in place of the national currency *official dollarisation*.

Official dollarisation can be seen as a currency board taken one step further. Under a currency board a government commits itself to keeping the exchange rate *vis-à-vis* another currency stable at all times and to subordinating monetary and fiscal policies to this one end. Difficulties may arise if wealth holders nonetheless get cold feet and a flight out of the country's currency occurs. Under official dollarisation a flight out of the country's currency cannot occur, because the country's currency no longer exists. Official dollarisation is a radical and effective method to put paid to foreign-exchange crises.

It is, of course, still possible for banking crises to occur under official dollarisation. As under a currency board, there is no domestic lender of last resort that can come to the rescue (though of course the Ministry of Finance could step in) and the central bank of the country whose currency has been adopted is not likely to be willing to fulfil this role. It should, however, in general not be too difficult to maintain financial stability. If foreign banks are free to set up shop in the dollarised country, it is easy for residents to shift their deposits from domestic to foreign banks. No general banking panic will occur, and the threat of deposits flowing away to foreign banks will act as a spur to domestic banks to try and build up a good reputation. Moreover, banks can establish lines of credit with foreign banks, as Panamanian banks indeed do (Bogetic 1999).

The archetypal example of a dollarised economy is Panama, where the US dollar became legal tender in 1904. There is a national currency, the *balboa*, but that exists only in the form of silver coins, besides being used as a unit of account. There is no central bank and access for foreign banks is unimpeded. Apart from the benefit of low inflation, Panama appears not to have been affected by upheavals such as the Mexican peso crisis in 1994–95 (Moreno-Villalaz 1999). The absence of any fear of inflation is such that 30-year fixed-rate mortgages are offered by private lenders, which, apart from

Puerto Rico, is totally unthinkable in other Latin American countries (Joint Economic Committee 2000). On 1 April 2000, Ecuador adopted the US dollar as its official currency, after a precipitous fall of the *sucre* from 6,825 to more than 21,000 in the dollar during 1999 (Instituto Ecuatoriano de Economía Politica 2000). On 1 January 2001, the US dollar became legal tender in El Salvador. The national currency, the *colon*, was gradually phased out over the next few years. In this case, however, there was no runaway inflation. The rationale behind the measure was rather that the government hoped in this way to reduce borrowing costs. One step on the way to full dollarisation was taken in Guatemala on 19 December 2000, when Congress approved a measure that made the dollar legal tender alongside the national currency, the *quetzal*. Other cases are the Balkan states or areas of Montenegro and Kosovo, which have used the euro as legal tender since 1 January 2002, after first having used the D-Mark, and East Timor, which adopted the US dollar as its official currency in early 2000.

Official dollarisation implies that the monetary authorities use their foreign-exchange reserves to buy dollar banknotes or sell these to commercial banks that want to build up balances in the accounts they hold with foreign banks. These balances bring in interest income, but the government of the dollarising country loses its seigniorage income. For a country such as Argentina, which had a currency board holding American Treasury Bills, the interest income from these investments was estimated in 1999 to run to between \$700 and \$750 million a year, or roughly 2 per cent of government revenue (Kiguel 1999). Other estimates of the seigniorage loss that results from giving up one's own notes and coins and adopting foreign money are of the order of 0.2–0.3 per cent of GDP (Haussmann and Powell 1999; Joint Economic Committee 2000). If calculations are based on total base money rather than only on notes and coins, higher percentages result of course (Bogetic 1999).[8] In order to make a changeover to the US dollar more attractive, some US Congressmen have proposed restoring seigniorage to officially dollarised countries (Joint Economic Committee 2000). After all, the United States receives more seigniorage income if other countries dollarise (if the dollarising country's official reserves are used to buy US banknotes, the United States stops paying interest to that country). This would not be something totally new, as South Africa has been sharing seigniorage with Lesotho and Namibia for some decades already (Bogetic 1999).

Dollarisation may be an effective answer to some problems, but it is no panacea. Creditors may, for instance, fear banking crises after a shift to full dollarisation, as there is no longer a lender of last resort that can come to the rescue in times of need (Chang 2000). It has been observed, for instance, that Panama, fully dollarised for a long time, was far from immune to swings in market sentiments towards emerging economies generally (Berg and Borensztein 2000, p. 8). Other research has been unable to find significant differences between dollarised and comparable non-dollarised countries as regards macroeconomic stability. Nor have lower interest rates systematically led to faster growth, possibly because dollarised countries have more difficulty absorbing external shocks (Edwards and Magendzo 2001).

6.7   FINAL OBSERVATIONS

The European Monetary Union is a unique phenomenon, being a currency union without full political union. The closest thing in history was perhaps the Austrian–Hungarian twin monarchy (see case 6 in the Appendix to this chapter). Other currency unions evolved into single national states (Germany, case 5 in the Appendix) or followed upon national unification (Switzerland and Italy in the nineteenth century; see Vanthoor 1996). Monetary unions without a single currency apparently have to be dominated by a hegemonic state in order not to fall apart as a result of uncoordinated monetary policies. Such a hegemonic state had to be able to restrain the other member states from pursuing monetary policies that would have been incompatible with the dominant country's own policy. Unions that have failed have suffered from lack of an authority that could guarantee sufficient policy coordination, if and when the restrictions imposed by a metallic standard became inoperative. Currency unions, such as the European Monetary Union, do not suffer from this problem, as they have a common currency, a common central bank and a common monetary policy.

One curious aspect of the European Monetary Union is that some of the convergence criteria do not seem to be well grounded in economic theory, whereas the theory of optimum currency areas in its turn has left hardly a trace in the Maastricht Treaty, as De Grauwe (1994, 1996) points out. The Delors Report duly noted that a high degree of wage and price flexibility is a prerequisite for a well-functioning monetary union, but prospective members of EMU did not and do not have to meet any requirements as to labour mobility and flexibility of wages and prices; or as to diversification of the industrial structure, for that matter. It is political considerations that have been decisive. It is tacitly assumed that institutional reform and the sheer force of circumstances will bring about the required flexibility of prices and wages, and in labour markets in general. As there is hardly a way back, governments and the European Commission have no choice but to sort out problems as they crop up and make sure the currency union goes on working.

APPENDIX 6.1   MONETARY UNIONS IN HISTORY

There have been several cases of monetary union in history. Some have failed, some have had a fair measure of success. In this Appendix we provide a survey of these monetary unions (apart from the literature cited below, this Appendix builds on Graboyes 1990; see also Mazzaferro 1992; Vanthoor 1996; Joint Economic Committee 2000). In Section 6 above we have drawn some conclusions from the historical experience.

A. Unions that Failed

1. *Colonial New England*   For nearly a century up to 1751, Connecticut, Massachusetts Bay, New Hampshire and Rhode Island accepted each others' paper money. The dominant economic power was Massachusetts. Things turned sour when the other three no longer adapted to Massachusetts' monetary policy and began to over-issue currency. In 1751, Massachusetts switched to a silver standard and ceased accepting the paper money issued by the other three states.

2. The *Latin Monetary Union*   (Posthuma 1982; on early attempts to transform the Latin Monetary Union into a kind of European Monetary Union, see Einaudi 2000.) On 23 December 1865, France, Belgium, Italy and Switzerland formed the Latin Monetary Union. Greece joined the union on 1 January 1869. The Union was on a bimetallic standard and it was the aim of France in particular to make bimetallism work by increasing the number of countries under bimetallism as much as possible. Gold and silver union coins could be freely minted in all member countries and were legal tender across the union. Each country could, in addition, mint limited amounts of smaller-denomination silver subsidiary coins. These had a lower silver content than union coins and were legal tender only in the country of issue. Nevertheless, public offices in one country were required to accept up to 100 francs of the other countries' subsidiary coins, in individual transactions. The Union's gold–silver price ratio, implicit in the metal content of its coins, grew out of line with the world market price ratio in the 1870s when many countries, including Germany, the Netherlands, Norway, Sweden and Denmark, adopted the gold standard.

Silver became overvalued and the Latin Monetary Union had to suspend silver convertibility, that is, silver coins could no longer be freely minted. Outstanding silver coins remained legal tender and subsidiary coins were virtually treated as legal tender. To complicate matters, Italy and Greece issued paper money that was traded at a discount in foreign-exchange markets. Profits could be made by changing Italian or Greek coins into

French or Swiss money, selling it against depreciated Italian or Greek paper money and trading that paper in at par for coins at the Italian or Greek national bank. The Union had to give up the fixed exchange rate for subsidiary coins. During World War I, all member countries' currencies except Switzerland's depreciated heavily against gold. Debased silver coins poured into the member country that happened to have the least depreciated currency, Switzerland. The Union ceased to exist for all practical purposes at the end of 1920 when Switzerland gave up buying other members' currencies at a fixed rate of exchange, though it ended formally only with Belgium's official withdrawal on 31 December 1926.

3. The *Scandinavian Monetary Union*   This union was formed in 1873 by Sweden and Denmark, Norway acceding in 1875 (Bergman, Gerlach and Jonung 1993). Gold coins and subsidiary coins circulated as legal tender in the Union and by 1900 banks in any Union country accepted banknotes issued in the other Union countries. During World War I Denmark and Norway saw their exports expand more than Sweden. Their money supply increased and Norwegian and Danish currency showed a tendency to fall relative to the Swedish krona. Danish and Norwegian coins and notes found their way into Sweden. Furthermore, the Swedish central bank, Sveriges Riksbanken, was under an obligation to buy gold from Norway and Denmark at par against Swedish banknotes.

On the advice of Knut Wicksell and Gustav Cassel, Sweden had restricted the trading of gold in general, but Denmark and Norway continued shipping gold to Sweden. In international markets gold could be bought more cheaply. Sweden forced the other two countries in 1917 to accept a ban on gold exports, but token coins were still legal tender at the pre-war parity across the Union. When around 1920 the Danish and Norwegian currencies had fallen significantly *vis-à-vis* the Swedish krona and the authorities had prohibited the export of token coins, large-scale smuggling took place. Sweden, therefore, forced Denmark and Norway to wind up what remained of the union in 1921.

4. The *East African Currency Area*   In 1922 British East Africa adopted a common currency, the East African shilling, which a currency board stood ready to convert into sterling. This arrangement continued after independence, helped by British subsidies. In 1966 Kenya, Uganda and Tanzania each introduced its own local shilling. These remained legal tender in all three countries, and also remained convertible into sterling. The Sterling Area was dismantled in 1972 and the East African countries now felt free to pursue more independent monetary policies, resulting in diverging inflation rates. 1977 saw the end of the East African Currency Area.

B. Unions that Endure(d)

5. The *Zollverein*   (See also Holtfrerich 1989.) The German Zollverein, established in 1834, soon evolved into a kind of monetary union. In 1838 most of the 35 principalities and four free cities chose one of two currencies, the Thaler and the Gulden, as their monetary standard. This substantially reduced transaction costs, as up till then the monetary circulation consisted of a great diversity of German and foreign coins. The Prussian Bank, established in 1846, soon became the dominant note-issuing bank. German political unification took place in 1871, but full currency union was not reached until 1 January 1876. On that date the Prussian Bank became the Reichsbank and the paper money issued by individual states was officially withdrawn from circulation. The success, in terms of durability, of the monetary union before unification can be ascribed to, first, the dominance of one state (Prussia), and second, the introduction of metallic standards that in effect prevented inflationary monetary policies. It is to be noted that monetary harmonisation started before political unification, but full currency union was only attained after political unification.

6. *Austria–Hungary*   From 1867 until the end of World War I, Austria and Hungary were two countries that were autonomous in many respects, with their own national parliaments and their own budgets. They had, however, joint foreign policy, armed forces and money. Austria and Hungary formed a customs union that came up for renewal every ten years. There was a union central bank, with capital, profits and the nationality of officials meticulously divided between the two countries according to a 70:30 rule. The central bank issued paper money with the wording in German on one side and in Hungarian on the other (Mazzaferro 1992; see also Goodhart 1988b, pp. 138–44 on the functioning of the Austro-Hungarian Bank). The lack of attention given to this set-up in economic history texts (such as Milward and Saul 1977, ch. 5) or period economics texts (Pierson 1912, pp. 471–3) suggests that it functioned smoothly.

7. The *CFA Franc Zone*   (Communauté Financière Africaine; see Bhatia 1985; Boughton 1992; Honohan 1992.) After France left Africa as a colonial power, two central banks were formed, the Banque Centrale des États de l'Afrique de l'Ouest and the Banque des États de l'Afrique Centrale. The former acts as the central bank for the West African Monetary Union, including Benin, Burkina Faso, Ivory Coast, Mali, Niger, Senegal and Togo, and the latter as the central bank for Cameroon, the Central African Republic, Chad, the Congo (Brazzaville), Equatorial Guinea and Gabon. Each group, plus the Comoros, has its own currency. The three

currencies are collectively known as the CFA franc, which was pegged to the French franc and after 1999 to the euro. Foreign-exchange reserves are pooled in the French Treasury, which also guarantees convertibility by an overdraft facility.

Inflation has been kept low (the unweighted average of annual consumer price increases in the 1980s was only 4.2 per cent; Boughton 1992, p. 36), largely as a result of strict limits on lending to governments, which, however, have been circumvented to some extent through lending to state-owned companies that are not technically government entities. Relatively low inflation could not prevent the CFA franc from becoming seriously overvalued, which was reflected in growing deficits on the French Treasury accounts of the three central banks. After having been pegged for 45 years to the French franc at the rate of 50 CFA francs to the French franc, the CFA franc was forced to devalue by 50 per cent to 100 CFA francs to one French franc in January 1994. The Comorian franc, which had been pegged to the French franc at the same rate as the CFA franc since 1988, devalued by 33.3 per cent to 75 Comorian francs to one French franc (Clément 1994). Clearly, the system is held together by France.

8. *Belgium–Luxembourg* These countries had their own currencies, which were linked at par and were legal tender in both countries, following the establishment of the Belgian–Luxembourg Economic Union in 1944, which thereby became a *de facto* monetary union. In actual practice, Belgian money circulated in Luxembourg, but Luxembourg money did not circulate in Belgium. A joint agency managed exchange regulations, but the Belgians were effectively free as to their monetary policy. Luxembourg had to adjust its monetary policy to Belgium and to accept Belgium's exchange-rate decisions. This became painfully apparent in 1982, when Belgium requested a meeting of ECOFIN in order to propose a devaluation of the Belgian franc and consulted Luxembourg just before the event, without taking its views into account (Gros and Thygesen 1992, p. 76).

9. *Other European Combinations of Large and Small Countries* Liechtenstein uses the Swiss franc. Monaco and Andorra used the French franc and switched to the euro. In Italy, Vatican City and San Marino used the Italian lira and switched to the euro but also strike their own coins. Northern Cyprus uses the Turkish lira.

10. *The Rand Monetary Area* (Honohan 1992.) Lesotho, Namibia and Swaziland have their own currencies, which are, however, freely exchangeable

against the South African rand one to one. In addition, the rand circulates freely in Lesotho, Namibia and Swaziland.

Note that cases 9 and 10 are cases of dollarisation. Recent cases of dollarisation are mentioned in Section 6.6 of this chapter. Most islands and other countries with less than 100,000 inhabitants have been left out of this listing (for further details, see Joint Economic Committee 2000).

NOTES

1. Curiously, an econometric correlation between growth and inflation has not been easy to establish. This field of empirical research abounds with pitfalls (see Temple 2000 for a discussion). Bruno and Easterly (1996) found a clear negative correlation only from 40 per cent inflation upwards. Barro (1996) could only find a very slight negative correlation between inflation and growth, but notes that the negative effect cumulates over the years. Motley (1998) on the other hand found that a 5 per cent reduction of inflation in a number of countries in the 1970s and 1980s was associated with an increase in the growth rate of real per capita GDP by 0.1 to 0.5 per cent. Extensive research by Ghosh and Phillips (1998) for IMF member countries over the period 1960–96 revealed a significant negative relationship between inflation and growth, except at very low inflation rates (below 3 per cent). This relationship is nonlinear, in the sense that an increase in inflation from, say, 10 per cent to 20 per cent is associated with a much larger decline in growth than an increase in inflation from 40 to 50 per cent. The negative relationship holds both in cross-section and in time series analysis. Ghosh and Phillips (1998, p. 687) suspect that other studies have failed to show a robust negative relationship because they did not allow for nonlinearities. Gylfason and Herbertsson (2001) specify the various ways in which inflation may affect growth and find, using data for 170 countries from 1960 to 1992, that inflation in excess of 10 to 20 per cent is generally detrimental to growth. Fernández (2003) finds a negative relation between inflation and long-run growth.
2. Seigniorage and inflation tax as percentages of GNP are calculated in different ways by different authors. The World Bank, for instance, defines inflation tax as the decline in purchasing power of average reserve money (or base money), but, like Click (1998), does not seem to take into account interest payments by the central bank to commercial banks on balances held with the central bank, which Gros does explicitly (see also Van Ewijk and Scholtens 1992). Generally, no account is taken of the costs of creating additional money (printing banknotes) or the costs of maintaining the money supply (the continuous checking of banknotes by the central banks and replacing worn notes), which should be subtracted from seigniorage yields.
3. The evidence about supply shocks is less clear. Demertzis, Hughes Hallett and Rummel (2000) found that even among Germany, France, the Benelux and Denmark, supply shocks (shifts in supply curves) showed a very low correlation. Verhoef (2003), using a different statistical technique, was more positive about the level and development of supply shocks in core EMU countries. See Demertzis, Hughes Hallett and Rummel for the difficulties of separating demand shocks, supply shocks and monetary policy shocks in empirical research.
4. Lucas (1976) argues that econometric models that may be useful for short-term forecasting give no clue as to the outcomes of changes in policy rules, as they take no account of changes in behaviour by economic agents.
5. See the *Protocol on the Convergence Criteria Referred to in Article 109j of the Treaty Establishing the European Community* and the *Protocol on the Excessive Deficit Procedure*,

      Article 1, on http://europa.eu.int/eur-lex/en/treaties/ or in Church and Phinnemore (1994, pp. 416–18).
6. The first President of the ECB, Dr W. Duisenberg, revealed, when still President of the Dutch central bank, that these fiscal criteria were based on the actual average government budget deficit of 3 per cent when the Delors Committee prepared its report, and an expected annual real growth rate of 2.5 per cent to 3 per cent at an inflation rate of between 0 per cent and 2 per cent (*NRC Handelsblad*, 25 January 1996). A 3 per cent deficit at a growth rate of nominal income of 5 per cent is compatible with a 60 per cent debt ratio (see Buiter, Corsetti and Roubini 1993, pp. 62–3).
7. The Pact consists of a European Council resolution and two regulations of the ECOFIN Council, available on http://ue.eu.int, where assessments by ECOFIN can also be found.
8. Bogetic calculates seigniorage by multiplying the base-money supply by the annual rate of inflation. This shows the reduction in real debt faced by the central bank and may result in considerably higher estimates of the loss of seigniorage after full dollarisation – no less than 7.4 per cent of GDP in the case of Ecuador.

References

Adler, M., and B. Lehmann (1983), 'Deviations from PPP in the Long Run', *Journal of Finance*, **38** (5).

Agénor, P.-R. (1992), *Parallel Currency Markets in Developing Countries: Theory, Evidence, and Policy Implications*, Princeton Essays in International Finance no. 188, Princeton: International Finance Section, Princeton University.

Agénor, P.-R. (2003), 'Benefits and Costs of International Financial Integration: Theory and Facts', *The World Economy*, **26** (8).

Aghevli, B.B., M.S. Khan and P.J. Montiel (1991), *Exchange Rate Policy in Developing Countries: Some Analytical Issues*, Occasional Paper 78, Washington, DC: IMF.

Aguilar, J., and S. Nydahl (2000), 'Central Bank Intervention and Exchange Rates: The Case of Sweden', *Journal of International Financial Markets, Institutions & Money*, **10** (3–4).

Alam, I.M.S., and A.R. Morrison (2000), 'Trade Reform Dynamics and Technical Efficiency: The Peruvian Experience', *World Bank Economic Review*, **14** (2).

Aldcroft, D.H., and M.J. Oliver (1998), *Exchange Rate Regimes in the Twentieth Century*, Cheltenham: Edward Elgar.

Alexius, A., and J. Nilson (2000), 'Real Exchange Rates and Fundamentals: Evidence from 15 OECD Countries', *Open Economies Review*, **11** (4).

Amiti, M. (1999), 'Specialization Patterns in Europe', *Weltwirtschaftliches Archiv*, **135** (4).

Amitrano, A., P. De Grauwe and G. Tullio (1997), 'Why Has Inflation Remained So Low after the Large Exchange Rate Depreciation of 1992?', *Journal of Common Market Studies*, **35** (3).

Angeloni, I., C. Cottarelli and A. Levy (1994), 'Cross-Border Deposits, Aggregation, and Money Demand in the Transition to EMU', *Journal of Policy Modeling*, **16** (1).

Angeloni, I., and M. Ehrmann (2003), 'Monetary Transmission in the Euro Area: Early Evidence', *Economic Policy*, no. 37, October.

Anker, P. (1999), 'Pitfalls in Panel Tests of Purchasing Power Parity', *Weltwirtschaftliches Archiv*, **135** (3).

Arestis, P., and M. Sawyer (1997), 'How Many Cheers for the Tobin Transactions Tax?', *Cambridge Journal of Economics*, **21** (6).

Argy, V. (1981), *The Postwar International Money Crisis*, London: George Allen & Unwin.

Ariyoshi, A., K. Habermeier, B. Laurens, İ. Ötker-Robe, J.I. Canales-Kriljenko and A. Kirilenko (2000), *Capital Controls: Country Experiences with their Use and Liberalization*, IMF Occasional Paper 190, Washington, DC: IMF.

Azali, M., M.S. Habibullah and A.Z. Baharumshah (2001), 'Does PPP Hold between Asian and Japanese Economies? Evidence using Panel Unit Root and Panel Cointegration', *Japan and the World Economy*, **13** (1).

Bagehot, W. (1920), *Lombard Street*, 14th edn, London: John Murray. First edition 1873.

Baillie, R.T., and W.P. Osterberg (1997), 'Why Do Central Banks Intervene?', *Journal of International Money and Finance*, **16** (6).

Baker, D. (2000), 'Taxing Financial Speculation: Shifting the Tax Burden from Wages to Wagers', Washington: Center for Economic and Policy Research, http://www.cepr.net/Wages_to_Wagers.htm.

Bakker, A.F.P. (1996), *The Liberalization of Capital Movements in Europe; The Monetary Committee and Financial Integration, 1958–1994*, Dordrecht: Kluwer.

Bakker, A.F.P. (2003), 'Advanced Country Experiences with Capital Account Liberalization', ch. 2 in Bakker and Chapple (2003).

Bakker, A.F.P., and B. Chapple (eds) (2003), *Capital Liberalization in Transition Countries*, Cheltenham: Edward Elgar.

Balassa, B. (1964), 'The Purchasing-Power Parity Doctrine: A Reappraisal', *Journal of Political Economy*, **72** (6).

Baliño, T.J.T., C. Enoch et al. (1997), *Currency Board Arrangements: Issues and Experiences*, Occasional Paper 151, Washington, DC: IMF.

Barro, R.J. (1996), 'Inflation and Growth', *Federal Reserve Bank of St. Louis Review*, **78** (3).

Bartolini, L., and A. Prati (1997), 'Soft versus Hard Targets for Exchange Rate Intervention', *Economic Policy*, no. 24, April.

Batten, D.S., and R.W. Hafer (1984), 'Currency Substitution: A Test of Its Importance', *Federal Reserve Bank of St. Louis Review*, **66** (7).

Bautista, R.M. (1982), 'Exchange Rate Variations and Export Competitiveness in Less Developed Countries under Generalized Floating', *Journal of Development Studies*, **18** (3).

Beetsma, R., and H. Uhlig (1999), 'An Analysis of the Stability and Growth Pact', *Economic Journal*, **109** (458), October.

Begg, D. (1997), 'The Design of EMU', in *Staff Studies for the World Economic Outlook*, Washington, DC: International Monetary Fund.

Bennett, A.G.G. (1994), 'Currency Boards: Issues and Experiences', in T.J.T. Baliño and C. Cottarelli (eds), *Frameworks for Monetary Stability*, Washington, DC: IMF.

Berg, A., and E. Borensztein (2000), *Full Dollarization: The Pros and Cons*, Economic Issues no. 24, Washington, DC: IMF.

Berg, A., E. Borensztein and P. Mauro (2003), 'Opciones de régimen monetario para América Latina', *Finanzas & Desarrollo*, **40** (3).

Bergman, M., S. Gerlach and L. Jonung (1993), 'The Rise and Fall of the Scandinavian Currency Union 1873–1920', *European Economic Review*, **37** (2/3).

Berk, J.M., and K.H.W. Knot (2001), 'Testing for Long Horizon UIP using PPP-based Exchange Rate Expectations', *Journal of Banking and Finance*, **25** (2).

Berkeley, G. (1951), *Of Motion* (trans. A.A. Luce), in A.A. Luce and T.E. Jessop (eds), *The Works of George Berkeley, Bishop of Cloyne*, vol. 4, London: Thomas Nelson and Sons. Originally published in 1721 as *De Motu*.

Bhagwati, J.N. (1982), 'Directly Unproductive, Profit-seeking (DUP) Activities', *Journal of Political Economy*, **90** (5).

Bhagwati, J.N. (1983), 'DUP Activities and Rent Seeking', *Kyklos*, **36** (4).

Bhatia, R.J. (1985), *The West African Monetary Union*, Occasional Paper 35, Washington, DC: IMF.

Bikker, J.A. (1994), 'Demografische onevenwichtigheid, nationale besparingen en lopende rekening', *Maandschrift Economie*, **58** (3).

Bilson, J.F.O. (1978), 'Rational Expectations and the Exchange Rate', in J.A. Frenkel and H.G. Johnson (eds), *The Economics of Exchange Rates: Selected Studies*, Reading, Mass.: Addison-Wesley.

Bilson, J.F.O. (1979), 'Recent Developments in Monetary Models of Exchange Rate Determination', *IMF Staff Papers*, **26** (2).

Bird, G. (1999), 'Crisis Averter, Crisis Lender, Crisis Manager: The IMF in Search of a Systemic Role', *The World Economy*, **22** (7).

BIS (2002), *Triennial Central Bank Survey; Foreign Exchange and Derivatives Market Activity in 2001*, March, on http://www.bis.org.

Bladen Hovell, R., and C. Green (1989), 'Crowding-out and Pulling-in of Fiscal Policy under Fixed and Flexible Exchange Rates', in R. MacDonald and M.P. Taylor (eds), *Exchange Rates and Open Economy Macroeconomics*, Oxford: Basil Blackwell.

Blanchard, O.J. (1979), 'Speculative Bubbles, Crashes and Rational Expectations', *Economics Letters*, **3**.

Blanchard, O.J., and F. Giavazzi (2002), 'Current Account Deficits in the Euro Area: The End of the Feldstein–Horioka Puzzle?', *Brookings Papers on Economic Activity* no. 2.

Blinder, A.S., and R.M. Solow (1974), 'Analytical Foundations of Fiscal Policy', in A.S. Blinder, R.M. Solow et al., *The Economics of Public Finance*, Washington, DC: Brookings Institution.

Boertje, B., and J.P. Verbruggen (1988), 'De ontwikkeling van het netto kapitaal-verkeer: een eenvoudige empirische analyse', *Maandschrift Economie*, **52** (3).

Bofinger, P. (2003), 'The Stability and Growth Pact Neglects the Policy Mix between Fiscal and Monetary Policy', *Intereconomics*, **38** (1).

Bogetic, Z. (1999), *Official or 'Full' Dollarization: Current Experiences and Issues*, http://users.erols.com/kurrency/bogdllr.htm

Boland, L.A. (1982), *The Foundations of Economic Method*, London: George Allen and Unwin.

Boonstra, W.W. (1990), 'Het Spaanse bankwezen (I)', *Bank- en Effectenbedrijf*, **39** (3).

Booth, G.G., and C. Ciner (2001), 'The Relationship between Nominal Interest Rates and Inflation: International Evidence', *Journal of Multinational Financial Management*, **11** (3).

Borenszstein, E.R. (1987), 'Alternative Hypotheses about the Excess Return on Dollar Assets, 1980–84', *IMF Staff Papers*, **34** (1).

Boughton, J.M. (1992), 'El franco CFA: Zona de estabilidad endeble en Africa', *Finanzas y Desarrollo*, **29** (4).

Boughton, J.M. (2003), 'On the Origins of the Fleming–Mundell Model', *IMF Staff Papers*, **50** (1).

Boyd, D., G.M. Caporale and R. Smith (2001), 'Real Exchange Rate Effects on the Balance of Trade: Cointegration and the Marshall–Lerner Condition', *International Journal of Finance and Economics*, **6** (3).

Branson, W.H. (1985), 'The Dynamic Interaction of Exchange Rates and Trade Flows', in T. Peeters, P. Praet and P. Reding (eds), *International Trade and Exchange Rates in the Late Eighties*, Amsterdam: North-Holland and Brussels: Editions de l'Université de Bruxelles.

Branson, W.H., and D.W. Henderson (1985), 'The Specification and Influence of Asset Markets', in R.W. Jones and P.B. Kenen (eds), *Handbook of International Economics vol. II*, Amsterdam: North-Holland.

Brown, R.P.C. (1990), *Sudan's Debt Crisis*, The Hague: Institute of Social Studies. Ph.D. dissertation, Groningen State University.

Bruno, M., and W. Easterly (1996), 'Inflation and Growth: In Search of a Stable Relationship', *Federal Reserve Bank of St. Louis Review*, **78** (3).

Buiter, W.H. (2000a), 'Optimal Currency Areas', *Scottish Journal of Political Economy*, **47** (3).

Buiter, W.H. (2000b), *Exchange Rate Regimes for Accession Countries*, address given at the EBRD Annual General Meeting in Riga, Latvia, 21 May; on http://www.nber.org/wbuiter.

Buiter, W., G. Corsetti and N. Roubini (1993), 'Maastricht's Fiscal Rules', *Economic Policy*, no. 16.

Buiter, W.H., and C. Grafe (2001), *Central Banking and the Choice of Currency Regime in Accession Countries*, Vienna: SUERF.

Buiter, W.H., and C. Grafe (2002), *Patching Up the Pact: Some Suggestions for Enhancing Fiscal Sustainability in an Enlarged European Union*, CEPR Discussion Paper 3496.

Calderón, C., and K. Schmidt-Hebbel (2003), 'Macroeconomic Policies and Performance in Latin America', *Journal of International Money and Finance*, **22** (7).

Calvo, G.A. (1986), 'Fractured Liberalism: Argentina under Martínez de Hoz', *Economic Development and Cultural Change*, **34** (3).

Calvo, G.A., L. Leiderman and C.M. Reinhart (1995), 'Capital Inflows to Latin America with Reference to the Asian Experience', in S. Edwards (ed.), *Capital Controls, Exchange Rates and Monetary Policy in the World Economy*, Cambridge: Cambridge University Press.

Calvo, G.A., L. Leiderman and C.M. Reinhart (1996), 'Inflows of Capital to Developing Countries in the 1990s', *Journal of Economic Perspectives*, **10** (2).

Calvo, G.A., and C.M. Reinhart (2002), 'Fear of Floating', *Quarterly Journal of Economics*, **117** (2).

Caprio, Jr, G., and A. Demirgüç-Kunt (1998), 'The Role of Long-Term Finance: Theory and Evidence', *World Bank Research Observer*, **13** (2).

Carrizosa, M., D.M. Leipziger and H. Shah (1996), 'El efecto tequila y la reforma bancaria en la Argentina', *Finanzas & Desarrollo*, **33** (1).

Cavallo, D.F., and G. Mondino (1996), 'Argentina's Miracle? From Hyperinflation to Sustained Growth', *Annual World Bank Conference on Development Economics 1995*, Washington, DC: World Bank.

Chandavarkar, A. (1996), *Central Banking in Developing Countries*, Basingstoke: Macmillan.

Chang, R. (2000), 'Dollarization: A Scorecard', Federal Reserve Bank of Atlanta *Economic Review*, **85** (3); http://www.frbatlanta.org/publica/eco-rev/rev_abs/3rd00/html.

Choudhry, T. (1999), 'Purchasing Power Parity in High-Inflation Eastern European Countries: Evidence from Fractional and Harris-Index Cointegration Tests', *Journal of Macroeconomics*, **21** (2).

Choudhury, A.R. (1991), 'The Relationship between the Inflation Rate and its Variability', *Applied Economics*, **23**.

Church, C.H., and D. Phinnemore (1994), *European Union and European Community: A Handbook and Commentary on the Post-Maastricht Treaties*, Hemel Hempstead: Harvester Wheatsheaf.

Clark, P., L. Bartolini, P. Bayoumi and S. Symansky (1994), *Exchange Rates and Economic Fundamentals*, Occasional Paper 115, Washington, DC: IMF.

Clément, J.A.P. (1994), 'Rationale for the CFA Franc Realignment', *IMF Survey*, 7 February.

Click, R.W. (1998), 'Seigniorage in a Cross-section of Countries', *Journal of Money, Credit, and Banking*, **30** (2).

Clinton, K. (1988), 'Transactions Costs and Covered Interest Arbitrage: Theory and Evidence', *Journal of Political Economy*, **96** (2).

Cody, B.J. (1991), 'Seigniorage and European Monetary Union', *Contemporary Policy Issues*, **9** (2).

Coes, D.V. (1994), 'Macroeconomic Stabilisation and Trade Liberalisation: Brazilian Experience and Choice', *The World Economy*, **17** (4).

Cole, D.C., and B.F. Slade (1992), 'Indonesian Financial Development: A Different Sequencing?', in D. Vittas (ed.), *Financial Regulation: Changing the Rules of the Game*, Washington, DC: World Bank.

Collier, P., and J.W. Gunning (1994), 'Trade and Development: Protection, Shocks and Liberalization', in D. Greenaway and L.A. Winters (eds), *Surveys in International Trade*, Oxford: Basil Blackwell.

Collier, P., A. Hoeffler and C. Pattillo (2001), 'Flight Capital as a Portfolio Choice', *World Bank Economic Review*, **15** (1).

Connolly, M., and D. Taylor (1976), 'Testing the Monetary Approach to Devaluation in Developing Countries', *Journal of Political Economy*, **84** (4), part 1.

Cooper, R.N. (1973), 'An Analysis of Currency Devaluation in Developing Countries', in M.B. Connolly and A.K. Swoboda (eds), *International Trade and Money*, London: George Allen & Unwin.

Cooper, R.N. (1986), 'Economic Interdependence and Coordination of Economic Policies', in R.N. Cooper, *Economic Policy in an Interdependent World: Essays in World Economics*, Cambridge, Mass.: MIT Press. First published in R.W. Jones and P.B. Kenen (eds), *Handbook in International Economics, vol. 2*, Amsterdam: Elsevier, 1985.

Cooper, R.N., and J.D. Sachs (1986), 'Borrowing Abroad: The Debtor's Perspective', in R.N. Cooper, *Economic Policy in an Interdependent World: Essays in World Economics*, Cambridge, Mass.: MIT Press. First published in G.W. Smith and J.T. Cuddington (eds), *International Debt and the Developing Countries*, Washington, DC: World Bank, 1985.

Coppock, L., and M. Poitras (2000), 'Evaluating the Fisher Effect in Long-term Cross-country Averages', *International Review of Economics and Finance*, **9** (2).

Corbo, V. (1985), 'Reforms and Macroeconomic Adjustments in Chile during 1974–84', *World Development*, **13** (8).

Corbo, V., and J. de Melo (eds) (1985), *Scrambling for Survival; How Firms Adjusted to the Recent Reforms in Argentina, Chile, and Uruguay*, Working Paper 764, Washington, DC: World Bank.

Corbo, V., and J. de Melo (1987), 'Lessons from the Southern Cone Policy Reforms', *World Bank Research Observer*, **2** (2).

Corbo, V., and S. Fischer (1994), 'Lessons from the Chilean Stabilization and Recovery', in B.P. Bosworth, R. Dornbusch and R. Labán (eds), *The Chilean Economy: Policy Lessons and Challenges*, Washington, DC: The Brookings Institution.

Corbo, V., and L. Hernández (1996), 'Macroeconomic Adjustment to Capital Inflows: Lessons from Recent Latin American and East Asian Experience', *World Bank Research Observer*, **11** (1).

Corden, W.M. (1971), *The Theory of Protection*, Oxford: Oxford University Press.

Corden, W.M. (1978), *Inflation, Exchange Rates, and the World Economy*, Oxford: Oxford University Press.

Corden, W.M. (1984), 'Booming Sector and Dutch Disease Economics: Survey and Consolidation', *Oxford Economic Papers*, **36** (3).

Corden, W.M. (1991), 'Macroeconomic Policy and Growth: Some Lessons of Experience', *Proceedings of the World Bank Annual Conference on Development Economics 1990*.

Cottarelli, C. et al. (1998), *Hungary: Economic Policies for Sustainable Growth*, Occasional Paper 159, Washington, DC: IMF.

Cram, L. (2001), 'Integration Theory and the Study of the European Policy Process', ch. 3 in J. Richardson (ed.), *European Union: Power and Policy-making*, 2nd edn, London: Routledge.

Cuddington, J.T. (1983), 'Currency Substitution, Capital Mobility and Money Demand', *Journal of International Money and Finance*, **2** (2).

Culbertson, Jr, W.P. (1975), 'Purchasing Power Parity and Black-Market Exchange Rates', *Economic Inquiry*, **13** (2).

Culver, S.E., and D.H. Papell (1999), 'Long-run Purchasing Power Parity with Short-run Data: Evidence with a Null Hypothesis of Stationarity', *Journal of International Money and Finance*, **18** (5).

Cushman, D.O. (2000), 'The Failure of the Monetary Exchange Rate Model for the Canadian–U.S. Dollar', *Canadian Journal of Economics*, **33** (3).

D'Amato, E. (2001), 'Analysts of Euro Weakness Look to the East', *Euromoney*, October.

Dalsgaard, T., J. Elmeskov and C.-Y. Park (2002), *Ongoing Changes in the Business Cycle – Evidence and Causes*, SUERF Studies no. 20, Vienna: SUERF.

Danthine, J.-P., F. Giavazzi and E.-L. von Thadden (2000), *European Financial Markets after EMU: A First Assessment*, NBER Working Paper 8044.

Davidson, P. (1997), 'Are Grains of Sand in the Wheels of International Finance Sufficient to Do the Job When Boulders are Often Required?', *Economic Journal*, **107** (442).

Davutyan, N., and J. Pippenger (1985), 'Purchasing Power Parity Did Not Collapse During the 1970's', *American Economic Review*, **75** (5).

Dawson, T. (2002), 'The IMF in Asia: Part of the Problem or Part of the Solution?', *IMF Survey*, **31** (14).

de Brouwer, G. (1999), *Financial Integration in East Asia*, Cambridge: Cambridge University Press.

De Grauwe, P. (1989), *International Money: Post-war Trends and Theories*, Oxford: Oxford University Press.

De Grauwe, P. (1992), *The Economics of Monetary Integration*, Oxford: Oxford University Press.

De Grauwe, P. (1994), 'Towards European Monetary Union without the EMS', *Economic Policy*, no. 18.

De Grauwe, P. (1996), 'The Economics of Convergence: Towards Monetary Union in Europe', *Weltwirtschaftliches Archiv*, **132** (1).

De Grauwe, P. (2000), 'Controls on Capital Flows', *Journal of Policy Modeling*, **22** (3).

De Grauwe, P., and M. Grimaldi (2001), 'Exchange Rates, Prices and Money: A Long-Run Perspective', *International Journal of Finance and Economics*, **6** (4).

de Gregorio, J., S. Edwards and R.O. Valdés (2000), 'Controls on Capital Inflows: Do They Work?', *Journal of Development Economics*, **63** (1), October.

de Jong, E. (1983), 'Wisselkoersfluctuaties op korte termijn en recente wissel-koerstheorieën; een beknopt overzicht', *Maandschrift Economie*, **47** (5).

de Jong, E. (1997), 'Exchange Rate Determination: Is There a Role for Macroeconomic Fundamentals?', *De Economist*, **145** (4).

De Nederlandsche Bank (2000), *Kwartaalbericht*, September.

De Nederlandsche Bank (2002), 'What Do We Understand about Exchange Rates?', *Quarterly Bulletin*, March.

de Roos, F. (1985), *De vorming van de wisselkoers*, Amsterdam: Noord-Hollandsche Uitgevers Mij. (Mededelingen der Koninklijke Nederlandse Akademie van Wetenschappen, afd. Letterkunde, Nieuwe reeks, deel 48 no. 2.)

Dell'Ariccia, G. (1999), 'Exchange Rate Fluctuations and Trade Flows: Evidence from the European Union', *IMF Staff Papers*, **46** (3).

Delors Report (1989), or: Committee for the Study of Economic and Monetary Union, *Report on Economic and Monetary Union in the European Community*; reprinted as a supplement to *ECU Newsletter*, Instituto Bancario San Paolo di Torino, no. 28.

Demertzis, M., A. Hughes Hallett and O. Rummel (2000), 'Is the European Union a Natural Currency Area, or Is It Held Together by Policy Makers?', *Weltwirtschaftliches Archiv*, **136** (4).

Denoon, D.B.H. (1986), *Devaluation under Pressure: India, Indonesia, and Ghana*, Cambridge, Mass.: MIT Press.

Detken, C., and P. Hartmann (2002), 'Features of the Euro's Role in International Financial Markets', *Economic Policy*, no. 35, October.

Diamandis, P.F. (2003), 'Market Efficiency, Purchasing Power Parity, and the Official and Parallel Markets for Foreign Currency in Latin America', *International Review of Economics and Finance*, **12** (1).

Diboglu, S., and F. Koray (2001), 'The Behavior of the Real Exchange Rate under Fixed and Floating Exchange Rate Regimes', *Open Economies Review*, **12** (2).

Diebold, F.X., and P. Pauly (1988), 'Endogenous Risk in a Portfolio-balance Rational-expectations Model of the Deutschemark–Dollar Rate', *European Economic Review*, **32** (1).

Dijkstra, A.G. (1995), 'Inflatie in Latijns Amerika', *Financiële en Monetaire Studies*, **14** (1).

Ding, Jianping (1998), 'China's Foreign Exchange Black Market and Exchange Flight: Analysis of Exchange Rate Policy', *The Developing Economies*, **36** (1).

Dixon, H. (1997), 'Controversy: Finance and Development', *Economic Journal*, **107** (442), May.

Dobrev, D. (1999), *The Currency Board in Bulgaria: Design, Peculiarities and Management of Foreign Exchange Cover*, Discussion Paper DP/9/1999, Bulgarian National Bank, http://www.bnb.bg.

Donovan, D.J. (1981), 'Real Responses Associated with Exchange Rate Action in Selected Upper Credit Tranche Stabilization Programs', *IMF Staff Papers*, **28** (4).

Doornbosch, R., and C. Brzeski (2002), 'Risico asymmetrische schokken neemt af', *ESB*, 27 September.

Dornbusch, R. (1976), 'Expectations and Exchange Rate Dynamics', *Journal of Political Economy*, **84** (6).

Dornbusch, R. (1980), *Open Economy Macroeconomics*, New York: Basic Books.

Dornbusch, R. (1987), 'Exchange Rate Economics: 1986', *Economic Journal*, **97** (385).

Dornbusch, R. (1989), 'Real Exchange Rates and Macroeconomics: A Selective Survey', *Scandinavian Journal of Economics*, **91** (2).

Dornbusch, R., and L. Tellez Kuenzler (1993), 'Exchange Rate Policy: Options and Issues', in R. Dornbusch (ed.), *Policymaking in the Open Economy*, New York: Oxford University Press.

Doroodian, K., C. Jung and R. Boyd (1999), 'The J-curve Effect and US Agricultural and Industrial Trade', *Applied Economics*, **31** (6).

Douven, R. and H.M.M. Peeters (1998), 'GDP-spillovers in Multi-country Models', *Economic Modelling*, **15** (2).

Drabek, Z., and S. Laird (1998), 'The New Liberalism: Trade Policy Developments in Emerging Markets', *Journal of World Trade*, **32** (5).

Ducker, M., and K. Wesche (2003), 'European Business Cycles: New Indices and their Synchronicity', *Economic Inquiry*, **41** (1).

Dufey, G., and I.H. Giddy (1978), *The International Money Market*, Englewood Cliffs, NJ: Prentice Hall.

ECB (1999), *Euro Banknotes and Coins* (July). On http://www.ecb.int.

Edgren, G., K.O. Faxén and C.E. Odhner (1969) 'Wages, Growth and the Distribution of Income', *Swedish Journal of Economics*, **71** (3).

Edwards, S. (1983), 'Floating Exchange Rates, Expectations and New Information', *Journal of Monetary Economics*, **11** (4).

Edwards, S. (1989), 'Exchange Controls, Devaluations, and Real Exchange Rates: The Latin American Experience', *Economic Development and Cultural Change*, **37** (3).

Edwards, S. (1993), 'Openness, Trade Liberalization, and Growth in Developing Countries', *Journal of Economic Literature*, **31** (3).

Edwards, S. (2002), *The Great Exchange Rate Debate after Argentina*, NBER Working Paper no. 9257.

Edwards, S., and I.I. Magendzo (2001), *Dollarization, Inflation and Growth*, NBER Working Paper no. 8671.

Eichengreen, B. (1990), 'One Money for Europe? Lessons from the US Currency Union', *Economic Policy*, no. 10.

Eichengreen, B. (1996), *A More Perfect Union? The Logic of Economic Integration*, Essays in International Finance 198, Princeton, NJ: International Finance Section, Princeton University.

Eichengreen, B. (2000), 'The Euro One Year On', *Journal of Policy Modeling*, **22** (3).

Eichengreen, B. (2001), 'Capital Account Liberalization: What Do Cross-Country Studies Tell Us?', *World Bank Economic Review*, **15** (3).

Eichengreen, B., A.K. Rose and C. Wyplosz (1995), 'Exchange Market Mayhem: The Antecedents and Aftermath of Speculative Attacks', *Economic Policy*, no. 21.

Eichengreen, B., J. Tobin and C. Wyplosz (1992), 'Two Cases for Sand in the Wheels of International Finance', *Economic Journal*, **105** (428), January.

Eichengreen, B., and C. Wyplosz (1998), 'The Stability Pact: More Than a Minor Nuisance?', *Economic Policy*, no. 26, April.

Eijffinger, S.C.W., and J. de Haan (1996), *The Political Economy of Central-Bank Independence*, Princeton Special Papers no. 19.

Einaudi, L. (2000), 'From the Franc to the "Europe": The Attempted Transformation of the Latin Monetary Union into a European Monetary Union, 1865–1873', *The Economic History Review*, **53** (2).

Engel, C., and J.H. Rogers (2001), 'Deviations from Purchasing Power Parity: Causes and Welfare Costs', *Journal of International Economics*, **55** (1).

Enoch, C., and A.-M. Gulde (1998), 'Las cajas de conversión, ¿una panacea para todos los problemas monetarios?', *Finanzas & Desarrollo*, **35** (4).

European Commission (1995), *Green Paper on the Practical Arrangements for the Introduction of the Single Currency*; http://europea.eu.int/en/record/green/gp9505/index.htm.

Evans, G.W. (1986), 'A Test for Speculative Bubbles in the Sterling–Dollar Exchange Rate', *American Economic Review*, **76** (4).

Expert Group on the changeover to the single currency (1995), *Progress Report on the Preparation of the Changeover to the Single European Currency*, submitted to the European Commission on 10 May 1995.

Faraque, H. (1995), 'Long-Run Determinants of the Real Exchange Rate: A Stock-Flow Perspective', *IMF Staff Papers*, **42** (1).

Fatum, R. (2000), *On the Effectiveness of Sterilized Foreign Exchange Intervention*, Working Paper no. 10, Frankfurt: European Central Bank, http://www.ecb.int.

Fatum, R., and M.M. Hutchison (2003), *Effectiveness of Official Daily Foreign Exchange Market Intervention Operations in Japan*, NBER Working Paper no. 9648.

Fauri, F. (1996), 'The Role of Fiat in the Development of the Italian Car Industry in the 1950s', *Business History Review*, **70** (2).

Feldstein, M., and C. Horioka (1980), 'Domestic Saving and International Capital Flows', *Economic Journal*, **90**, June.

Fernández Valdovinos, Carlos G. (2003), 'Inflation and Economic Growth in the Long Run', *Economic Letters*, **80** (2).

Fernández-Arias, E., and P.J. Montiel (1996), 'The Surge in Capital Inflows to Developing Countries: An Analytical Overview', *World Bank Economic Review*, **10** (1).

Fischer, S. (1998), 'Capital-Account Liberalization and the Role of the IMF', in *Should the IMF Pursue Capital-Account Convertibility?*, Essays in International Finance 207, Princeton, NJ: International Finance Section, Princeton University.

Fischer, S. (2001), *Exchange Rate Regimes: Is the Bipolar View Correct?*, www.imf.org/external/np/speeches/2001/010601a.htm.

Fisher, I. (1930), *The Theory of Interest*, New York: Macmillan (repr. A.M. Kelley, New York, 1967).

Fleming, J.M. (1962), 'Domestic Financial Policies under Fixed and under Floating Exchange Rates', *IMF Staff Papers*, **9** (3). Reprinted in R.N. Cooper (ed.), *International Finance*, Harmondsworth: Penguin, 1969.

Fleming, J.M. (1971), 'On Exchange Rate Unification', *Economic Journal*, **81** (323), September.

Fleming, J.M. (1974), 'Dual Exchange Markets and Other Remedies for Disrupted Capital Flows', *IMF Staff Papers*, **21** (1).

Flood, R.P., and A.K. Rose (1999), 'Understanding Exchange Rate Volatility without the Contrivance of Macroeconomics', *Economic Journal*, **109** (459).

Flood, R.P., and A.K. Rose (2001), *Uncovered Interest Parity in Crisis: The Interest Rate Defence in the 1990s*, CEPR Discussion Paper no. 2943.

Fonseca, G. (1992), 'Économie de la drogue: taille, caractéristiques et impact économique', *Revue Tiers Monde*, **33** (131).

Ford, J.L. (1990), *Current Issues in Open Economy Macroeconomics: Paradoxes, Policies and Problems*, Aldershot: Edward Elgar.

Frankel, J.A. (1979), 'On the Mark: A Theory of Floating Exchange Rates Based on Real Interest Differentials', *American Economic Review*, **69** (4).

Frankel, J.A. (1992), 'Measuring International Capital Mobility: A Review', *American Economic Review*, **82** (2), Papers and Proceedings.

Frankel, J.A. (1993), *On Exchange Rates*, Cambridge, Mass.: MIT Press.

Frankel, J.A. (1995), 'Monetary Regime Choice for a Semi-open Economy', in S. Edwards (ed.), *Capital Controls, Exchange Rates, and Monetary Policy in the World Economy*, Cambridge: Cambridge University Press.

Frankel, J.A. (1999), *No Single Currency Regime is Right for All Countries or at All Times*, Essays in International Finance no. 215, Princeton, NJ: International Finance Section, Princeton University.

Frenkel, J.A. (1978), 'A Monetary Approach to the Exchange Rate: Doctrinal Aspects and Empirical Evidence', in J.A. Frenkel and H.G. Johnson (eds), *The Economics of Exchange Rates: Selected Studies*, Reading, Mass.: Addison-Wesley. First published in *Scandinavian Journal of Economics*, **78** (2), 1976.

Frenkel, J.A. (1981a), 'Flexible Exchange Rates, Prices, and the Role of "News": Lessons from the 1970s', *Journal of Political Economy*, **89** (4).

Frenkel, J.A. (1981b), 'The Collapse of Purchasing Power Parities during the 1970's', *European Economic Review*, **16** (1).

Frenkel, J.A., and M.L. Mussa (1985), 'Asset Markets, Exchange Rates and the Balance of Payments', in R.W. Jones and P.B. Kenen (eds), *Handbook of International Economics, vol. II*, Amsterdam: Elsevier.

Frey, B.S. (1984), *International Political Economics*, Oxford: Basil Blackwell.

Friedman, M. (1953), 'The Methodology of Positive Economics', Part I in M. Friedman, *Essays in Positive Economics*, Chicago: University of Chicago Press.

Friedman, M. (1974), *Monetary Correction*, London: Institute of Economic Affairs.

Fujii, E., and M. Chinn (2001), 'Fin de Siècle real interest parity', *Journal of International Financial Markets, Institutions & Money*, **11** (3–4).

Gale, D. (1982), *Money: In Equilibrium*, Cambridge: Cambridge University Press.

Garber, P., and M.P. Taylor (1995), 'Sand in the Wheels of Foreign Exchange Markets: A Sceptical Note', *Economic Journal*, **105** (428), January.

Garretsen, H., K.H.W. Knot and E. Nijsse (1998), 'Learning about Fundamentals: The Widening of the French ERM Bands in 1993', *Weltwirtschaftliches Archiv*, **134** (1).

Genberg, H. (1978), 'Purchasing Power Parity under Fixed and Flexible Exchange Rates', *Journal of International Economics*, **8** (2).

Ghosh, A., and S. Phillips (1998), 'Warning: Inflation May Be Harmful to Your Growth', *IMF Staff Papers*, **45** (4).

Ghosh, A.R. (1995), 'International Capital Mobility amongst the Major Industrialised Countries: Too Little or Too Much?', *Economic Journal*, **105** (428), January.

Ghosh, A.R., A.-M. Gulde and H.C. Wolf (2000), 'Currency Boards: More than a Quick Fix?', *Economic Policy*, no. 31, October.

Ghosh, A.R., and J.D. Ostry (1995), 'The Current Account in Developing Countries: A Perspective from the Consumption-Smoothing Approach', *World Bank Economic Review*, **9** (2).

Goldstein, M. and P. Isard (1992), 'Mechanisms for Promoting Global Monetary Stability', in M. Goldstein, P. Isard, P.R. Masson and M.P. Taylor, *Policy Issues in the Evolving International Monetary System*, Occasional Paper 96, Washington, DC: IMF.

Goodhart, C.A.E. (1988a), 'The Foreign Exchange Market: A Random Walk with a Dragging Anchor', *Economica*, **55** (220).

Goodhart, C.A.E. (1988b), *The Evolution of Central Banks*, Cambridge, Mass.: MIT Press.

Graboyes, R.F. (1990), 'The EMU: Forerunners and Durability', *Economic Review*, Federal Reserve Bank of Richmond, **76** (4).

Grahl, J., and P. Lysandrou (2003), 'Sand in the Wheels or Spanner in the Works? The Tobin Tax and Global Finance', *Cambridge Journal of Economics*, **27** (4).

Greenaway, D. (1998), 'Does Trade Liberalisation Promote Economic Development?', *Scottish Journal of Political Economy*, **45** (5).

Greenaway, D., W. Morgan and P. Wright (2002), 'Trade Liberalisation and Growth in Developing Countries', *Journal of Development Economics*, **67** (1).

Greer, M.R. (1999), 'Assessing the Soothsayers: An Examination of the Track Record of Macroeconomic Forecasting', *Journal of Economic Issues*, **33** (1).

Grieve Smith, J. (1997), 'Exchange Rate Instability and the Tobin Tax', *Cambridge Journal of Economics*, **21** (6).

Groen, J.J.J. (2000), 'The Monetary Exchange Rate Model as a Long-Run Phenomenon', *Journal of International Economics*, **52** (2).

Gros, D. (1990), 'Seigniorage and EMS Discipline', in P. De Grauwe and L. Papademos (eds), *The European Monetary System in the 1990s*, Harlow: Longman.

Gros, D., and N. Thygesen (1992), *European Monetary Integration*, London: Longman.

Gros, D., and G. Vandille (1995), 'Seigniorage and EMU: The Fiscal Implications of Price Stability and Financial Market Integration', *Journal of Common Market Studies*, **33** (2).

Grosser, G. (1988), 'Empirical Evidence of Effects of Policy Coordination among Major Industrial Countries since the Rambouillet Summit of 1975', in W. Guth (ed.), *Economic Policy Coordination*, Washington, DC: IMF.

Grubel, H.G. (1968), 'Internationally Diversified Portfolios: Welfare Gains and Capital Flows', *American Economic Review*, **58**. Reprinted in J.H. Dunning (ed.), *International Investment*, Harmondsworth: Penguin, 1972.

Gruijters, A.P.D. (1991), 'De efficiëntie van valutamarkten: een overzicht', *Maandschrift Economie*, **55** (4).

Gulde, A.-M. (1999), *The Role of the Currency Board in Bulgaria's Stabilization*, Policy Discussion Paper 99/3, Washington, DC: IMF.

Gupta, S. (1984), 'Unrecorded Trade at Black Exchange Rate: Analysis, Implications and Estimates', *Aussenwirtschaft*, **39** (1/2).

Gupta-Kapoor, A., and U. Ramakrishnan (1999), 'Is There a J-Curve? A New Estimation for Japan', *International Economic Journal*, **13** (4).

Gylfason, T., and T.T. Herbertsson (2001), 'Does Inflation Matter for Growth?', *Japan and the World Economy*, **13** (4).

Haas, E. (1972), 'International Integration: The European and the Universal Process', in M. Hodges (ed.), *European Integration: Selected Readings*, Harmondsworth: Penguin. Excerpt from E. Haas, *International Political Communities*, Anchor Books, 1966.

Habermeier, K., and A.A. Kirilenko (2002), *Securities Transaction Taxes and Financial Markets*, paper for the Third Annual IMF Research Conference, Washington, DC, 7–8 November, www.imf.org/external/pubs/ft/staffp/2002/00–00/arc.htm.

Hallwood, C.P., and R. MacDonald (2000), *International Money and Finance*, 3rd edn, Oxford: Blackwell.

Handa, J., and I.M. Bana (1990), 'Currency Substitution and Transactions Costs', *Empirical Economics*, **15** (3).

Hanson, J. (1995), 'Opening the Capital Account: Costs, Benefits, and Sequencing', in S. Edwards (ed.), *Capital Controls, Exchange Rates, and Monetary Policy in the World Economy*, Cambridge: Cambridge University Press.

Harberger, A.C. (1950), 'Currency Depreciation, Income and the Balance of Trade', *Journal of Political Economy*, **58** (1).

Harrod, R.F. (1957), *International Economics*, 3rd edn, Digswell Place: Nisbet, and Cambridge: Cambridge University Press. First edn 1933.

Harvey, J.T. (1996), 'Orthodox Approaches to Exchange Rate Determination: A Survey', *Journal of Post Keynesian Economics*, **18** (4).

Harvey, J.T. (2001), 'Exchange Rate Theory and "the Fundamentals"', *Journal of Post Keynesian Economics*, **24** (1).

Haskel, J., and H. Wolf (2001), 'The Law of One Price – A Case Study', *Scandinavian Journal of Economics*, **103** (4).

Hau, H., W. Killeen and M. Moore (2002), 'How Has the Euro Changed the Foreign Exchange Market?', *Economic Policy*, **17** (34), April.

Haudeville, B., and J. Lama (1988), 'Contribution à l'analyse des marchés parallèles de change en Afrique de l'Ouest', *Revue d'économie politique*, **98** (3).

Haussmann, R., and A. Powell (1999), *Dollarization: Issues and Implementation*, working paper, Inter-American Development Bank, http://www.iadb.org/oce/exchange_rate/implement.pdf.

Heitger, B. (1987), 'Purchasing Power Parity under Flexible Exchange Rates – The Impact of Structural Change', *Weltwirtschaftliches Archiv*, **123** (1).

Heston, A., and R. Summers (1996), 'International Price and Quantity Comparison: Potentials and Pitfalls', *American Economic Review*, **86** 92), Papers and Proceedings.

Hill, B.E. (1984), *The Common Agricultural Policy: Past, Present and Future*, London: Methuen.

Hoffman, D.L., and D.E. Schlagenhauf (1983), 'Rational Expectations and Monetary Models of Exchange Rate Determination', *Journal of Monetary Economics*, **11** (3).

Hoffmann, J., and S. Homburg (1990), 'Explaining the Rise and Decline of the Dollar', *Kyklos*, **32** (1).

Holtfrerich, C.-L. (1989), 'The Monetary Unification Process in 19th-century Germany: Relevance and Lessons for Europe Today', in M. de Cecco and A. Giovannini (eds), *A European Central Bank?*, Cambridge: Cambridge University Press.

Honohan, P. (1992), 'Price and Monetary Convergence in Currency Unions: The Franc and Rand Zones', *Journal of International Money and Finance*, **11** (4).

Hoogduin, L.H., and G. Korteweg (1993), 'Monetary Policy on the Road to EMU', in S.C.W. Eijffinger and J.L. Gerards (eds), *European Monetary Integration and the Financial Sector*, Amsterdam: NIBE.

Husted, S., and R. MacDonald (1999), 'The Asian Currency Crash: Were Badly Driven Fundamentals to Blame?', *Journal of Asian Economics*, **10** (4).

IMF (1990), *World Economic Outlook*, October.

IMF (1993), *Articles of Agreement*.

IMF (1994), 'Assigning a Policy Role for the Exchange Rate: A Case Study in Cape Verde', *IMF Survey*, 10 January.

IMF (1995), *International Capital Markets*, World Economic and Financial Surveys, August.

IMF (1996a), *World Economic Outlook*, May.

IMF (1996b), *International Capital Markets*, September.

IMF (1997a), *World Economic Outlook*, May.

IMF (1997b), *World Economic Outlook*, October.

IMF (1998a), 'Financial Crises: Characteristics and Indicators of Vulnerability', ch. IV in *World Economic Outlook*, May.

IMF (1998b), *International Capital Markets*, September.

IMF (1999a), 'IMF Tightens Defenses against Financial Contagion by Establishing Contingent Credit Lines', Press Release No. 99/14 (25 April), http://www.imf.org/external/np/sec/pr/1999/PR9914.

IMF (1999b), *Exchange Rate Arrangements and Currency Convertibility*, World Economic and Financial Surveys.

IMF (1999c), *Greece: Selected Issues*, IMF Staff Country Report no. 99/138.

IMF (2000), *World Economic Outlook*, October.

IMF (2001), *The IMF's Contingent Credit Lines: A Factsheet*, http://www.imf.org/external/np/exr/facts/ccl.htm.

IMF (2002), *World Economic Outlook*, April.

IMF (2003a), *Collective Actions Clauses: Recent Development and Issues*, on www.imf.org.

IMF (2003b), *Annual Report 2003*.

Ingram, J.C. (1969), 'Comment' (on Kenen 1969), in R.A. Mundell and A.K. Swoboda (eds), *Monetary Problems of the International Economy*, Chicago: University of Chicago Press.

Ingram, J.C. (1973), *The Case for European Monetary Integration*, Essays in International Finance 98, Princeton, NJ: International Finance Section, Department of Economics, Princeton University.

Instituto Ecuatoriano de Economía Politica (2000), *Dolarización Oficial en Ecuador*, http://www.his.com/~ieep/dolrznec.htm.

International Financial Statistics, IMF, various issues.

Isaac, A.G., and S. de Mel (2001), 'The Real-interest-differential Model after 20 Years', *Journal of International Money and Finance*, **20** (4).

Ishiyama, Y. (1975), 'The Theory of Optimum Currency Areas: A Survey', *IMF Staff Papers*, **22** (2).

Jager, H., and R. Pauli (2001), 'Anti-inflatoir wisselbeleid via een currency board; De Walters-kritiek doorbroken?, *Maandschrift Economie*, **65** (6).

James, H. (1996), *International Monetary Cooperation since Bretton Woods*, New York: Oxford University Press.

Jansen, W.J. (1998), 'Interpreting Saving–Investment Correlations', *Open Economies Review*, **9** (3).

Jeanne, O., and J. Zettelmeyer (2001), 'International Bailouts, Moral Hazard and Conditionality', *Economic Policy*, no. 33, October.

Johnson, H.G. (1972a), 'The Monetary Approach to Balance-of-Payments Theory', in H.G. Johnson, *Further Essays in Monetary Economics*, London: George Allen & Unwin. Reprinted in J.A. Frenkel and H.G. Johnson (eds), *The Monetary Approach to the Balance of Payments*, London: George Allen & Unwin, 1976 and in M.B. Connolly and A.K. Swoboda (eds), *International Trade and Money*, London: George Allen & Unwin, 1973.

Johnson, H.G. (1972b), 'Theoretical Problems of the International Monetary System', in H.G. Johnson, *Further Essays in Monetary Economics*, London: George Allen & Unwin. Earlier published in *The Pakistan Development Review*, **7** (1), 1967 and in *Journal of Economic Studies*, **2** (2), 1968.

Joint Economic Committee (2000), *Basics of Dollarization*, Staff Report July 1999, updated January 2000; http://www.senate.gov/~jec/basics.htm.

Kamin, S.B. (1988), *Devaluation, External Balance, and Macroeconomic Performance: A Look at the Numbers*, Princeton Studies in International Finance no. 62, Princeton, NJ: International Finance Section, Princeton University.

Kaminsky, G. (1993), 'Is There a Peso Problem? Evidence from the Dollar/ Pound Exchange Rate, 1976–1987', *American Economic Review*, **83** (3).

Kapur, I., et al. (1991), *Ghana: Adjustment and Growth, 1983–91*, Occasional Paper 86, Washington, DC: IMF.

Kempa, B., and M. Nelles (1999), 'The Theory of Exchange Rate Target Zones', *Journal of Economic Surveys*, **13** (4).

Kenen, P.B. (1969), 'The Theory of Optimum Currency Areas: An Eclectic View', in R.A. Mundell and A.K. Swoboda (eds), *Monetary Problems of the International Economy*, Chicago: University of Chicago Press.

Keynes, J.M. (1919), *The Economic Consequences of the Peace*, London: Macmillan.

Keynes, J.M. (1929), 'The German Transfer Problem', *Economic Journal*, **39** (153). Reprinted in H.S. Ellis and L.S. Metzler (eds), *Readings in the Theory of International Trade*, London: George Allen and Unwin, 1950.

Keynes, J.M. (1961), *The General Theory of Employment, Interest and Money*, London: Macmillan. First published 1936.

Kiguel, M. (1999), in *IMF Economic Forum; Dollarization: Fad or Future for Latin America?*, 24 June; http://www.imf.org/external/np/tr/1999/ TR990624.HTM.

Kiguel, M., and S.A. O'Connell (1995), 'Parallel Exchange Rates in Developing Countries', *World Bank Research Observer*, **10** (1).

Kilian, L., and M.P. Taylor (2003), 'Why Is It So Difficult to Beat the Random Walk Forecast of Exchange Rates?', *Journal of International Economics*, **60** (1).

Kindleberger, C.P. (1978), *Manias, Panics, and Crashes: A History of Financial Crises*, London: Macmillan.

Kindleberger, C.P. (1987), *The World in Depression 1929–1939*, 2nd edn, Harmondsworth: Penguin.

King, A. (1998), 'Uncovered Interest Parity: New Zealand's Post-deregulation Experience', *Applied Financial Economics*, **8** (5).

Koedijk, K.G., B. Mizrach, P.A. Stork and C.G. de Vries (1995), 'New Evidence on the Effectiveness of Foreign Exchange Market Intervention', *European Economic Review*, **39** (3/4).

Kong, Q. (2000), *Predictable Movements in Yen/DM Exchange Rates*, Working Paper WP/00/143, Washington, DC: IMF.

Kontolemis, Z.G. (2002), *Money Demand in the Euro Area: Where Do We Stand (Today)?*, Working Paper WP/02/185, Washington, DC: IMF.

Kouretas, G.P., and L.P. Zarangas (2001), 'Black and Official Exchange Rates in Greece: An Analysis of their Long-Run Dynamics', *Journal of Multinational Financial Management*, **11** (3).

Krasker, W.S. (1980), 'The "Peso Problem" in Testing Forward Exchange Markets', *Journal of Monetary Economics*, **6** (2).

Krause, L.A. (1991), *Speculation and the Dollar*, Boulder, Col.: Westview Press.

Kravis, I.B., and R.E. Lipsey (1983), *Toward an Explanation of National Price Levels*, Princeton Studies in International Finance no. 52, Princeton: International Finance Section, Department of Economics, Princeton University.

Krueger, A.O. (1974), 'The Political Economy of the Rent-Seeking Society', *American Economic Review*, **64** (3).

Krueger, A.O. (1978), *Liberalization Attempts and Consequences*, Cambridge, Mass.: Ballinger.

Krugman, P.R., and M. Obstfeld (2003), *International Economics*, 6th edn, New York: Harper Collins.

Kuo, B.-S., and A. Mikkola (2001), 'How Sure Are We About Purchasing Power Parity? Panel Evidence with the Null of Stationary Exchange Rates', *Journal of Money, Credit, and Banking*, **33** (3).

Labán, R., and F. Larraín B. (1994), 'The Chilean Experience with Capital Mobility', in B.P. Bosworth, R. Dornbusch and R. Labán (eds), *The Chilean Economy: Policy Lessons and Challenges*, Washington, DC: The Brookings Institution.

Lane, P.R. (2001), 'The New Open Economy Macroeconomics: A Survey', *Journal of International Economics*, **54** (2).

Lane, P.R., and G.M. Milesi-Ferretti (2000), *The Transfer Problem Revisited: Net Foreign Assets and Real Exchange Rates*, Working Paper WP/00/123, Washington, DC: IMF.

Lane, P.R., and G.M. Milesi-Ferretti (2002), 'External Wealth, the Trade Balance, and the Real Exchange Rate', *European Economic Review*, **46** (6).

Lane, P.R., and G.M. Milesi-Ferretti (2003), *International Financial Integration*, CEPR Discussion Paper no. 3769, February.

Lane, T., A. Ghosh, J. Hamann, S. Phillips, M. Schultze-Ghattus and T. Tsikata (1999), *IMF-Supported Programs in Indonesia, Korea, and Thailand: A Preliminary Assessment*, http://www.imf.org/external/pubs/ft/op/opasia/index/htm, January.

Laney, L.O., C.D. Radcliffe and T.D. Willett (1984), 'Currency Substitution: Comment', *Southern Economic Journal*, **50** (4).

Lange, C., and F. Nolte (1998), 'Konsequenzen der europäischen Währungsunion für den Geldschöpfungsgewinn der Mitgliedsländer', *Kredit und Kapital*, **31** (4).

Lanjouw, G.J., and M.M. Wielinga (1994), 'De politieke economie van protectie en anti-protectie', *Maandschrift Economie*, **58** (2).

Laursen, S., and L.A. Metzler (1950), 'Flexible Exchange Rates and the Theory of Employment', *Review of Economics and Statistics*, **32** (4).

Lee, M.A. (1975), *Excess Inflation and Currency Depreciation*, Ph.D. thesis, University of Chicago, cited in A.B. Laffer, 'The Phenomenon of Worldwide Inflation: A Study in International Market Integration', in D.I. Meiselman and A.B. Laffer (eds), *The Phenomenon of Worldwide Inflation*, Washington, DC: American Enterprise Institute for Public Policy Research.

Lensink, R., N. Hermes and V. Murinde (2000), 'Capital Flight and Political Risk', *Journal of International Money and Finance*, **19** (1).

Levich, R.M. (1978), 'Tests of Forecasting Models and Market Efficiency in the International Money Market', in J.A. Frenkel and H.G. Johnson (eds), *The Economics of Exchange Rates: Selected Studies*, Reading, Mass.: Addison-Wesley.

Levich, R.M. (1985), 'Empirical Studies of Exchange Rates: Price Behavior, Rate Determination and Market Efficiency', in R.W. Jones and P.B. Kenen (eds), *Handbook of International Economics, Vol. II*, Amsterdam: North-Holland.

Levin, J.H. (1981), 'The Niehans Paradox, Flexible Exchange Rates, and Macroeconomic Stability', *Journal of International Economics*, **11** (2).

Lindert, P.H., and C.P. Kindleberger (1982), *International Economics*, 7th edn, Homewood, Ill.: Irwin.

Losee, J. (2001), *A Historical Introduction to the Philosophy of Science*, 4th edn, Oxford: Oxford University Press.

Loth, W. (1990), *Der Weg nach Europa; Geschichte der europäischen Integration 1939–1957*, Göttingen: Vandenhoeck & Ruprecht.

Lothian, J.R. (1998), 'Some New Stylized Facts of Floating Exchange Rates', *Journal of International Money and Banking*, **17** (1).

Lothian, J.R., and Y. Simaan (1998), 'International Financial Relations under the Current Float: Evidence from Panel Data', *Open Economies Review*, **9** (4).

Lucas, R.E. (1976), 'Econometric Policy Evaluation: A Critique', in K. Brunner and A.H. Meltzer (eds), *The Phillips Curve and Labor Markets*, Carnegie-Rochester Conference Series on Public Policy, Vol. 1.

Lüdiger, M. (1989), 'Wechselkursovershooting contra effiziente Devisenmärkte', *Kredit und Kapital*, **22** (2).

Lutz, F.A. (1970), 'The Agricultural Regulations of the European Economic Community as an Obstacle to the Introduction of Greater Flexibility of Exchange Rates', in G.N. Halm (ed.), *Approaches to Greater Flexibility of Exchange Rates: The Bürgenstock Papers*, Princeton, NJ: Princeton University Press.

Maasoumi, E., and J. Pippenger (1989), 'Transaction Costs and the Interest Parity Theorem: Comment', *Journal of Political Economy*, **97** (1).

MacDonald, R. (1988a), *Floating Exchange Rates: Theories and Evidence*, London: Unwin Hyman.

MacDonald, R. (1988b), 'Purchasing Power Parity: Some "Long Run" Evidence from the Recent Float', *De Economist*, **136** (2).

MacDonald, R. (1999), 'Exchange Rate Behaviour: Are Fundamentals Important?', *Economic Journal*, **109** (459).

MacDonald, R., and P. Swagel (2000), 'Business Cycle Influences on Exchange Rates: Survey and Evidence', ch. IV in *World Economic Outlook Supporting Studies*, Washington, DC: IMF.

MacDougall, G.A.D. (1958), 'The Benefits and Costs of Private Investment from Abroad: A Theoretical Approach', *Economic Record*, **36**. Reprinted in J. Bhagwati (ed.), *International Trade*, Harmondsworth: Penguin, 1969.

Maes, I. (1992), 'Optimum Currency Area Theory and European Monetary Integration', *Tijdschrift voor Economie en Management*, **37** (2).

Malkiel, B.G. (2003), 'The Efficient Market Hypothesis and its Critics', *Journal of Economic Perspectives*, **17** (1).

Manzur, M. (1993), *Exchange Rates, Prices and World Trade*, London: Routledge.

Mark, N.C. (2001), *International Macroeconomics and Finance: Theory and Econometric Methods*, Malden, Mass.: Blackwell.

Mark, N.C., and Y.-K. Moh (2003), *Official Interventions and Occasional Violations of Uncovered Interest Parity in the Dollar-DM Market*, NBER Working Paper no. 9948.

Masson, P.R. (1981), 'Dynamic Stability of Portfolio Balance Models of the Exchange Rate', *Journal of International Economics*, **11** (4).

Masson, P.R., and M.P. Taylor (1992), 'Issues in the Operation of Monetary Unions and Common Currency Areas', in M. Goldstein, P. Isard, P.R. Masson and M.P. Taylor, *Policy Issues in the Evolving International Monetary System*, Occasional Paper 96, Washington, DC: IMF.

Mazzaferro, F. (1992), 'Unity through Diversity', *ECU Newsletter* no. 40, San Paolo Bank Holding.

McCauley, R.N., and W.R. White (1997), *The Euro and European Financial Markets*, Working Paper 41, Basel: BIS.

McCloskey, D.N. (1994), *Knowledge and Persuasion in Economics*, Cambridge: Cambridge University Press.

McKinnon, R.I. (1969), 'Optimum Currency Areas', in R.N. Cooper (ed.), *International Finance: Selected Readings*, Harmondsworth: Penguin. First published in *American Economic Review*, **53**, 1963.

McKinnon, R.I. (1979), *Money in International Exchange*, New York: Oxford University Press.

McKinnon, R.I. (1981), 'The Exchange Rate and Macroeconomic Policy: Changing Postwar Perceptions', *Journal of Economic Literature*, **19** (2).

McKinnon, R.I. (1982), 'Currency Substitution and Instability in the World Dollar Standard', *American Economic Review*, **72** (3).

McKinnon, R.I. (1984), *An International Standard for Monetary Stability*, Washington, DC: Institute for International Economics.

McKinnon, R.I. (1993a), *The Order of Economic Liberalization*, 2nd edn, Baltimore: Johns Hopkins University Press.

McKinnon, R.I. (1993b), 'International Money in Historical Perspective', *Journal of Economic Literature*, **31** (1).

Meese, R.A., and K. Rogoff (1983), 'Empirical Exchange Rate Models of the Seventies: Do They Fit Out of Sample?', *Journal of International Economics*, **14** (1/2).

Melvin, M., and B. Peiers (1996), 'Dollarization in Developing Countries: Rational Remedy or Domestic Dilemma?', *Contemporary Economic Policy*, **14** (3).

Meredith, G., and Y. Ma (2002), *The Forward Premium Puzzle Revisited*, Working Paper WP/02/28, Washington, DC: IMF.

Metzler, L.A. (1948), 'The Theory of International Trade', in H.S. Ellis (ed.), *A Survey of Contemporary Economics*, Philadelphia: Blakiston.

Micco, A., E. Stein and G. Ordoñez (2003), 'The Currency Union Effect on Trade: Early Evidence from EMU', *Economic Policy*, no. 37.

Mill, J.S. (1917), *Principles of Political Economy* (Ashley edn), London: Longmans, Green and Co. First published 1848.

Milner, C., P. Mizen and E. Pentecost (2000), 'A Cross-Country Panel Analysis of Currency Substitution and Trade', *Economic Inquiry*, **38** (2).

Milward, A.S., and S.B. Saul (1977), *The Development of the Economies of Continental Europe, 1850–1914*, London: George Allen and Unwin.

Minford, P. (1989), 'Do Floating Exchange Rates Insulate?', in R. MacDonald and M.P. Taylor (eds), *Exchange Rates and Open Economy Macroeconomics*, Oxford: Basil Blackwell.

Montiel, P., and C.M. Reinhart (1999), 'Do Capital Controls and Macroeconomic Policies Influence the Volume and Composition of

Capital Flows? Evidence from the 1990s', *Journal of International Money and Finance*, **18** (4).

Moosa, I.A. (2000), 'A Structural Time Series Test of the Monetary Model of Exchange Rates under the German Hyperinflation', *Journal of International Financial Markets, Institutions & Money*, **10** (2).

Moreno-Villalaz, J.L. (1999), 'Lessons from the Monetary Experience of Panama: A Dollar Economy with Financial Integration', *Cato Journal*, **18** (3).

Motley, B. (1998), 'Growth and Inflation: A Cross-country Study', Federal Reserve Bank of San Francisco *Economic Review*, no. 1.

Mundell, R.A. (1961), 'A Theory of Optimum Currency Areas', *American Economic Review*, **51** (4).

Mundell, R.A. (1962), 'The Appropriate Use of Monetary and Fiscal Policy for Internal and External Stability', *IMF Staff Papers*, **9** (1).

Mundell, R.A. (1963), 'Capital Mobility and Stabilization Policy under Fixed and Flexible Exchange Rates', *Canadian Journal of Economics and Political Science*, **29** (4). Reprinted in R.E. Caves and H.G. Johnson (eds), *Readings in International Economics*, London: George Allen & Unwin.

Murray, C.J., and D.H. Papell (2002), 'The Purchasing Power Parity Persistence Paradigm', *Journal of International Economics*, **56** (1).

Mussa, M.L. (1990), *Exchange Rates in Theory and in Reality*, Essays in International Finance no. 179, International Finance Section, Princeton, NJ: Princeton University Press.

Mussa, M., P. Masson, A. Swoboda, E. Jadresic, P. Mauro and A. Berg (2000), *Exchange Rate Regimes in an Increasingly Integrated World Economy*, Occasional Paper 193, Washington, DC: IMF.

Myers, S.C. (2001), 'Capital Structure', *Journal of Economic Perspectives*, **15** (2).

Myrdal, G. (1963), *Economic Theory and Under-developed Regions*, London: Methuen. First published by Gerald Duckworth, 1957.

Nadal-De Simone, F., and P. Sorsa (1999), *A Review of Capital Account Restrictions in Chile in the 1990s*, Working Paper WP/99/52, Washington, DC: IMF.

Neely, C.J. (1997), 'Technical Analysis in the Foreign Exchange Market: A Layman's Guide', *Federal Reserve Bank of St. Louis Review*, **79** (5).

Neely, C.J., and L. Sarno (2002), 'How Well Do Monetary Fundamentals Forecast Exchange Rates?', *Federal Reserve Bank of St. Louis Review*, **84** (5).

Ngama, V.L. (1994), 'A Re-examination of the Forward Exchange Rate Unbiasedness Hypothesis', *Weltwirtschaftliches Archiv*, **130** (3).

Niehans, J. (1975), 'Some Doubts about the Efficacy of Monetary Policy under Flexible Exchange Rates', *Journal of International Economics*, **5** (3).

Nsouli, S.M., S. Eken, P. Duran, G. Bell and Z. Yücelik (1993), *The Path to Convertibility and Growth: The Tunisian Experience*, Occasional Paper 109, Washington, DC: IMF.

Obstfeld, M. (1985), 'Floating Exchange Rates: Experience and Prospects', *Brookings Papers on Economic Activity*, no. 2.

Obstfeld, M., and K. Rogoff (1996), *Foundations of International Macroeconomics*, Cambridge, Mass.: MIT Press.

Ohlin, B. (1929), 'The Reparation Problem: A Discussion', *Economic Journal*, **39** (154). Reprinted in H.S. Ellis and L.S. Metzler (eds), *Readings in the Theory of International Trade*, London: George Allen and Unwin, 1950.

Olson, M. (1971), *The Logic of Collective Action*, 2nd edn, Cambridge, Mass.: Harvard University Press.

'One Market, One Money' (1990), *European Economy*, no. 44.

Osugi, K. (1990), *Japan's Experience of Financial Deregulation since 1984 in an International Perspective*, BIS Economic Papers 26.

Otto, G. (2003), 'Terms of Trade Shocks and the Balance of Trade: There is a Harberger–Laursen–Metzler Effect', *Journal of International Money and Finance*, **22** (2).

Pakko, M.R., and P.S. Pollard (2003), 'Burgernomics: A Big Mac™ Guide to Purchasing Power Parity', *Federal Reserve Bank of St. Louis Review*, **85** (6).

Pakko, M.R., and H.J. Wall (2001), 'Reconsidering the Trade-creating Effects of a Currency Union', *Federal Reserve Bank of St. Louis Review*, **83** (5).

Papell, D.H., and H. Theodorakis (1998), 'Increasing Evidence of Purchasing Power Parity over the Current Float', *Journal of International Money and Finance*, **17** (1).

Pareto, V. (1909), *Manuel d'Économie Politique* (trans. A. Bonnet), Paris: Giard & Brière.

Parsley, D., and S.-J. Wei (2003), *A Prism into the PPP Puzzles: The Micro-foundations of Big Mac Real Exchange Rates*, NBER Working Paper 10074.

Pauli, R. (2002), 'Loont flexibiliteit?', *ESB*, **87** (4376), 27 September.

Persson, T. (2001), 'Currency Unions and Trade: How Large is the Treatment Effect?', *Economic Policy*, no. 33, October.

Pierson, N.G. (1912), *Leerboek der Staathuishoudkunde*, 3rd edn, Haarlem: Erven Bohn.

Pilat, D., and D.S. Prasada Rao (1996), 'Multilateral Comparison of Output, Productivity, and Purchasing Power Parities in Manufacturing', *Review of Income and Wealth*, **42** (2).

Pilbeam, K. (1995a), 'The Profitability of Trading in the Foreign Exchange Market: Chartists, Fundamentalists, and Simpletons', *Oxford Economic Papers*, **7** (3).

Pilbeam, K. (1995b), 'Exchange Rate Models and Exchange Rate Expectations: An Empirical Investigation', *Applied Economics*, **27** (11).

Pollard, P.S. (2001), 'The Creation of the Euro and the Role of the Dollar in International Markets', *Federal Reserve Bank of St. Louis Review*, **83** (5).

Porojan, A. (2001), 'Trade Flows and Spatial Effects: The Gravity Model Revisited', *Open Economies Review*, **12** (3).

Posthuma, S. (1982), 'De Latijnsche Muntunie 1 Januari 1866–31 December 1926', in S. Posthuma, *Analyses en beschouwingen in retrospect*, Leiden: Stenfert Kroese. First published in *Economisch-Statistische Berichten*, **12** (594), 1927.

Prasad, E., K. Rogoff, S.-J. Wei and M.A. Kose (2003), *Effects of Financial Globalization on Developing Countries: Some Empirical Evidence*, Washington, DC: IMF.

Pringle, R. (1989), 'Foreign Lending Revisited 1880–1980', in D.E. Fair and C. de Boissieu (eds), *The International Adjustment Process: New Perspectives, Recent Experience and Future Challenges for the Financial System*, Dordrecht: Kluwer.

Protopapadakis, A.A., and H.R. Stoll (1986), 'The Law of One Price in International Commodity Markets: A Reformulation and Some Formal Tests', *Journal of International Money and Finance*, **5** (3).

Quirk, P.J., B.V. Christensen, K.-M. Huh and T. Sasaki (1987), *Floating Exchange Rates in Developing Countries: Experience with Auction and Interbank Markets*, Occasional Paper 53, Washington, DC: IMF.

Quirk, P.J., O. Evans et al. (1995), *Capital Account Convertibility; Review of Experience and Implications for IMF Policies*, Occasional Paper 131, Washington, DC: IMF.

Ramaswamy, R., and H. Samiei (2000), *The Yen–Dollar Rate: Have Interventions Mattered?*, Working Paper WP/00/95, Washington, DC: IMF.

Ramírez-Rojas, C.L. (1986), 'La sustitución monetaria en países en desarrollo', *Finanzas y Desarrollo*, **23** (2).

Reinhart, C.M., and V.R. Reinhart (1999), 'On the Use of Reserve Requirements in Dealing with Capital Flow Problems', *International Journal of Finance and Economics*, **4** (1).

Reinhart, C.M., and V.R. Reinhart (2002), 'Una banda cambiaria en el G-3 ¿Es lo mejor para los mercados emergentes?', *Finanzas y Desarrollo*, **39** (1).

Reinhart, C.M., and R.T. Smith (2001), *Temporary Controls on Capital Inflows*, NBER Working Paper 8422.

Reisen, H. (2002), 'Tobin Tax: Could it Work?', *OECD Observer*, 29 March, http://www.oecdobserver.org/news/print...id/664/Tobin_tax:_could_it_work_html.

Roberts, M.A. (1995), 'Imperfect Information: Some Implications for Modelling the Exchange Rate', *Journal of International Economics*, **38** (3–4).

Robinson, J. (1950), 'The Foreign Exchanges', in H.S. Ellis and L.S. Metzler (eds), *Readings in the Theory of International Trade*, London: George Allen and Unwin. Earlier published in J. Robinson, *Essays in the Theory of Employment*, 2nd edn, Oxford: Basil Blackwell, 1947, vol. III, ch. 1.

Rogoff, K. (1996), 'The Purchasing Power Parity Puzzle', *Journal of Economic Literature*, **34** (2).

Rogoff, K. (1999), 'Monetary Models of Dollar/Yen/Euro Nominal Exchange Rates: Dead or Undead?', *Economic Journal*, **109** (459).

Rogoff, K. (2002), *Dornbusch's Overshooting Model after Twenty-Five Years*, Working Paper WP/02/39,Washington, DC: IMF.

Romer, P. (1994), 'New Goods, Old Theory, and the Welfare Costs of Trade Restrictions', *Journal of Development Economics*, **43**.

Rose, A.K. (2000), 'One Money, One Market: Estimating the Effect of Common Currencies on Trade', *Economic Policy*, no. 30, April.

Rose, A.K., and E. van Wincoop (2001), 'National Money as a Barrier to International Trade: The Real Case for Currency Union', *American Economic Review*, **91** (2).

Sabirin, S. (1993), 'Capital Account Liberalization: The Indonesian Experience', in S. Faruqi (ed.), *Financial Sector Reforms in Asian and Latin American Countries*, Washington, DC: World Bank.

Sachs, J., and C. Wyplosz (1986), 'France under Mitterrand', *Economic Policy*, no. 2.

Sahay, R., and C.A. Végh (1995), 'La dolarización en las economías en transición', *Finanzas y Desarrollo*, **32** (1).

Salter, W.E.G. (1959), 'Internal and External Balance: The Role of Price and Expenditure Effects', *Economic Record*, **35** (71).

Samuelson, P.A. (1964), 'Theoretical Notes on Trade Problems', *Review of Economics and Statistics*, **46** (3).

Sarantis, N. (1987), 'A Dynamic Asset Market Model for the Exchange Rate of Pound Sterling', *Weltwirtschaftliches Archiv*, **123** (1).

Sarno, L., and M.P. Taylor (2001), 'Official Intervention in the Foreign Exchange Market: Is It Effective and, If So, How Does It Work?', *Journal of Economic Literature*, **39** (3).

Sarno, L., and M.P. Taylor (2002), *The Economics of Exchange Rates*, Cambridge: Cambridge University Press.

Scheerlinck, I., and M. Pans (2000), 'Flexibiliteit van arbeidsmarkten in de Europese Unie: concepten en statistieken', *Maandschrift Economie*, **64** (6).

Schnabl, G. (2001), 'Purchasing Power Parity and the Yen/Dollar Exchange Rate', *World Economy*, **24** (1).

Scitovsky, T. (1962), *Economic Theory and Western European Integration*, 2nd printing, London: George Allen and Unwin. First published 1958.

Scitovsky, T. (1967), 'Theory of Balance-of-Payments Adjustment', *Journal of Political Economy*, **75** (4), Part II.

Shleifer, A., and L.H. Summers (1990), 'The Noise Trader Approach to Finance', *Journal of Economic Perspectives*, **4** (2).

Singh, A. (1995), *Corporate Financial Patterns in Industrializing Countries: A Comparative International Study*, Washington, DC: IFC.

Singh, A. (1997), 'Financial Liberalisation, Stockmarkets and Economic Development', *Economic Journal*, **107** (442), May.

Solomon, R. (1979), 'A Quantitative Perspective on the Debt of Developing Countries', in L.G. Franko and M.J. Seiber (eds), *Developing Country Debt*, New York: Pergamon Press.

Spahn, P.B. (1996), 'El impuesto de Tobin y la estabilidad cambiaria', *Finanzas y Desarrollo*, **33** (2).

Spiro, J. Edelman (1992), *The Politics of International Economic Relations*, 4th edn, London: Routledge.

Spitäller, E. (1980), 'Short-run Effects of Exchange Rate Changes on Terms of Trade and Trade Balance', *IMF Staff Papers*, **27** (2).

Sriram, S.S. (1999), *Survey of Literature on Demand for Money: Theoretical and Empirical Work with Special Reference to Error-Correction Models*, Working Paper 99/64, Washington, DC: IMF.

Steinherr, A. (1998), *Derivatives: The Wild Beasts of Finance*, Chichester: John Wiley & Sons.

Stockman, A.C. (1998), 'New Evidence Connecting Exchange Rates to Business Cycles', Federal Reserve Bank of Richmond *Economic Quarterly*, **84** (2).

Stockman, A.C. (1999), 'Choosing an Exchange-rate System', *Journal of Banking & Finance*, **23** (10).

Stockman, A.C., and L.E.O. Svensson (1987), 'Capital Flows, Investment, and Exchange Rates', *Journal of Monetary Economics*, **19** (2).

Swagel, P. (1999), 'The Contribution of the Balassa–Samuelson Effect to Inflation: Cross-country Evidence', Ch. III in *Greece: Selected Issues*, Staff Country Report no. 99/138, Washington, DC: IMF.

Szász, A. (1988), *Monetaire diplomatie; Nederlands internationale monetaire politiek 1958–1987*, Leiden: Stenfert Kroese.

Szász, A. (1999), *The Road to European Monetary Union*, London: Macmillan.

Tagaki, S. (1991), 'Exchange Rate Expectations', *IMF Staff Papers*, **38** (1).

Takayama, A. (1972), *International Trade*, New York: Holt, Rinehart and Winston.

Taylor, A.M., and J.G. Williamson (1994), 'Capital Flows to the New World as an Intergenerational Transfer', *Journal of Political Economy*, **102** (2).

Taylor, M.P. (1995), 'The Economics of Exchange Rates', *Journal of Economic Literature*, **33** (1).

Taylor, M.P., and P.C. McMahon (1988), 'Purchasing Power Parity in the 1920s', *European Economic Review*, **32** (1).

Temple, J. (2000), 'Inflation and Growth: Stories Short and Tall', *Journal of Economic Surveys*, **14** (4).

Theron, N. (1998), 'Can South Africa Afford Full Liberalisation of Exchange Controls? Some Lessons from International Experience', *South African Journal of Economics*, **66** (1).

Tille, C., N. Stoffels and O. Gorbachev (2001), 'To What Extent Does Productivity Drive the Dollar?', *Current Issues in Economics and Finance*, **7** (8) (Federal Reserve Bank of New York).

Tobin, J. (1974), *The New Economics One Decade Older*, Princeton, NJ: Princeton University Press.

Tsiang, S.C. (1989), 'The Role of Money in Trade-Balance Stability: Synthesis of the Elasticity and Absorption Approaches', in S.C. Tsiang, *Finance Constraints and the Theory of Money, Selected Papers edited by M. Kohn*, San Diego: Academic Press. First published in *American Economic Review*, **51** (5), 1961.

ul Haq, M., I. Kaul and I. Grunberg (eds) (1996), *The Tobin Tax: Coping with Financial Volatility*, New York: Oxford University Press.

Ulan, M.K. (2000), 'Review Essay: Is a Chilean-Style Tax on Short-Term Capital Inflows Stabilizing?', *Open Economies Review*, **11** (2).

van der Wal, D. (1992), 'De verdediging van het pond sterling en het Ierse punt', *ESB*, **77** (3885).

van Ewijk, C.J. and L.J.R. Scholtens (1992), 'The Distribution of Seigniorage in the Netherlands', *De Economist*, **140** (4).

van Hoek, T.H. (1992), 'Explaining Mark/Dollar and Yen/Dollar Exchange Rates in the 1980s', *Economics Letters*, **38**.

Vander Kraats, R.H., and L.D. Booth (1983), 'Empirical Tests of the Monetary Approach to Exchange-rate Determination', *Journal of International Money and Finance*, **2** (3).

Vanthoor, W.F.V. (1996), *European Monetary Union since 1848*, Cheltenham: Edward Elgar.

Vataja, J. (2000), 'Should the Law of One Price be Pushed Away? Evidence from International Commodity Markets', *Open Economies Review*, **11** (4).

Verhoef, B.A. (2003), *The (A)symmetry of Shocks in the EMU*, Staff Report 106/2003, The Netherlands Bank.

Visser, H. (1996), 'The Exchange Rate as an Export-stimulation Mechanism', in R. Buitelaar and P. van Dijck (eds), *Latin America's New Insertion in the World Economy: Comparative Analyses of Structural Change*, Basingstoke: Macmillan.

Visser, H., and J. ter Wengel (1999), 'The Asian Crisis, the IMF and Dr Mahathir', *Intereconomics*, **34** (4).

Visser, H. and I. van Herpt (1996), 'Financial Liberalisation and Financial Fragility: The Experiences of Chile and Indonesia Compared', in N. Hermes and R. Lensink (eds), *Financial Development and Economic Growth: Theory and Experiences from Developing Countries*, London: Routledge.

Wagner, H. (2000), 'Which Exchange Rate Regimes in an Era of High Capital Mobility?', *North American Journal of Economics and Finance*, **11** (2).

Williamson, J. (1985), *The Exchange Rate System*, 2nd edn, Washington, DC: Institute for International Economics.

Wilson, P. (2001), 'Exchange Rates and the Trade Balance for Dynamic Asian Economies – Does the J-Curve Exist for Singapore, Malaysia, and Korea?', *Open Economies Review*, **12** (4).

World Bank (1990), *Trends in Developing Economies 1990*, Washington, DC.

World Bank (1995), *Workers in an Integrating World*, World Development Report 1995, New York: Oxford University Press.

World Bank (1999), *Entering the 21st Century*, World Development Report 1999/2000, New York: Oxford University Press.

World Bank (2001), *Global Economic Prospects and the Developing Countries 2001*, Washington, DC.

Wyplosz, C. (2002), 'How Risky is Financial Liberalization in the Developing Countries?', *Comparative Economic Studies*, **44** (2).

Zis, G. (1988), 'Theories of Balance of Payments and Exchange Rate Determination', in G. Zis, R. Vaubel, S. Baker, T. Hitiris and N. Peera, *International Economics*, Harlow: Longman.

Index